BEST WATERSIDE PUBS

THE BEST
Waterside
PUBS
IN ENGLAND & WALES

Chris Rowland and John Simpson

ALMA
BOOKS

IN ASSOCIATION WITH THE
CAMPAIGN FOR REAL ALE

Authors: **Chris Rowland and John Simpson**

Illustrations: **John Simpson**

Maps: **Perrott Cartographics**

Cover photograph of the Boat, Berkhamsted, Herts:
Reuben Foster, Bridgewater Boats

Typeset and printed by: **Cambridge University Press**

ISBN 1-85249-109-4

Published by **Alma Books Ltd.,** *a wholly-owned
subsidiary of the Campaign for Real Ale Ltd., 34 Alma Road,
St Albans, Herts.*

© *Alma Books Ltd 1992*

CONTENTS

INTRODUCTION

Chris Rowland and John Simpson have produced a voyage of discovery. There can be no better way to see the rural delights and industrial heritage of Britain than along the country's canals and rivers. But even the most idyllic rustic scene or finest example of urban architecture needs, if you will pardon the pun, to be watered and so the authors have dotted the landscape with their choice of good pubs.

Their guide, it must be stressed, is not just for boating people. It is a *waterside* guide, not a waterways one. It is aimed at all those who enjoy being beside a canal or river, which is why the authors also offer pubs "off the towpath." But there is no doubt that the finest way to enjoy the pubs in the guide is to take to the waters themselves and gently cruise them with frequent stops for beer and victuals.

You will find in the pubs chosen for the guide an enormous choice and variety of beers. If you were to take a similar voyage in France you would be likely to find that the choice of beer in cafés would be Kronenbourg, Kronenbourg or Kronenbourg. That is because France is predominantly a wine-producing country. Britain, on the other hand, has a great brewing tradition. That tradition is still alive thanks to the efforts of regional brewers who continue to supply beers rich with taste and character.

The comparison with France is useful. It produces a wide variety of wines, from the fruity whites of Alsace, to the deep, earthy clarets of Bordeaux, the smooth and rounded whites and reds of Burgundy and the deep, sun-ripened reds of the Rhone. Britain has a similar rich diversity of beers. If you travel the land in the company of Messrs Rowland and Simpson you will find and relish an astonishing range of beers for such a small and compact country.

Yorkshire and the North-east is famous for ales that are tart and yet creamy, due to the drinkers' passion for a thick collar of foam on their pints. In the North-west, beers have an uncompromising bitterness while the brews of the East Midlands have a legendary sulphur characteristic from the gypsum-rich waters that made the production of pale ale possible in the 19th century. The West Midlands' tradition is for malty, lightly hopped yet quenching brews that refreshed generations of workers involved in the heavy industries of Birmingham and the Black Country. The beers of South Wales are not dissimilar for the same reason.

To the east lies the great grain basket of East Anglia where brewers are generous with their malt, a tradition that also imbues the beers of the Thames Valley with a good fruity character. London's beers are influenced by their proximity to the hops farms of Kent and you will find a spicy, herbal tang and bite in the beers of Fuller's and Youngs. In the West Country the tradition is for beers with a massive fruity note, most forcibly expressed in the ales of St Austell. which have a ripe peardrops character.

None of these beers and styles can be enjoyed without the British pub. Uniquely among the beer-drinking nations of the world, the British consume most of their beer on draught. The pub is where we drink draught beer and the pub has become an endangered species.

As a result of a report from the Monopolies and Mergers Commission in 1989, massive changes have been taking place in the pub trade. The MMC did not like the state of British brewing and found a "complex monopoly" at work controlled by the six giant national brewing groups. Although the MMC's proposals were considerably watered down by the government, new rules have allowed tenants of national brewers to take a "guest ale" in their outlets. The nationals have also been told to turn half their pubs above a two thousands ceiling into free houses offering a wider and genuine choice of beers to customers.

The guest beer rule has been widely abused. Only a handful of independent brewers have gained new business from it. The national brewers have arranged beer swaps between themselves or have widened the scope of trading deals they have had with a few independents for many years. Whitbread has produced a list of some 26 "guest ales" with which it generously offers to supply its tenants but 23 of those beers, including Boddingtons, Flowers, Higsons and Strongs, are brands directly owned by the giant.

On the pub front, the national brewers have reacted with horror to the notion they should provide more choice. They have preferred to sell pubs rather than turn them into free houses. Many of the pubs sold have been disposed of in blocks to non-brewing free house chains. They are excluded from the requirement to sell guest ales and can sign cosy deals with the former owners to provide them with beers. Plus ça change...

The biggest sale has been a two-way one between Grand Metropolitan, owner of Watneys, Wilsons and Websters, and Courage. GrandMet has left brewing, selling all its plants to Courage while Courage sold its pubs to GrandMet. At a stroke GrandMet became the biggest pub retailing group in Britain and has a seven-year supply deal with Courage. Very neat, very legal and very much against the spirit of the MMC report.

The biggest threat to the future of the pub lies in the new, hard-faced and profit-driven nature of the giant brewers and the new pub chains. Pubs are no longer seen as essential parts of the community. They are called "profit centres"; the customers are "traffic". As with a petrol station, the essential thing is to get as much traffic into the profit centre as possible and get it out the other end as fast as possible. It all fits uneasily with the image of the British pub as a warm and inviting place for people of all ages and backgrounds.

Pubs that do not stack up the cash are in danger of the axe. Many of the pubs in this guide are at risk because they are in isolated places, are not busy twelve hours a day and are difficult to reach with delivery trucks. They can and will survive if enough people care about them, use them, support them and make a fuss if the axe is sharpened. CAMRA has been caring about good beer and pubs for twenty-one years and has scored many successes. Most of the beers you will drink in the pubs in this guide would not exist but for the Campaign's endeavours.

So enjoy the beers and the pubs. But do more than that. Care about them. Talk about them. And don't let the faceless and profit-hungry marketing tyrants consign them to oblivion.

In the meantime I have great pleasure in launching this waterside guide. May Bacchus bless all who sail with her.

Roger Protz

HOW TO USE THIS GUIDE

 food is available as specified. This always means full meals unless otherwise indicated. Many pubs do not serve meals late in the evening, so check by phone if you wish to eat late. Prices given were correct at time of surveying in 1990.

V many pubs have the odd vegetarian dish, but these pubs make a real effort to provide imaginative vegetarian food.

 a garden, or where specified, other outdoor area for drinking – occasionally this will just be tables on the pavement.

 a family room or area without a bar is provided where the licensee will allow children accompanied by a parent or other responsible adult. In pubs where meals are served, children may be confined to the dining area, and thus be expected to have a meal. Check with staff.

 the type of accommodation is specified, but no prices are given. Check by phone for availability.

CC credit cards

 real ales are listed with beers from independent breweries and national brands. For full details of beers consult CAMRA's Good Beer Guide.

 frequent live entertainment either theatre or music.

 nearest underground station. This will be just a few minutes walk unless otherwise stated.

 nearest British Rail station.

WHAT IS REAL ALE?

Real ale is a definition accepted by the Concise Oxford Dictionary. It is also known as traditional draught beer or cask-conditioned beer. Real ale is brewed from malted barley, using pure water and hops, and fermented by top-fermenting yeast. At the end of fermentation the beer is allowed to condition for a few days and is then racked into casks, often with the addition of priming sugar and a handful of dry hops for aroma. The beer continues to "work" or ferment in the cask while a clearing agent called finings drags the yeasty deposits to the floor of the cask. The beer is neither filtered nor pasteurised and must not be served by any method using applied gas pressure.

Real ale can be served straight from the cask and many country pubs still use this method, while some special winter brews in town pubs are often dispensed from a cask on the bar. But most real ale is drawn – hence the word "draught" – by a suction pump from the pub cellar. The pump is operated either by a handpump, a tall lever on the bar, or by an electric pump. Electric pumps are rare in the south of England but are used widely in the Midlands and the North.

Real ale should be served at a temperature of 55–56 degrees F (12–13 degrees C). This is a cool temperature that brings out the best character-istics of a top-fermented beer. It is a higher temperature than those used for serving lager beers, but it is pure mythology that real ale is "warm".

PUB HOURS

In August 1988 the British Government made long-overdue changes to pub licensing laws, which had been severely restricted since the First World War. Pubs can now open Monday to Saturday from 11 am until 11 pm. But individual licensees can choose which hours they wish to open between 11 in the morning and 11 at night. They will choose their hours to suit their trade. Many pubs now display their opening hours on the exterior. It is likely that pubs in tourist areas or areas of high urban concentration will stay open in the afternoon, especially in the summer. During the winter months it is likely that many pubs will keep to the old hours and will close between 3 pm and 5.30 or 6 pm. Sunday hours have been only slightly extended: the standard hours are 12 noon to 3 pm and 7 pm to 10.30 pm.

The changes in licensing laws also had an effect on the times food is served, but where a pub is now open all day on the whole hot meals are still served lunchtimes and evenings only, with snacks during the rest of the day, unless otherwise stated. Phone numbers of pubs are included, so if you are planning to eat out it would be wise to phone first to check the exact times meals are served, and to book a table in establishments where they take bookings.

CHILDREN IN PUBS

You cannot drink alcohol in a pub below the age of eighteen years (although at sixteen, children accompanied by an adult may drink beer, wine or cider with a meal). You can go into a pub at fourteen but you can drink only non-alcoholic products. Licensees tend to be extremely strict on "under-age drinking" as they can be prosecuted and lose their licences to trade. Children of all ages can go into pubs that have rooms set aside as "family rooms". Where a pub has a separate restaurant children are allowed in to eat with their parents unless specified otherwise; in cases where food is only served in the bars the guide has tried to indicate if children are permitted. If a pub in this guide is shown to have a beer garden then children can use this facility but if the garden is reached via the pub it is wise for parents or guardians to ask permission to take the children through the licensed area.

The Rising Sun, Berkhamsted

GRAND UNION CANAL

AIRE & CALDER

The Aire & Calder heads eastwards from its junction with the Leeds & Liverpool Canal in Leeds, sharing some of its course with the River Aire. At Castleford the River Calder is joined, in turn merging with the Calder & Hebble on the outskirts of Wakefield. Many notable Yorkshire towns and cities are accessible by water, including Dewsbury, Brighouse, Elland and Sowerby Bridge where the navigation terminates. The Huddersfield Broad Canal leaves the Calder & Hebble at Cooper Bridge for the short journey into Huddersfield.

ALLERTON BYWATER
Boat

Main Street, Allerton Bywater, W. Yorks, waterside at Allerton Bywater on the Aire & Calder. NB: passing craft create a considerable wash, so moor with care

---

✗ lunchtime

🍴

☺

🍺 **Stones Best Bitter**

This attractive brick-built terraced pub on the river bank has a good, solid, dependable look about it, oddly picturesque against the mining village beyond. From the river it must look especially welcoming with its whitewashed frontage, slate roof and beer terrace. A Bass cask hangs invitingly above the front door.

The narrow, low-ceilinged bar is not, however, how you might expect it to be. It has a haphazard, makeshift feel about it, faintly reminiscent of a beach cabin with its cheap wood panelling and Formica-topped tables. Indeed there is much here that is plastic or fake, cheap and cheerful, yet the overriding impression is of its raucous good humour amid the clatter of dominoes and the babble of conversation. There is a dartboard and mini TV to add to the mix.

Off the bar and up a few steps is a good separate family room, while the lounge to the rear of the pub is plush and predictable, with comfortable seating, subdued lighting and no surprises. It's adequate though.

The Boat caters well with starters, steaks, scampi, fish, pies, all with a choice of chips, jackets or roast potatoes, curry, chicken, salads including prawn platter, chip butties and other sandwiches, daily specials chalked on the blackboard and some kids' specials – assuming kids only eat burgers, sausages or fish fingers. Sunday lunches are particularly good value and popular with the locals.

Somehow the Boat just sort of clicks, its overall effect greater than the sum of its parts.

BROOKFOOT
Red Rooster

OFF THE TOWPATH
Tel: (0484) 713737
*123 Elland Road (A6025),
Brookfoot, Brighouse, W. Yorks,
100 yards from the Calder &
Hebble, midway between Ganny
and Brookfoot locks. Accessible
from both*

✗   rolls lunchtime

🛏

🍺   **Marstons Pedigree Bitter,
Merrie Monk; Theakstons Best
Bitter, XB; Samuel Smith's
Museum Ale; Old Mill
Traditional Bitter; Clarks
Burglar Bill's Bitter; Timothy
Taylor's Landlord, Ram Tam;
guest beers; Thatchers Cider
(H)**

Compact and friendly roadside local, over 100 years old, part of the TFC Inns group. Mini beer festival and Good Beer Guide regular, with beers chalked on blackboard with gravities and prices. Purists' pub, landlord once assistant to Timothy Taylor's head brewer. Extension planned, including restaurant.

CALDER GROVE
Navigation

Tel: (0924) 274361
*Broad Cut Road, Calder Grove,
nr. Wakefield, W. Yorks;
canalside, just below Short Cut
Top Lock, Calder & Hebble*

✗   lunchtime

🛏

🍺   **Tetley Mild, Bitter; Trough
Wild Boar**

Although the city of Wakefield has many fine pubs, most are not particularly close to the canal. The Navigation, just outside the city, is a fine canal pub and a pleasant oasis between the rather grey and drab environs of Horbury and Wakefield itself.

This simple one-room pub is situated in the shadows of a handsome, imposing railway viaduct, and heralded by an attractive tree-lined stretch of canal and a lock. Its well-developed canal frontage features an extensive beer garden which runs down to the water's edge and contains swings and slides for children. Originally the navigation's course ran to what is now the rear of the pub, so the front door was once the back.

Today the Navigation is a good, reassuringly traditional pub, sturdy of build and chunky of beam. To the right as you enter is a pleasant little corner bar with a set of handpumps. Tucked

ELLAND
Barge and Barrel

Tel: (0422) 373623
*Park Road (A6025), Elland, W.
Yorks. Canalside opposite Elland
Wharf, Calder & Hebble*

✗ lunchtime

🍴

◎

🍺 **Marstons Pedigree Bitter,
Owd Rodger; Timothy
Taylor's Landlord; Oak Best
Bitter, Tyke Bitter, Old Oak;
guest beers**

This is a large, plush, four-roomed Victorian-style free house, comfortable and roomy, with a central island bar with lots of polished wood and leaded glass. A separate room leads off from the main concourse, and canal maps and paintings adorn the walls. There is a fine fireplace in the front room, and a bar billiards table stands in the public bar. However, what makes the pub really special is its commitment to tradition and its typical Yorkshire brand of homespun warmth and friendliness, nowhere better demonstrated than its fine range of traditional beers – often as many as ten of them (six regulars and four guest beers). West Riding Tyke Bitter, the "house" beer, is brewed under licence by the Oak Brewery at Heywood.

The Barge and Barrel is well aware of its historical and trade links with the canal, unlike some canal pubs which fail to acknowledge its existence. It is reflected in the menu. "Tom Puddings" was the name given to the scores of small tow boats which once carried coal from the great coalfields of Yorkshire to the power stations. The name lives on at the Barge and Barrel, but not in marine form. Instead it now appears on the menu and describes another proud tradition – two big Yorkshire puddings with slices of roast beef, all covered in thick onion gravy. You can also tuck into a Lock Keeper's Lunch or Bargee's Tea. Hot meals are available every lunchtime, and every evening between 5 and 8 pm, except Sundays. Traditional Sunday lunches are also served.

The Barge and Barrel doesn't forget families either – unlike the austere station waiting rooms which pass for children's rooms in many pubs, this one is thoughtful and well appointed, and even contains a "ball pool" which turns out to be a bed of soft spongy balls piled high upon which kids with energy to burn and a kamikaze instinct can hurl themselves like lemmings on speed, until sated and without fear of injury.

Colliers Arms

Tel: (0422) 372007
66 Park Road (A6025), Elland, W. Yorks. Canalside between Elland and Park Nook locks, Calder & Hebble

✗ lunchtime and evening

🕮

◉

🍺 **Samuel Smith's Old Brewery Bitter, Museum Ale**

The Colliers is a smart, two-roomed cottage pub, beamy and low ceilinged, with a canalside extension at the rear. The bar is traditional though quite plush for a bar, fully carpeted with wooden tables and lots of dark wood finish. An open stone fireplace, stained glass windows and lots of old black and white prints of the navigation add to the ambience. Bar stools line the wood-panelled bar, with a collection of water jugs for added embellishment. There is a TV in one corner and a small games area with a dartboard tucked away in the other.

The lounge is similar, perhaps a touch lighter and airier, with a collection of plates, pottery and bric-à-brac. Lighter and airier still is the small conservatory recently added to the back of the pub alongside the canal, ideal for the family. It has a "pine and cane" feel to it, and framed Lockmaster canal maps on the walls. It also contains the only poster I've ever seen, hand-written, advertising crisps, peanuts and snacks, under the dubious heading "Be a devil – have a nibble". It didn't really strike me as that sort of pub.

Alongside the conservatory is a small water-side beer garden with parasols and pleasant views, although the busy road at the front of pub means there's no prospect of a quiet drink.

The Colliers Arms has something for everyone. The beers of Sam Smiths are very tasty, the food excellent and reasonably priced. Available at lunchtimes (12–2) and on certain evenings (Thurs, Fri, Sat, Mon, 6–8), it includes sandwiches, starters and sweets, cold buffet, main courses and home made specials like steak and potato pie, vegetable lasagne, bacon and vegetable quiche and the ubiquitous chili. The three-course Sunday lunches are ludicrously cheap, with further reductions for kids.

FERRYBRIDGE
Golden Lion

Tel: (0977) 82132/83527
*The Square (off A1 on B6136),
Ferrybridge, W. Yorks. Canalside
by Ferrybridge lock and A1
viaduct, Aire & Calder*

✕ lunchtime and evening

🍴

⛵

🍺 **Tetley Bitter**

Standing defiantly in the vast shadows of the mighty A1 flyover across the River Aire, this imposing and interesting pub was once a coaching inn on the old Great North Road. Its multi-roomed interior is distinctive and quite unusual, refreshingly different from the open plan uniformity which we are increasingly being asked to accept.

The Golden Lion has at its heart a central island-style bar with leaded glass screens, serving most of the other rooms at various points. Surrounding the bar is a foyer, a kind of dark wood-panelled inner sanctum in which people can sit or stand and drink. It has a piano at one end, an organ and fruit machines at the other and wrought iron gates in the middle. Off the foyer lead a host of other rooms. At the back of the pub is the tap room, basic, airy and clean, with lino floor and a TV.

A room at the front does a splendid impersonation of a TV lounge/guest room in a seaside B&B. It has a ship's wheel and, of course, a TV. There is a dining room often housing a mini carvery, and a separate restaurant. You may have correctly deduced that food plays a significant part in life at the Golden Lion, with excellent hot and cold food available lunchtimes and evenings. Sunday lunchtimes are hectic, with two separate sittings. Advance booking is essential.

The gents' toilets (of which there are two, although one seemed purely decorative) are worthy of note, with white porcelain urinals and ornate marble tiles, reminiscent of the older parts of the London Underground.

The outdoor drinking area presents striking contrasts between the wide expanse of tranquil river in the foreground, the A1's ceaseless roar above and the menacing grey bulk of Ferrybridge power station's cooling towers beyond.

MIRFIELD
Navigation

Tel: (0924) 492476
Off Station Road, Mirfield, W.
Yorks. Canalside, near Bridge 18,
Calder & Hebble

✖ lunchtime

☺

⊟ **Whitbread Castle Eden,**
   Trophy Bitter

This lively, friendly two-roomed local has an atmosphere more reminiscent of a club than a pub. The main lounge is plush, comfortable, almost intimate if you discount the loud juke box. It has artexed walls, unusually ornate ceiling and yet more mulberry-coloured dralon upholstery, though this seems sturdier than most.

The other room leads off this, lets kids in and ought to be a lot nicer than it is. It looks beamy, cosy and inviting but suffers from being disconnected from any serving area. What ought to be disconnected are the juke box and the battery of fruit machines which line its walls and make it more like a trashy amusement arcade than a bar. This room is used by families and as an overspill for the lounge.

Predictable but good value pub grub is on offer, including grills, steak, chicken, chili (is there a pub that doesn't?), burgers, all with chips.

The Navigation is the best choice for boaters in Mirfield, with moorings right outside by its rear car park.

SOWERBY BRIDGE
Moorings

Tel: (0422) 833940
No. I Warehouse, Canal Basin
(off A58), Sowerby Bridge, W.
Yorks. Situated in Sowerby Bridge
basin, the terminus of the Calder
& Hebble navigation

✖ lunchtime and evening

☗

☺

⊟ **McEwan 80/−, Youngers**
   Scotch Bitter, Theakston XB;
   Moorhouse's Premier Bitter;
   regular guest beers and
   comprehensive range of
   foreign beers, mostly Belgian

The Moorings was opened in March 1978 following a lengthy and extensive restoration and conversion of formerly derelict canal warehousing originally dating from 1790. The result has been a spectacular success, as the Moorings has quickly established itself as one of the finest pubs on the northern canal network, host to the local canal society and CAMRA branch and with something to please or interest just about everyone. It's a regular in both the Good Beer Guide and the Good Pub Guide.

Distinctive from the outside, spacious and airy inside, the Moorings is comfortable and relaxing, with exposed stone walls, tile-top tables, rush seated stools and fabric covered seats.

It possesses an air of calm and timelessness, enhanced by high ceilings and big patio windows with views of the boatyard and canal basin outside. The bar contains a well-designed integral family room, sectioned off with a glass partition.

The pub serves a fine selection of handpulled traditional beers, hosts an annual "Beers from around the world" evening, and has built a reputation for its astonishingly wide range of bottled continental speciality beers, mostly Belgian, including Duvel, Chimay and other Trappist beers, Hoegaarden Wit, Liefmans Goudenband, De Koninck, Rodenbach and a host of lambic beers including kriek (cherry beer), frambozen (raspberries), cassis (blackcurrant) and a peach beer. There is a specially printed Belgian beer menu. The foreign beers are available for take-out. Meanwhile discerning whisky drinkers can choose from more than sixty single malt whiskies. You're equally well catered for if you want to eat, with imaginative bar food every lunchtime and evening including a "Lock Keeper's Lunch", consisting of a choice of three cheeses and a help-yourself selection of pickles, salads, fruits and wholemeal bread. At least one vegetarian meal is always available, and a kiddies' menu is also offered. Upstairs, a small but charming restaurant is open evenings except Sundays, and offers more panoramic views of the canal basin and surrounding hillside scenery.

Navigation

Tel: (0422) 831636
47 Chapel Lane, Sowerby Bridge, W. Yorks. Canalside at Bridge 1, just before the terminus

✕ lunchtime and evening

🕯

🍺 Tetley Bitter

If you're looking for a pub with real canal flavour, check out this splendidly "pubby" pub. From the car park beer garden overlooking the water, its benches dotted haphazardly around, to the delightfully traditional bar, it's a proper pub: warm, cosy and friendly with more than a whiff of canal atmosphere, enhanced by its popularity and long associations with canal travellers and its collection of Buckby cans and roses 'n' castles decor.

Although converted to a pub around 1770, the fine old stone building is considerably older than that. It has a beamed ceiling, some nice old wooden settles and lots of dark wood. A row of bar chairs – they're not really stools – faces the wood-panelled bar. The tiled floor here gives way to carpeting for the tables and seating area. The upholstery is, for once, not wine coloured but a very effective snooker-table green. The whole bar is lit by hanging lamps and miners' lanterns, and fairly bristles with character.

There is also a small and quite unusual side room, with a high step up to a bank of seating which serves as a tiny grandstand for watching epic encounters on the pool table in the pit below.

The menu is excellent and varied, with a wide range to suit all tastes and including one or two highly innovative options. It is divided into several sections: sandwiches including steak, chip butties and half pound of sausages such as Ellandale (beef and herb) and Pennine (lamb and mint); substantial snacks featuring Sri Lankan chicken curry, spare ribs and garlic rabbit; vegetarian including Many Bean stew, aubergine and cashew nut bake, Aviyal vegetable curry and others; and proper meals such as steaks and "Boeuf à la Tetleys" with Yorkshire pudding. On Tuesdays and Wednesday, steak and bake is an excellent value package for two people, with a choice of starters, 10 oz steak with baked potato and salad, and half litre of wine. Traditional Sunday lunches are also available and even the coffee – espresso and cappuccino – is "real".

TV's "Stay Lucky" with Dennis Waterman and Jan Francis was filmed in the basin, and the Navigation was the pub used in the series. With two fine (though very different) pubs and an Indonesian restaurant selling traditional beers including Timothy Taylors, the area around the terminus of the Calder & Hebble navigation at Sowerby Bridge is a place for enthusiasts of fine food and beer to linger and savour.

Puzzle Hall Inn

Tel : (0422) 835547
Hollins Mill Lane (off A58),
Sowerby Bridge, W. Yorks.
Rochdale canal, adjacent to
towpath close to terminus

✗ lunchtime and evening

🍴

🍺 **Wards Mild, Thorne Best Bitter, Kirby Strong Beer, Sheffield Best Bitter; Vaux Double Maxim**

The ambitious restoration of the Rochdale canal, from Sowerby Bridge across the Pennines into Manchester, will eventually complete a new canal ring to rival the best – a ring o' Roses. The major obstacle remains the few hundred obstinate yards of concrete that separate the termini of the Rochdale canal and the Calder & Hebble navigation.

As it is, the Puzzle Hall is stranded alongside the Rochdale's towpath overlooking a slightly run-down industrial part of this charming Calderdale town. Nevertheless, this historic local, reputedly the oldest pub in town, is worth a visit for its good beer and relaxed informal atmosphere. The building itself dates from the early seventeenth century, when it was a dwelling house. It became a licensed premises a century later, for the consumption of home-brewed ale. In 1905, Mrs Sylvia Platt had a brewery tower built for the brewing of Platt's of Sowerby Bridge's labelled beers. In the 1930s the pub was taken over by Wards brewery of Sheffield, which in turn became part of Vaux as did Darleys of Thorne, Yorkshire, whose beers are also available.

The Puzzle Hall is primarily a boozers' pub, plain and friendly. It has a small basic bar with a hotch-potch of different styles of decor and furnishing, including some wood panelling (in the plank rather than dark oak style), patterned top tables, burgundy upholstery and a TV in the corner. The lounge is removed from the serving area and contains a piano. There is a small car park beer garden. The Puzzle Hall hosts a folk club on Monday nights.

Bar snacks and hot meals include soup, garlic mushrooms, chili, chicken Kiev and various sandwiches and toasties. Traditional beers are, of course, central to the pub's appeal and it offers a fine (though varying) range of Vaux group beers which are not too easily found along the towpaths of England – a good enough reason for a visit.

STANLEY FERRY
Ferry Boat

Stanley Ferry, nr. Wakefield, W. Yorks. Canalside at Stanley Ferry marina, Aire & Calder

✗ lunchtime and evening, seven days a week

🍴

🍺 **Theakstons Best Bitter, XB, Old Peculier, Youngers No. 3, Scotch Bitter**

Built on the same principle (if not the same scale) as Sydney Harbour bridge, which it predates by a century, Stanley Ferry aqueduct is a monumental structure which was first traversed by boat in 1839. Although the canal is now diverted over the new concrete aqueduct, opened in 1981, the original and much more impressive one still stands alongside in all its gaudily-painted glory, its intricate metallic lacework still intact.

With a swing bridge, fine marina and boatyard, museum and pub, Stanley Ferry is an interesting point at which to moor and explore. The Ferryboat Inn was skilfully and sympathetically fashioned from an old canal warehouse, with great attention to detail. The split level barn-like (in size and style) interior is decidedly bucolic, with lots of exposed brickwork and wood finish. Bar meals are served from an old market-style cart in the corner. Hot beef baguettes, salads, lasagne, vegetarian meals, filled jacket potatoes, starters and sweets all appear on the menu but its real heart are the wonderful Yorkshire pudding dinners – puddings eight inches in diameter filled to overflowing with a choice of roast meats, hotpot, chicken chasseur and onion gravy. There is also a delightful informal restaurant upstairs – the Tom Puddings restaurant – with a good reputation locally.

The pub also has a nautical feel about it. A ship's wheel hangs from the ceiling, with others mounted above the bar, illuminated by lamps sunk into portholes and the fully carpeted drinking area is lit by ship's lanterns. Giant poster-size sepia prints recall bygone days on the waterways. Outside there are pleasant views of the river, marina and aqueducts from the pleasant riverside beer garden.

The Ferryboat is extremely popular with all ages, catering well for the beer drinker, diner and family alike. At the time of visiting there was uncertainty over its future management. As with so many of these warehouse conversions (of which this is a particularly good example), there is a thin line between integrity and the total exclusion zone of crass commercialism. It is to be hoped that whoever ultimately winds up with the tiller manages to steer well away from the lamentable latter course.

The George Inn,
Bathampton

John Simpson

KENNET & AVON CANAL

ASHBY CANAL

The Ashby leaves the Coventry canal at Marston Junction near Bedworth and winds aimlessly north on a fairly rural course to its terminus north of Snarestone, skirting Hinckley and Market Bosworth on the way.

MARSTON JABBETT
Corner House Hotel

OFF THE TOWPATH
Nuneaton Road (B4112)

✗

🏠

☺

🍺 Marston Burton Best Bitter,
Pedigree Bitter, Owd Rodger

One hundred and fifty yards south of Bridge 5, the Corner House Hotel is a large pub with a public bar, vast wood-panelled lounge and small garden with assorted pets. There are good bar meals. The games room doubles as a family room, and houses bar billiards and table football.

HINCKLEY
Lime Kilns

Tel : (0455) 631158
Watling Street (A5), nr Hinckley,
Leics. Canalside at Bridge 15

✗ lunchtime and evening

🏠

☺

🍺 Marstons, Burton Best Bitter,
Pedigree Bitter

At the turn of the century, this handsome pub was known as the Plough. But the adjoining bridge was already known as Lime Kilns Bridge in recognition of the lime extracted from the surrounding fields, and soon the pub too adopted the name.

Its frontage, originally old cottages, has remained more or less intact, unlike the interior which was converted to a single L-shaped brick-finish bar in major alterations six years ago, as it single-mindedly targeted the family market. Fortunately it is large enough to accommodate several distinct areas including a lively friendly bar, which rescues it from the open-plan anonymity which afflicts many single-room pubs. Access from the rear of the pub and its large, splendid canalise garden is somewhat unusual – up a flight of stairs.

The Waterside Restaurant downstairs over-looks the canal and offers high quality English/ French cuisines, while good home-cooked bar food is also available at all times except Sunday evenings, and features steam and grills, chilis and curries, fish dishes and a self-serve salad bar.

The Lime Kilns caters for a very broad trade. With an almost total lack of housing nearby, it relies on the canal and, principally, the A5 trunk road by which it stands for its custom. The outcome is usually plenty of space for mooring but precious little for car parking. Families are welcome at the pub and in the garden.

The Dundas Arms, Kintbury

KENNET & AVON CANAL

RIVER AVON

The Avon is divided administratively into the Lower and Upper Avon, the boundary being the Bridge Inn at Offenham. The river leaves the Severn at Tewkesbury and heads eastwards through Evesham and Pershore towards Stratford upon Avon, where the Stratford canal is joined.

BARTON
Cottage of Content

OFF THE TOWPATH
Barton, Warwicks

✖ lunchtime and evening

🍺 **Whitbread Flowers Original
and IPA**

Look for the permanent caravan site on the south bank. The pub is just beyond it, one hundred yards from the river. It is a picturesque fifteenth century cottage pub with low beams and flagstone floor. There is varied and interesting food at all times. Ideally, drink at the Bull's Head and eat at the Cottage of Content – they're less than a mile apart.

BIDFORD-ON-AVON
Bull's Head

OFF THE TOWPATH
High Street, Bidford-on-Avon,
Warwicks

✖ lunchtime

🛏

🍺 **Whitbread Best Bitter, Flowers
Original**

Five minutes walk from rare free moorings below Bidford Bridge. It's a friendly, clean, comfortable pub with low ceiling, front snug, larger rear bar and garden. Excellent pub, recommended stop.

PERSHORE
Millers Arms

OFF THE TOWPATH
8 Bridge Street,
(0386) 553864

✖

🍺 **Adnams Broadside; Hall &
Woodhouse Badger Best
Bitter; Wadworth 6X**

Two hundred yards from Pershore Old Bridge in Bridge Street is the Millers Arms, an open-plan multi-level pub with lots of wooden dividers and a good range of beers. Lunchtime food includes curry and chips and vegetable spring rolls. Evening meals in summer only.

STRATFORD-UPON-AVON
Dirty Duck

Tel: (0789) 297312
Waterside. On the north bank in central Stratford

✗ lunchtime and evening

🍴

🍺 **Whitbread Flowers Original**

Famous theatrical pub now officially known as the Dirty Duck rather than the Black Swan, although both names are displayed outside. The building is part-Elizabethan, and the mulberry tree outside is reputedly over three hundred years old. Supposedly the Bard himself sat beneath it while musing over a sonnet or two, but then there's hardly anywhere in Stratford where he didn't.

The pub's proximity to the Royal Shakespeare Theatre is reflected in its clientele (a mixture of actors both famous and aspiring, stage staff and tourists), in its decor, especially in the Theatre Bar which is plastered with framed signed black-and-white photos of actors, and even in the menu, which starts outrageously with "Prologue" (which turns out to be a good selection of starters), continues with "Act I" and "Act II", the main courses, and ends preposterously with "All's Well that Ends Well", the grandest title yet devised for a list of desserts! The whole is grouped under the claim "Theatre of the Gastronomic Arts". You may be more interested to know that it consists of bar snacks including sandwiches, pies and macaroni cheese, and a restaurant menu featuring steaks, chicken chasseur, various fish dishes and house specials like smoked salmon and scrambled eggs. Food is available at all times, and there is a separate split-level wood-panelled restaurant.

Otherwise the pub has just two rooms: the Theatre Bar with wooden pews, tapestry-effect seat covers, oak panelling and an open fire with a brass canopy and a small centre bar with a wooden floor and chunky cross-beam. It seats only eight or nine, although there is standing room. The raised servery spans the full width of the room and faces the double doors which lead out to the splendid patio overlooking the river. Moorings are on the opposite bank, so you either have to cross at the bridge or use the old chain ferry to cross the river. Hardy down-to-earth canal folk with lingering doubts about being swamped by precious theatrical "dahlings" should be reassured; the Dirty Duck attracts a much broader mix than that.

TEWKESBURY

OFF THE TOWPATH

At the junction of the rivers Avon and Severn, the historic town of Tewkesbury has many fine pubs, with the town centre just a short walk from the rivers. The **Berkeley Arms** in Church Street is a seventeenth century pub of real character, offering Wadworths 6X, Farmers Glory and in winter Old Timer, along with lunchtime food.

The **Black Bear**, said to be the oldest inn in Gloucestershire and dating back to 1308, is a rambling rabbit warren of a pub, low beamed and half-timbered, with family room and a garden leading down the river. It offers Whitbread WCPA, Flowers Original and PA, guest beers in summer and food from snacks to full meals lunchtimes and evenings. Other historic inns worth visiting include the **Bell** in Church Street, a twelfth century pub opposite the abbey, and the **Hop Pole**, associated with Dickens' Pickwick Papers.

WELFORD-ON-AVON
Four Alls

Tel: (0789) 750228
Binton Road, Welford-on-Avon, Warwicks. Riverside at Binton Bridges

✗ lunchtime and evening

🍴

◎

🍺 Marstons Pedigree Bitter; Flowers Original; Hook Norton Best Bitter

A King I rule over all
A parson I pray for all
A soldier I fight for all
A farmer I pay for all

Thus is explained this old pub's name, preserved in the stained glass of the bar. Built in the middle seventeenth century, it began as a farmhouse, becoming a tollhouse for traffic passing over the bridge. The tollkeeper was known as the Lord of the Isles after the three islands in the river. It only became a licensed house at the turn of the century, and before the war was apparently known as "The Knees and Nipples", in reference to the licensee's four desirable daughters.

In recent times the pub has become more famous as a family pub, and for its first class though slightly pricy food. A complete range is available, all day every day, from sandwiches to three-course meals and including a vegetarian selection, good children's menu and Sunday lunches. Dishes like steak au poivre and escalope of pork in cider sauce are characteristic of the menu.

The large rear "family garden", not riverside, has wooden tables and children's play equipment starring a large bouncy castle. The dimly-lit interior consists of a central bar flanked by two dining areas. A grandfather clock acts as doorman inside the front door, and shelves sag under learned tomes. Assorted prints and photos share the wall space with artifacts like saws and a musket. Light wood panels, wooden settles and mock rustic exposed brickwork do their best to make it pub-like, but there's no disguising that food rules here. Nevertheless, there is a good choice of beers, and you won't feel out of place if you don't eat.

WYRE PIDDLE
Anchor Inn

Tel: (0386) 552799
Evesham Road (B4084), Wyre Piddle, nr Pershore, Worcs. Riverside north bank at Wyre Piddle

✘ lunchtime and evening

🍴

🍺 **Whitbread Flowers Original, IPA**

The Anchor actually reverses the trend by being even better inside than the exterior suggests. It's a quaint, vibrant little pub dating from the seventeenth century and providing beautiful views from its dining area across the river and Vale of Evesham beyond. Its pretty garden with white garden furniture slopes down to the Avon through a series of levels. The only moorings in the village are here and space can be quite competitive in summer when the pub is very popular.

The atmosphere in the Anchor is wonderfully friendly and homely, cosy and intimate, particularly in the delightful dim snug with its inglenook fireplace and low-beamed ceiling, sagging under more than three hundred years of service. It has a leaded glass door and seats about twenty or so, at a push. The walls are dotted with pen and ink drawings, pictures and heraldic shields and crests, and the servery crowned with an arrangement of hops, which adds aroma and colour to the room, and presumably acts as a preservative too.

Next door is a farmhouse cottage of a lounge, light, airy and comfortable. The pub's food has a deservedly good reputation, with a bar menu and restaurant menu, the latter confined to the restaurant. The bar menu includes sandwiches, ploughman's with assorted cheeses, home-made soups, pasta dishes and a range of desserts, while various steaks in sauces and fresh fish dishes using trout, salmon and halibut all appear on the full menu. The Anchor has earned places in the Good Beer Guide and the Good Pub Guide.

BIRMINGHAM CANAL NAVIGATIONS (BCN)

The BCN is the collective term for the fascinating and intricate complex of over 100 miles of waterways criss-crossing the heart of Birmingham and the Black Country. In addition to the Main Line from Birmingham to Wolverhampton, other canals include the Dudley No. 1 and No. 2 canals, the Titford, Wyrley & Essington, Tame Valley, Walsall and Rushall canals, plus a host of branches, arms, loops, tunnels and other contortions. Waterways giving access to the BCN are the Stratford canal, Worcester & Birmingham canal and Birmingham & Fazeley canal (all via central Birmingham), the Staffs & Worcester via Wolverhampton and the Stourbridge canal via the Dudley canal.

There can scarcely be a pub in the entire region that isn't close to a canal; yet the legendary quality of pubs in the Black Country generally is not reflected in its canalside pubs: most of the best and most famous examples are off the towpath.

BIRMINGHAM
Prince of Wales

OFF THE TOWPATH
Tel: (021) 643 9460
84 Cambridge Street,
Birmingham B1. Near Cambrian
Wharf at top of Farmers Bridge
locks. Moor at Cambrian Wharf,
walk straight past the Long Boat
pub, turn right onto Cambridge
Street. The pub is on the left

✗ lunchtime and early evening

🍺 **Ansells Mild, Bitter; Ind Coope Burton Ale; Tetley Bitter**

A classic Birmingham pub (and there aren't many), down-to-earth and unpretentious. Saved from demolition as all else around falls before the awesome new International Convention Centre complex. Now the only old building in a riot of redevelopment, it stands defiantly alone as part of the new complex's rear walls. Entry from the street via its side corridor transports you instantly into another world. Hot and cold snacks are available lunchtimes and early evenings. Close to the Birmingham Repertory Theatre.

BIRMINGHAM, WINSON GREEN
Bellefield

OFF THE TOWPATH
Tel: (021) 558 0647
Winson Street, Winson Green,
Birmingham. 100 yards south of
Main Line

✗ lunchtime and evening

🍺 **Davenports Mild, Bitter; occasional cider**

Basic Victorian back-street boozer with some interesting features including an unusual ceiling and tiled lounge. Derelict Samuel White's brewery at the rear. Asian licensee offers unusual range of Asian snacks (including samosas).

BRIERLEY HILL
Bell

Tel: (0384) 72376
Delph Road (B4172), Brierley
Hill, W. Midlands. Bottom of
Delph Nine locks, where Dudley
No. 1 canal joins the Stourbridge
canal

✗ lunchtime and evening

🏨

🍺 **Holt, Plant & Deakin Mild, Bitter, Entire, Celebration**

The Stourbridge and Dudley No. 1 canals join at Brierley Hill, the authentic Black Country, after which the latter canal climbs immediately through a flight of eight locks, known, of course, as the "Delph Nine", not for reasons of impenetrable Black County perversity but because the middle seven were replaced by a new line of six in 1858, and the old name simply stuck. With its bywashes tumbling over a series of waterfalls it must be one of the most appealing urban flights on the inland waterways network.

The Bell is located by the bottom lock of the

flight and mooring outside would be impossible, so a towpath walk will be necessary to enjoy the heartwarming Black Country welcome of this popular early Victorian pub. It's typical HP&D house, with open fires, bric-à-brac including old photographs and paintings, mirrors and figurines, and a cosy, narrow, "granny's front parlour" lounge with wooden tables and a wall-mounted collection of plates. The bar is especially popular with boating visitors, many of whom have enjoyed an evening of off-the-cuff entertainment when piano playing regulars have been coaxed to the pub's ivories.

The Bell features regularly in the CAMRA Good Beer Guide and the Good Pub Guide, as well as being listed by Routier. Its food is a firm favourite in the area and also available for take-out. It includes starters, home-made specialities like chili and lasagne, and Holt's famous hot sandwiches such as hot pork and stuffing on crusty bread. Food is available lunchtimes and evenings except Sundays.

There are a Post Office, telephone and water point nearby.

Just 400 yards east of the bottom of the Delph locks in Delph Road is The Vine (Bull & Bladder), a famous unspoilt Black Country boozer and the Batham's brewery tap. On its facade is the quotation, "Blessings of your heart, you brew good ale" from Shakespeare's "Two Gentlemen of Verona". Handpumped Batham's Mild and Bitter and food including seafood and snacks are available.

Woodside Inn

OFF THE TOWPATH
Pedmore Road (A4036), Brierley Hill. 200 yards from Woodside Bridge and visible from it, Dudley No. I canal. Near Merry Hill Centre

✕ lunchtime and evening

⋈
🍺 Fullers ESB; Marston Pedigree Bitter; Moorhouse's Pendle Witches Brew; Youngs Special

A pleasant but unexceptional building but superb beers and food. As well as the beers listed there is at least one traditional mild and other guest beers, including Belgian speciality brew Hoegaarden Wit on draught. Good value food includes mountainous portions and vegetarian options. Good moorings on the Netherton side of the bridge.

LANGLEY Brewery Inn

Tel: (021) 544 6467
Station Road (B4182), Langley, W. Midlands. Canalside at Langley Green Bridge, Titford Canal

✕ lunchtime
🍺 Holt Plant & Deakin Mild, Bitter, Entire (H)

Re-opened by Black Country brewers Holt Plant & Deakin in September 1984, the Brewery Inn is a familiar stopping-off point for users of the BCN, providing heart-warming relief from the grim surrounding moonscape of disused or flattened factories and monstrous heavy industry.

It dates back to 1860 when it was known as the Bridge, and then became the New Inn. It became the brewery tap for Holt Plant & Deakin, a formerly defunct Black Country brewery the name of which was revived by the Allied Breweries group to which it now belongs. Although the traditional mild and bitter have always been brewed at the group's Tetley Walker plant in Warrington, the flagship brew Entire used to be brewed here until the late 1980s when production was switched to their new Wolverhampton site – with some loss of quality according to some local drinkers.

The pub's restoration has been tastefully done in traditional Black Country style, all cluttered, cosy and country kitchen. It is a tribute to the care and attention taken in the renovation that it seems to have evolved naturally rather than being designed that way. It features a roomy tap room and a kitchen/parlour with an original cast iron kitchen range, Victorian furniture and bric-à-brac. Separated by ornate snob screens, the two rooms have open fires which are actually used in winter.

Lunchtime snacks include crusty sandwiches filled with hot pork, stuffing and gravy or hot beef or turkey, cold sandwiches like cheese, onion and black pudding double-deckers, and hot soup with crusty bread.

NETHERTON
Dry Dock

Tel: (0384) 235369
Windmill End, Netherton, Dudley. Canalside at Windmill End, between the Bumblehole Branch and the Boshboil Arm

✘ lunchtime and evening

🍺 **Ind Coope Burton Ale, Holt Plant & Deakin Mild, Lumphammer (H)**

The Dry Dock was one of the earlier ventures of the Little Pub Company's burgeoning chain of idiosyncratic theme pubs, first surfacing in the mid 1980s, and by comparison with some that followed (see the Pie factory at Tipton), seems almost staid and sober. Its theme is, of course, the canal which runs behind the pub. Perhaps the most immediate of its many striking aspects is the central serving area, cunningly fashioned from the hollowed out six-plank hull of a salvaged Runcorn narrowboat. But as in any LPC pub, the attention to detail is immense and the gimmicks fly thick and fast.

Regular features include Lumphammer, a traditional but unremarkable beer specially brewed for the group by Allied at Burton, and awesome, legendary Desperate Dan pies, monstrous concoctions full of meat, potato and vegetables and complete with pastry Viking horns. They are as much an endurance test as a meal, and finishing one will earn you a personalised Glutton Certificate. More conventional lines of catering are available at all times, including a Black Country speciality, faggots 'n' paes, as it is spoken and spelt locally. The printed menu urges "Please drink harder and faster. Thank you." Meanwhile, the "Noble and Ancient Society of Little People" are another fun part of the manufactured mystique surrounding the pub. They have their own secret sign language, enabling them to say things like "Hello" surreptitiously, "the wife is with me and I was not here earlier" and "the person to my right is a tax inspector" or similar. On the wall a poster proclaims "A pint of lump is yer only man", a customised adaptation of Flan O'Brien's famous ode to Irish stout. In mitigation the LPC's founder, one Colm "Mad" O'Rourke, is, in case you hadn't guessed, Irish.

The pub's two-room interior is home to ornate tiled walls, gaudy paintwork and a plethora of bizarre mechanical devices straight from the Heath Robinson catalogue which all add to the unique atmosphere. The pub is clearly visible from the canal, although direct access is via a steep and tricky grassy bank. The grand west portal of Netherton tunnel is close by, as is the tall tower of Cobb's Engine House, which used to pump water from the nearby mines to prevent flooding. It is said that if its engine ever missed a beat, a thousand women's hearts missed one too.

Make of the Dry Dock what you will. It's brash, unashamedly gimmicky and brazenly contrived but never dull, and you have to concede it's done with style, humour and a sense of fun. That something entirely original has been created is beyond dispute.

OLD HILL
Three Furnaces

OFF THE TOWPATH
Old Hill, W. Midlands. 100 yards
west of Waterfall Lane bridge,
Dudley No. 2 canal

🍺 **Banks's and Hanson's Mild**
and Bitter

Fine unspoilt Black Country pub with small rooms leading off a central passageway in the local idiom. Banks's real ales served by their ubiquitous metered electric pumps.

RUSHALL
Manor Arms

Tel: (0922) 24491
*Park Road, Daw End, Rushall,
Walsall. Canalside, Daw End
Bridge, Rushall canal*

✗ lunchtime and evening

🍴

🍺 **Banks's Mild, Bitter**

Tucked away among the soulless expanses of Walsall's northern approaches stands this gem of a pub, hidden from the sight of all but canal users in an oasis of rural tranquillity.

The Manor Arms is yet another "oldest pub in England" but its claim seems suspect even for this genre! In structure it is predominantly eighteenth century, and was first licensed in 1895, selling ale to passing bargees. Today it remains truly unspoilt, with an unhurried, timeless quality. Scrubbed-top tables, quarry tiles, beams, horse brasses and plates blend to create an intimate and inviting atmosphere. The low ceilings and irregular layout are a non-conformist's and traditional pub lover's delight (which must make it the worst nightmare of many a modern pub architect).

What's Brewing cartoonist Bill Tidy, a former Walsall resident and Manor Arms regular, featured the pub in a TV documentary and some examples of his work still adorn the bar walls. There is no bar counter as such, the staff stand among the customers, dispensing most of the beers from an unusual bank of handpumps mounted on a shelf in the end wall. The cosy bar leads off to a narrow corridor where drinkers often congregate, getting their drink through a serving hatch. The remaining rooms, all in harmony with the pub's old and rustic appeal, lead off the corridor.

Food is available at all times and the quality and quantity of meals are such that the dining areas (and their occupants) fill up very quickly. The steaks are particularly renowned locally, as is the speciality carvery on Fridays.

There is a canalside beer garden for summer time and no less than three real fires to make it glow in winter. At the terminus of the canal, via the Daw End and Anglesey branches, lies Chasewater reservoir, which has a number of attractions including a steam railway.

The pub is one of Bass's recent sell-offs, now offering the rare chance to drink Banks's beers from handpumps.

TIPTON
Fountain

Tel: (021) 520 8777
Owen Street, Tipton. Canalside near Factory Road and Owen Street bridges, BCN Main Line (Birmingham level). Moorings are limited outside the pub, so try Coronation Gardens on the other side of Owen Street bridge

✗ lunchtime

ᕍ **Holt Plant & Deakin Mild, Bitter, Entire (H)**

The Fountain was once the headquarters of William Perry, famed Black Country prize fighter known as the "Tipton Slasher". Originally a canal boatman, he became champion in 1850 and held the title for seven years. His print can be found in the lounge, ironically facing one of that paragon of serenity and beauty, the Mona Lisa. Neither, I feel, are the originals.

Small, cosy, narrow and dimly lit, this friendly Black Country pub bears all the typical Holt Plant & Deakin hallmarks, for those familiar with that praiseworthy Black Country operation. Its distinctive cluttered impression is enhanced by ornaments, prints, bric-à-brac and sections of exposed brickwork.

Good home-made food is available (lunchtimes only, except Sundays), from hot snacks like the Black Country institution of hot pork sandwiches with stuffing and crusty bread, to full meals like "Beef in Entire", a beef carbonnade utilising the locally brewed beer.

Unfortunately, redevelopment plans involving the closure of Factory Road and the creation of a new marina complex threaten the demolition of the old stables and other buildings, leaving this Grade II listed building standing alone like a last tooth in an empty gum.

OFF THE TOWPATH

While in the Tipton area, there is an astounding pub which everyone should at least witness. Five minutes walk from Factory Bridge on the BCN Main Line (at T-junction head south along Hurst Lane/Bloomfield Road) is **Mad O'Rourke's Pie Factory**, Hurst Street, Tipton (021 557 1402). It's way beyond mortal powers of description. One of the Little Pub Company chain (see the Dry Dock at Netherton), it is a shrine to pigs, pies and monumental attention to detail. Mad O'Rourke is the eccentric (and now extremely wealthy) Irish entrepreneur who set up the group. Food is available every session, and includes LPC's speciality, Desperate Dan pies. Lumphammer is brewed for the group by Allied at Burton.

The Pie Factory is an experience you should have, though not necessarily repeat. Make of it what you will.

WOLVERHAMPTON
Great Western

OFF THE TOWPATH
Tel: (0902) 351090
Sun Street (off A4124),
Wolverhampton. 50 yards from
the Main Line, close to Horseley
Fields junction with the Wyrley &
Essington canal, the main railway
station and the old BWB Broad
Street depot. Next to the old low
level station

✘ lunchtime

🍴

🍺 **Holden's Mild, Black Country
Bitter, Special Bitter, Stout
Batham Bitter**

Although close to the canal, access from the canal is via a covered, arched and tiled walkway which is easy to miss. Don't – this is THE stop for central Wolverhampton. Since its revitalisation in 1987, it has quickly established itself as a firm favourite, featured in the Good Beer Guide and finalist in CAMRA's 1988 national Pub of the Year awards. Good range of Black Country beers, excellent value, hearty, no frills home cooking. A recent extension has changed the atmosphere into something more akin to a working men's club.

The Ostrich Inn, Bristol

KENNET&AVON CANAL

BIRMINGHAM & FAZELEY CANAL

A short waterway running from central Birmingham where it connects with the Tame Valley canal at Salford Junction and the Grand Union via the Digbeth Branch at Aston Junction. Its course passes the sci-fi Gravelly Hill interchange (Spaghetti Junction) and Birmingham's northern suburbs, skirting Sutton Coldfield on its way to Fazeley near Tamworth and its junction with the Coventry canal.

BIRMINGHAM
Bartons Arms

OFF THE TOWPATH
High Street, Aston, Birmingham.
Three quarters of a mile west
of the bottom of Aston locks

✗ lunchtime

◁ **M&B Mild, Brew XI,**
   Springfield Bitter

A longish walk, but worth it to witness the splendour of one of the best-preserved Edwardian pubs in the country, sparkling in the bizarre setting of one of the more soulless concrete expanses of inner city. Stained glass, ornate tile work and snob screens stud the cavernous interior. The clientele is lively, friendly and cosmopolitan. Live music most evenings.

Altogether a magnificent specimen.

BODYMOOR HEATH
Dog and Doublet

Bodymoor Heath, Warwicks.
Canalside between Double Bridge
and Cheatles Farm Bridge, next
to the lock

✗ lunchtime and evening

🍴

☺

◁ **M&B Mild, Brew XI; Draught**
   Bass

Pubs on the Birmingham & Fazeley canal tend to reflect the canal itself – fairly bland and unremarkable. The Dog and Doublet is about the best of a pretty ordinary bunch, not least because the M&B beers (should your situation dictate that you stay away from the Bass) are, unusually, handpumped which helps raise them a smidgeon from their customary electric-pumped mediocrity.

Much of the pub's original eighteenth-century structure is retained, making it one of only a handful of surviving relics of pre-industrial Midlands in the area. The thick real beams are heavily outnumbered by the fake matchstick variety, but at least they're there. The pub is attractively located and does offer fine views of the canal and the lock, with its canalside drinking area.

Inside there appears to have been some kind of role reversal between the bar and lounge. That which is officially known as the bar is uneventful and lounge-like. It has some tacky but fairly unobtrusive taped muzak and an incredibly intrusive fruit machine desecrating a recess with its piercing, listener-unfriendly electronic warbling. I am unashamedly neo-Luddite about these wretched machines, and not just because I don't know how to play them.

The "lounge" is of course bar-like, and quite

pleasant, with leaded windows, more beams (both types), and a cosy wooden settle. It is marginally less prone to be swamped by diners, who tend to dominate proceedings, sometimes scanning the place in eagle-eyed pursuit of signs of a table becoming vacant, to swoop and await their meals. The food is good – steaks and all the usual grills with chips or jackets, daily specials, sweets, a vegetarian menu which offers more than just vegetable lasagne (eg lentil bake) and a separate children's menu.

Despite its isolated setting the Dog is close to Drayton Manor Park and Zoo, the Belfry complex and Aston Villa's training ground. On sunny weekends and at Bank Holidays the overspill from this unholy trinity can turn the pub into something approaching Heathrow during a July strike by air traffic controllers, adding significantly to the waiting time for food.

The Anchor Inn, Great Bayford

FENLAND WATERWAYS

BRIDGEWATER CANAL

Built by the third Duke of Bridgewater and engineered in part by James Brindley, the historic Bridgewater canal was the forerunner of all modern canals.

Its main line runs from Preston Brook in Cheshire to Stretford in Manchester via Lymm, the outskirts of Warrington, Altrincham and Sale. One arm (once the main line) leads to Runcorn, whilst the Leigh Branch passes through Wordsley and Leigh before meeting the Leeds and Liverpool canal at Wigan.

EAGLE BROW
LYMM
Spread Eagle

OFF THE TOWPATH
Eagle Brow (A6144)

✗ lunchtime

🍺 Lees GB Mild, Bitter,
   Moonraker

Two hundred yards from Lymm Bridge along the Main Street, or alternatively one hundred yards from Whitbarrow aqueduct via the Under Bridge, is the Spread Eagle. It offers the delicious traditional beers of J. W. Lees' Manchester brewery, a rare and welcome treat for canal customers. This ornate old pub with its delightful tiny cosy snug also offers the rich, dark and powerful Moonraker in winter.

ECCLES
Packet House

corner Liverpool Road/Barton Road, Patricroft, Eccles, Gtr. Manchester. Canalside at Bridge 47, Leigh Branch

✗ lunchtime

🍺 Boddingtons Mild, Bitter

For beer drinkers the Golden Mile refers not to the seafront at Blackpool but the insalubrious main thoroughfare of the Manchester suburb of Eccles. Here stands a whole succession of rough and ready town pubs, a long line heaving with Holts and bristling with Boddingtons. At the end furthest from the centre of Eccles is the Packet House, a raucous, cheerful street-corner drinking den that's unashamedly basic and bright. The public bar has plastic-tiled floor, fluorescent strip lighting, tables topped with real Formica and assorted sports trophies. A TV and juke box vie for aural supremacy. The games room, with pool tables, dartboard and gaming machines, is the meeting place for a cross section of local youth, while the sardine-packed occupants of the tiny vault resemble an illicit gathering during Prohibition. Indeed the pub becomes the Packed House at weekends as the locals gather en masse to down copious volumes of Boddies – lager is conspicuous by its rarity.

The Packet House is not, admittedly, the first type of pub that springs to mind when considering the stereotypical canalside hostelry, but it is a good example of its kind and, travelling north, a convenient stop after miles of Trafford Park Industrial Estate.

LITTLE BOLLINGTON
Swan With Two Nicks

OFF THE TOWPATH
Park Lane (off A56), Little
Bollington, Gtr. Manchester

✗

🍺 Whitbread Castle Eden Ale,
Chesters Mild, Bitter

Accessible via Bollington underbridge, about ten minutes walk from the canal, the small attractive village of Bollington is home to this fine old country pub with beams and good food.

LITTLE BOLLINGTON
Old No. 3

Tel: (0925) 756115
Lymm Road, Little Bollington,
Gtr. Manchester

✗ lunchtime and evening

🕭

🍺 Courage Directors Bitter, John
Smith's Bitter

The pub's name refers back to old coaching days, when it was the third stagecoach stop on the journey from Liverpool to London. Built in 1886, it retains much of its original charm, with its attractive white-painted frontage with its flowers and hanging baskets, and etched windows bearing the legends "Yates Ales and Stouts" – long since defunct – and "Magnet Ales". Gleaming, polished wooden tables and old black and white prints foster a cosy atmosphere, compromised only by an intrusive gaming machine, the bane of many an otherwise unspoilt pub.

A good range of home cooked meals including seafood, "grizzly bear" steaks, vegetarian options and children's menu are available seven days a week, lunchtimes and evenings until 9 pm. There is a canalside beer garden and kids' play area complete with swings, slides and junior goal posts. An attractive black and white beamed outbuilding, probably once stables, acts as a convenient serving area for the garden. As the Bridgewater is not exceptionally well blessed with water points, the presence of one outside this quaint old pub makes an added inducement to stop.

Of course, no old pub would be complete without a resident ghost, and Ye Old No. 3 doesn't miss out.

LYMM
Bull's Head

32 The Cross (A6144)
Tel: (0925) 752831

✖ lunchtime

🛏

🍺 Hydes Mild, Bitter

The canal passes through the heart of Lymm, a fine historic town with cobbled streets and replica wooden stocks at the seventeenth century Lymm Cross. The Bull's Head was about 100 years old when the canal arrived, and the road in front was raised to create the hump-backed bridge. It was a common lodging place for boatmen who could stable their horses at the rear. It gains inclusion here for offering water-ways users the rare opportunity to drink Hydes traditional beers, and in good condition too, as well as more than fifty malt whiskies. Unfortunately, having been knocked about over the years, the pub's interior is merely pleasant and wholly unremarkable which is, in view of its attractive original exterior, downright disappointing. The comfortable, run of the mill lounge is predictability itself, incorporating brass and copper knick-knacks and plenty of the ubiquitous burgundy dralon fabric that threatens to take over the country. There is a plain, bright saloon bar and commendable toilets with everything in full working order, blissful release if you're entombed in a narrowboat.

Home-made bar meals and snacks are served every lunchtime, good though fairly mainstream. There are the usual gammon, plaice, scampi, open sandwiches, salads, filled baked potatoes, hot beef or steak, plus cakes, pies and specials which change daily. There is a small courtyard for outdoor drinking.

MOORE
Red Lion

OFF THE TOWPATH
Moore, Cheshire. Five minutes
walk into village from Bridge 7
(Moore Bridge)

✖ lunchtime

🍺 Greenalls Mild, Bitter

Typical village local, friendly, homely and hearty. Good food.

SALE
Bridge Inn

Tel : (061) 969 7536
Dane Road, Sale, Gtr.
Manchester. Canalside, Bridge 36

≠

🍺 Boddingtons Mild, Bitter

Travelling north, this is the last convenient canalside stop for acceptable hop-based refreshment before Manchester and the bleak expanses of the Trafford Park Industrial Estate.

The public bar has been pleasingly refurbished in a rough-hewn sort of way. The wood is plain, unvarnished, untreated, un-everything, and the ceiling ready nicotine-stained to recreate the mellowing process; instant authenticity. Tiled floor and bric-à-brac complete the scene.

The lounge is part separated from the bar by an unusual chest-high (if you're exactly the right height) division. In style it is similar to the bar, but a touch plusher and more decorative with a carpeted floor.

Lunchtime meals and snacks are available, but the Bridge has the rare distinction of an in-house chippy, open during chip shop hours, so Boddies and chips are on the menu. There are shops, a laundrette and railway station nearby.

The Anchor and Hope, Upper Clapton

CALDON CANAL

More accurately described as the Caldon branch of the Trent & Mersey canal, the Caldon leaves the latter at Etruria in deepest Potteries and heads east into the beautiful and secluded scenery of the Staffordshire moorlands and Churnet Valley. At Hazlehurst Junction the main line joins the River Churnet whilst the Leek branch terminates at the edge of that town.

CHEDDLETON
Black Lion

OFF THE TOWPATH
Cheddleton, Staffs. 100 yards
south of Bridge 42

✗ snacks

🍺 **Marstons Burton Bitter,**
   Pedigree Bitter

Situated opposite the church, this is a lovely traditional single-room local, welcoming and good and pubby. Once owned by Walkers Brewery of Leek.

CONSALL FORGE
Black Lion

Tel: (0782) 550294
Canalside at Consall Forge

✗ lunchtimes, afternoon when
   open, early evening

🍴

🍺 **Marstons Pedigree Bitter;**
   Ruddles County

One of the best-known and most photographed pubs on the waterways, the Black Lion can thank its stunning location for much of its far-reaching reputation. With the steeply wooded Churnet Valley hillside as its dramatic backcloth, it gazes out upon the canal, the River Churnet complete with bubbling weir and ornate arched stone bridge, and the beautiful country park scenery of the Staffordshire Moorlands. It is one of few pubs inaccessible by motor car – drivers who have bumped and bounced their way through Nature Park and country track have to park on the opposite bank and cross the bridge on foot. It has to be easier by boat, and much more fun.

However, having battled through to the pub, any brave orienteer who approaches it expecting to devour a tranquil pint in splendid isolation could be in for a rude awakening. In summer, at weekends and at holiday times the Black Lion becomes a busy and raucous people-magnet. You may have to rub backpacks with ramblers and hikers and jostle with family units on manoeuvres to get your pint, and be prepared to be patient for your food, which is plain and basic (sandwiches, everything-with-chips).

The same could be said of the interior. There are three rooms, a front bar and side room with cheap and cheerful decor, pink-washed bare walls, tiled floors and the type of chairs you find in schools or seaside cafés. The side room has a dartboard. The small parlour at the rear is the posh bit, with carpet and a TV. Plush it ain't, nor commercialised, and therein lies its appeal – apart, of course, from its superb setting. What the Black Lion has in abundance is individuality and there aren't too many left you can say that about.

DENFORD
Holly Bush

Denford, Staffs. Canalside near Bridge 38, Caldon Main Line, south of cross-over aqueduct

✘ snacks and full pub menu, all day. Children's menu

🍴

🍺 **Ind Coope Burton Ale**

One of several delightfully situated pubs on the Caldon in the beautiful countryside of the Staffordshire Moorlands, this exquisite seventeenth-century hostel flags down passers-by with its quaint black-and-white exterior, and fulfils its promise with a cosy, welcoming interior.

Just inside the front door there's a tiny entrance porch with an old Singer sewing machine. In the main bar you will immediately be confronted by two banks of three gleaming handpumps, all six bearing the identical clip of Ind Coope's fragrant, potent flagship brew, Burton Ale. There is an authentic beamed ceiling, tiled floor, a long wooden table and some wood-panelling behind the seating. Mirrors and prints decorate the walls, along with a plaque, level with the counter, which indicates the high water mark of the Denford flood in August 1987. There is an open fireplace to one side.

The lounge area is quite similar to the bar, only with a touch more of the parlour about it, with its old typewriter, clocks, prints, piano and generally clustered and homely feel.

Children are well catered for, with a family room at the rear and a separate children's menu. The choice for hungry grown-ups is predictable and mid-priced, including rolls, ploughman's lunches, steaks, pies, fish, gammon, pizza and chili, all with chips, and a limited selection of starters and sweets. Food is available just about whenever the pub is open, which is likely to be all day on Saturdays, holidays or simply if the sun is shining.

The Holly Bush is easily accessible from both the main line of the canal by which its stands, and the Leek Branch one hundred yards up the hill in the village of Longsdon. Moorings are plentiful.

MILTON
Miners Arms

Tel: (0782) 545510
125 Millrise Road, Milton, Stoke-on-Trent, Staffs

✗ lunchtime (not Wed, Sun), evening till 8 pm

🍴

🍺 Five Towns Bursley Bitter;
Draught Bass; Ruddles
County; Courage Directors;
Taylors Landlord; regular
guest beers

The Miners is a simple terraced estate pub in a not especially pretty party of town, homely and uncomplicated (rather than basic), and geared principally to beer sales and local trade. It's not obsessed with food (evening food finishes at 8 pm so they can get on with the business of being a pub) or dominated by loud music, and if that makes it sound like a throwback to a different time then it is certainly not meant as a criticism. It just means that the way is left clear to enjoy the excellent choice of traditional beers without intrusion or distraction. It's a free house so the range varies constantly, but those listed are generally available, including the Potteries-based Five Towns Bitter. The beers attract people from way beyond the pub's local catchment area.

Most of the food at the Miners is home-made, ranging from curries and chilis to pies like steak or cheese and onion. There are steaks, sandwiches and the ever-popular sausage and chips, burger and chips end of the menu. No food is available on Wednesday or Sunday lunchtimes.

Otherwise there isn't much else to say about the pub. It has a small friendly bar with dartboard and a cosy lounge decorated with advertising mirrors and brasses and plates depicting country and canal scenes and maps. Children are allowed in until 8 pm provided they are well behaved. Outside there is a beer garden with a barbecue area and children's play area. There are shops and various utilities nearby in Milton village.

CHESTERFIELD CANAL

From its junction with the River Trent at Stockwith, the Chesterfield runs south-west through the Nottinghamshire towns of Retford and Worksop, terminating at the latter. It was extensively restored in the 1960s and has an active canal society.

DRAKEHOLES
Griff Inn

Tel: (0777) 817206
Drakeholes, near Doncaster, S. Yorks. Canalside by entrance to Drakeholes tunnel

✗ lunchtime and evening

🍴

🛏

🍺 **Tetley Bitter; Whitbread Castle Eden Ale**

Across the road from the entrance to Drakeholes tunnel, this handsome building with its ivy-clad, castellated façade and heraldic pub sign was designed to blend in with the buildings on the nearby Wiseton Hall estate. Another good example of the style can be seen on the Man Face bridge, which shows a bearded old man's face smiling on one side of the bridge and stern on the other.

Over two hundred years old, this unusually shaped pub probably housed the workers who dug the tunnel. It still offers accommodation but to a very different type – it's expensive. Until recently it was known as the White Swan until facing chipped away to reveal red paintwork. Entering the pub into a porch with chair, table and giant yucca, you have a three-way choice – left for a rather pink and peachy restaurant, right for a large, neat and tidy conservatory-style lounge with a commemorative map of the Chesterfield canal, and straight ahead for a small, unusual hexagonal bar with an open fireplace, comfortable bench seating, several contrasting styles of pictures and paintings. The ambience is set by hotel reception-type piped muzak.

You can also drink outside on the large lawn in front of the pub, or at some canalside tables on the opposite side of the road. There is a crafts shop next door.

Mouthwatering bar menus are chalked on blackboards in bar and lounge. There is a pies menu with steak and ale, game, chicken and vegetable, a good vegetarian menu including spicy vegetable crumble, a fish menu, hot meals like beef goulash, lamb bourgignon, Griff hotpot, steaks, chops, liver and bacon casserole, filled jacket spuds, a children's menu, sandwiches, starters and sweets. There is also a special carvery in the Wedgwood Room on Saturday evenings and Sunday lunchtimes. The Griff Inn also caters for weddings and private functions. Impeccable but impersonal service is provided by ever-so-polite and well-trained staff in white shirts and black bow ties, all programmed to call you "sir" or "madam".

The beers are no more than adequate and not particularly exciting, and a hardy drinking den it ain't, but if you like a bit of local history or interesting architecture, a hint of style and elegance and wondrous food, you'll be happy here.

HAYTON
Boat Inn

Tel: (0777) 700158
Main Road (B1403), Hayton, Notts. Canalside near Hayton Low Bridge

✗ lunchtime and evening

☕

🛏

🍺 **Draught Bass; Whitbread Castle Eden Ale; occasional guest beers**

Situated in pleasant country surroundings in the village of Hayton near Retford, the Boat is an attractive and popular canalside emporium with a broad appeal and good amenities wherever you look – traditional beers, lovely beer garden with excellent kids' play facilities, good wide-ranging food, wedding parties and private functions, its own moorings and even accommodation in "cottage suites" across the courtyard. The toilet facilities are good too.

Food is at the heart of this slick and successful business operation. There is a grill menu, a good vegetarian menu featuring mushroom and nut fettucine, spinach and mushroom lasagne and vegetable chili, a roast of the day, large Yorkshire puddings filled with roast meat, peas and onion gravy, seafood platter, home-made steak and kidney pie, chicken wings in spicy sauce, hot roast meats on French bread and numerous other options.

The open-plan interior is a blend of new and old, basically a modern kitting out of an old black-beamed shell – plush upholstery and carpets, bar stools, some exposed brickwork columns, plenty of brasses and canal paintings. There is a lower level games area with pool table, dartboard, old style jukebox and gaming machines and some canalware. At the other end of the pub through a set of saloon-style swing doors is the Gallery dining area.

Only one obvious criticism – although a free house and a thriving, enterprising one at that, it has clearly hitched its wagon to the big brewers. The beers are well kept but when so many small brewers of tasty local beers are desperate for outlets it seems a shame to waste a good free house. A wider and more interesting range of traditional beers would surely do nothing but boost trade and spread the pub's net still wider.

RETFORD

OFF THE TOWPATH

As the canal twists pleasantly through the town of Retford, there are at least a couple of pubs worth mooring up for. The **Black Boy** in Moorgate (tel: (0777) 702758) is a pleasant unspoilt locals' pub on the edge of the town centre, offering Wards Sheffield Best Bitter and accommodation. South of the town centre in Albert Road, the **Albert Hotel** (tel: (0777) 708694) is a superb traditional pub, again offering accommodation along with Websters and Whitbread real ales and wholesome food lunchtimes and evenings.

WORKSOP
Fisherman's Arms

OFF THE TOWPATH
Church Walk

ᕯ **Home Mild, Bitter**

The mining town of Worksop is friendly if hardly picturesque or inviting. Probably the best choice for beer and pub lovers is the **Fishermans Arms**, 100 yards south of the BWB yard. It's a real traditional old pub, hearty and homely. It's how pubs should be (and once were), a view obviously not shared by many of today's brewers and operators of pub chains.

COVENTRY CANAL

Beginning in a large and surprisingly attractive basin in the heart of Coventry, the canal passes through or close to the towns of Bedworth, Nuneaton, Atherstone and Tamworth before terminating at Fradley Junction near Lichfield where it joins the Trent & Mersey. It has junctions with the Oxford Canal at Hawkesbury, the Ashby Canal at Marston and the Birmingham & Fazeley at Fazeley.

AMINGTON Gate

Tel: (0827) 63189
*Tamworth Road, Amington,
Staffs. Canalside at Bridge 69*

✖ lunchtime and evening

🍴

🍺 Marstons Border Mild,
Pedigree Bitter

Although more than 200 years old, the most significant shift in the Gate's character has occurred in the last few years following some major, obvious and predictable refurbishments. It's now more foody and more comfortable, but somewhat anonymous, with a new conservatory backing on to the lounge, which has an area roped off for diners only. They can tuck into typical but quite good pub fayre, from sandwiches and burgers to grills, chili, lasagne, pies, fish, two or three daily specials and traditional Sunday lunches. There is a smallish garden between the canal and large car park, a telephone for customers' use – in short, it's strong on catering, comfort and amenities. However, that elusive character, quality, is best tracked down in the small saloon bar, the pub's saving grace and principal reason for its inclusion. It's a cool traditional haven with old black beams, some new wood panelling, vinyl floor covering and along the far wall a row of raised-edge wooden tables for pub games. It has a dartboard, fruit machine and a chaotic mixture of styles of prints and photos on the walls. The doors open out virtually over the water, where there are a number of mooring rings. The beer is in pretty good nick too, and it's your best bet for a decent pint before you skirt the ever-increasing sprawl that is Tamworth.

Apart from the fact that these modernised pubs are all just about identical with their brass fittings, floral upholstery, polished dark wood finish and mid-range food, they seem to parallel those endless, faceless, soulless modern private housing developments – pleasant enough and with all the amenities but somehow lacking that elusive sense of real identity, community or character.

HUDDLESFORD
Plough Inn

Tel : (0543) 432369
Huddlesford, nr. Lichfield, Staffs.
Canalside, Plough Bridge (no.
38), Huddlesford Junction

✗ lunchtime (not Sun.), evening
till 8 pm (not Sun or Mon)

🍴

🍺 **Ansells Mild, Bitter, Ind Coope**
Burton Ale

The disused Wyrley and Essington canal, which once linked the Coventry canal with the Birmingham canal network at Huddlesford Junction, is now the subject of ambitious restoration plans. The remains of its eastern end are now used for moorings by the local boat club.

The pub itself has a familiar canal history. Originally built to house, feed and water the navvies who dug the canal over 200 years ago, it then switched to catering for the boatmen and their horses. As the canal trade died, so did the pub's, and its isolated location helped little in attracting car-borne replacements (a marked contrast to today). By the 1960s it had become a rundown rural cottage pub on a downward spiral and with little apparent future. But things can turn. In the early 1980s enthusiastic new owners bought in, recognising the potential of the Plough's canalside location and the vast new housing estate rising a mile or two away on the edge of the cathedral city of Lichfield. Lots of hard work and cash later, they have success on their hands. The Plough has become an extremely busy, popular country pub.

Many are attracted by the food – there's a good range of hot meals and snacks, daily specials à la chili/curry/lasagne, excellent home-made steak, mushroom and Guinness pies, spicy sausage on French bread and plenty more besides. You get trains and boats too – the main London–North West rail line passes on an embankment to the side of the lovely canalside beer garden. The traditional beers have gained the pub Good Beer Guide inclusion and there's a choice of Guinness and Murphy's for lovers of Irish stout.

The L-shaped interior has a bar area with dartboard to the right and to the left an intimate lounge with lots of plates and brasses, a neatly-blended extension and some cosy seating by the window.

LONGFORD
Greyhound

Tel: (0203) 363046
*Sutton Stop, Longford (off A444
and near junction M6 Jct. 2), nr
Coventry. Canalside at
Hawkesbury Junction*

✖ lunchtime and evening

🍴

🍺 **Draught Bass, M&B Mild;**
guest beers

The Greyhound and the junction of the Oxford and Coventry canals by which it stands are famous and historically significant canal landmarks. Originally a farmhouse and then the pay office of the nearby pit, the building provided stabling for the pit horses and was extended to accommodate barge horses when the canal junction arrived. The office became a pub, first licensed in 1817, and the junction became known among the boatmen as Sutton Stop after a particularly long-serving nineteenth century toll keeper. The first landlord, one Thomas Hardy, hired out his biggest shires as ice breakers on the canals during winter.

Today the Greyhound still oozes character, with real old brick fireplaces and roaring log fires in winter, high-backed settles, collections of toby jugs and stuffed animals, a wonderfully haphazard little snug known as the Donkey Box, a tap room known as the Elbow Room because it's always packed, handpulled cask ales and occasional guest beers, newly-added adventure playground for kids and flower garden for adults, all floodlit at night, a menagerie of dogs and cats, chickens and turkeys, sheep, two geese called Port and Sherry and two goats called Mitchell and Butler!

Strong canal connections are still maintained, not least in the pub's splendid and interesting menu. It includes a famous Pie Parlour, which features specialities like Whispering Smith's Pie, named after a famous canal character and made of steak, kidney and Stilton in mild ale. Or you could try Isle of Skye pie, smoked fish in cheese and horseradish, and Nora Batty's Vegetarian Bake, which turns out to be a blend of root vegetables in herbs and spices. And the landlady who creates these masterpieces won the 1989 Pub Lunch of the Year with Wellington Pie, a mighty concoction involving beef, beer and pâté. On a cold winter's day though, the real crowning glory is the Brothpot, a vast vat of warm, thick, heartwarming and genuine broths like lamb and vegetable and oxtail, which sits on top of the counter in the Donkey Box and is, as far as I'm aware, unique to the Greyhound. It's served at all sessions and comes complete with a bread roll. Although food is available every lunchtime and evenings except Sundays and Mondays, it's best to book the dining room in advance at weekends. Two words of caution: firstly the Brothpot empties quickly, watched furtively by the wily locals who count the portions out of the pot and suddenly strike when there are just enough portions of extra thick, meat-heavy broth left in the bottom for them!

And secondly, hot meals are only served till 1.30 lunchtimes – as we discovered by arriving at 1.33 slavering for a pie.

EREWASH
CANAL

Leaving the Trent Navigation at Trent Lock, the Erewash bears north through Long Eaton and Ilkeston before terminating at Langley Mill, close to Eastwood, D. H. Lawrence country.

COTMANHAY
Bridge Inn

Tel: (0602) 322589
*Bridge Street, Cotmanhay (off
A6007), Ilkeston, Derbys.*
Canalside at Cotmanhay Bridge

✗ lunchtime

🍴

🍺 Hardys & Hansons Best Mild,
Best Bitter

The surroundings, admittedly, do not look promising. In one direction, a vast unsightly industrial plant towering about the canal like something out of "War of the Worlds". In the other, an unrelieved expanse of modern housing stretching away into the distance. For this is the harsh, gritty landscape of the Derbys/Notts borders, land of pits, quarries and foundries, and the canal provides some welcome relief on its surprisingly rural course.

This simple two-room local was built about the same time as the canal. The hump-back bridge next to it has been raised to make it easier for boats to pass, and the pub retains a little of the canal flavour as well as the earthiness that characterises the area. It's a simple brick building with an obvious more modern brick extension to the smoke room (or Botany Lounge), which is still quite small. The whole is plainly furnished and decorated, the smoke room with brocade-covered benches and stools, assorted pictures on the walls and a piano. A handwritten sign outside the door requests "those dressed in work attire to kindly use the bar". Well that's what bars were for, I suppose, and at least there is the option. The bar (known as the Bridge Bar) is very simple, basic and friendly, and popular with anglers. There is a small basic garden with swings. The landlord, who is a real character, permits no swearing in the bar.

The pub is open all day, every day, and serves electric-pumped beers in good condition, along with bar meals and snacks until 8 pm six days a week. Sense of community is what the pub is all about: it hosts several clubs including cricket and dominoes, holds cash draws and sells eggs off the counter.

ILKESTON

OFF THE TOWPATH

There are several interesting and worthwhile pubs in the market town of Ilkeston. The **Durham Ox** in Durham Street has appeared in every edition of the Good Beer Guide and is a busy, traditional back street local with an open-plan interior and cheap B&B. It sells Wards Mild and Sheffield Best Bitter as well as Choice Best Bitter, and lunchtime food.

The **Flowerpot** in Chapel Street near the Albion shopping centre is an old street-corner local worshipped by Shipstones lovers. The mild and bitter now come via Greenalls. It serves excellent lunches.

The King's Head, Wadenhoe

FENLAND WATERWAYS

FENLAND
WATERWAYS

The principal rivers of the Fens are the Nene and the Great Ouse. These are navigable from Northampton and Bedford respectively and end their seaward journey at the Wash after long tidal reaches. The chief tributary of the Great Ouse is the river Cam, navigable from Cambridge.

Between Peterborough and Ely the two main rivers are connected by a complex network of waterways known as the Middle level Navigations. Access to the main system of canals and rivers is via the Grand Union at Northampton.

BRANDON CREEK
Ship Inn

Tel: (035 376) 228
Brandon Creek, Norfolk.
Riverside at the confluence of the
Great and Little Ouse

✕ lunchtime and evening

🏨

☺

🍺 **Ruddles Best Bitter, County;**
Websters Yorkshire Bitter

Situated in a pleasant sylvan oasis in the featureless expanse of the Fens, the Ship is the kind of pub one could safely take one's maiden aunt to. Very much food and family orientated, it has an atmosphere that positively exudes tranquillity.

The surrounding and overhanging trees cast dappled shadows over the flint and pantiled exterior. A concrete bridge carrying the A10 across the river rather spoils the scene from some angles but, as this has diverted this busy road from in front of the pub, one can accept a minor visual intrusion. The river itself is only evident from ground level by the superstructures of boats taking advantage of copious moorings behind the high Fenland banks.

Inside, the pub is bright and airy with skylights illuminating any potentially dark corners. There is a restaurant and large saloon bar furnished in sturdy, attractive and traditional manner. Children are welcome in the restaurant and in a sunken area of the saloon which has as its central feature an elaborate flint and brick fireplace and chimney breast.

The Ship enjoys a supper licence allowing it to open all day on Sunday for meals. Rather confusingly the pub and the hamlet of Brandon Creek reside firmly in Cambridgeshire with the two rivers forming a clear and immovable boundary, except in the eyes of the Post Office who have placed them in the county of Norfolk.

CAMBRIDGE
Fort St. George

Tel: (0223) 354327
*Midsummer Common,
Cambridge. East bank below
Jesus Lock on the River Cam*

✖ lunchtime and evening (not
Sun, Mon)

🛇

◎ in food bar

🍺 **Greene King IPA, Abbot Ale**

This pub was once known as the Fort St. George *in England*, apparently to distinguish it from a real fort of that name in India. This may well no longer be a necessary qualification to the statement "just off to the Fort St. George, dear", but would certainly add to the pub's considerable charm if still in use today.

This was once a typical multi-purpose establishment sited on a lock island, but since the removal of the lock further upstream in the 1830s and the filling in of the channel, the Fort St. George has rejoined the mainland as if by continental drift. This gives it a rather remarkable situation, the river on one side, the green expanse of Midsummer Common on the other.

The pub itself is pleasantly tiled and weatherboarded, and unmistakably antique. There are some sympathetic modern outbuildings and a low wall with a lych gate separating the patio from the common. The interior is very well preserved with many original features. There is a nice little Victorian luncheon bar and a main bar covered in sporting paraphernalia. A rowing eight is suspended from the ceiling in some four parts and photos of the Light Blue Boat Race crews from the Victorian and Edwardian eras surround the walls. There is also a rack of ancient cricket bats, more my sport.

Having taken such trouble to preserve and improve a fine old pub it seems a crime that Greene King feel there is a place here (as certainly there is elsewhere) for a juke box and gaming machines. The garish appearance and flashing lights of the electronic gizmos and the intrusive din are totally at odds with the kind of pleasant ambience a pub like this ought to thrive on.

The fake handpumps and the issue of plastic glasses for outside drinking also rankle, but this latter may well be a necessary evil for the benefit of Midsummer Common's cow population. My first encounter with this herd was so surprising that I nearly bicycled into the brackish waters of the Cam.

Green Dragon

Tel: (0223) 355182
5 Water Street, Chesterton, Cambridge. West bank of the Cam, 400 yards below Elizabeth Bridge

✕ lunchtime meals, bar snacks

🏠

🍺 Greene King IPA, Abbot Ale

A genuinely old pub, the building dating from the 15th or 16th century. The exterior has a fine tiled roof, shuttered windows, doorways approached by stone steps with wrought iron railings and white painted walls, all very well looked after. The interior owes its character rather less to its age than to modernisation (or more properly antiquification) carried out by Greene King in 1975. The two walk-through bars are separated by a massive central chimney breast with large inglenooks exposed on either side. Additional subdivisions consist of the exposed timber framing of the original internal walls.

The Green Dragon is very much a no-frills community boozer, catering for the locals rather than the tourist hoardes that invade this historic city every summer. It also has a long association with the river despite being somewhat set back from the bank and separated from it by a roadway. The ferry that operated there, now replaced by a footbridge, was owned by the publicans of the Green Dragon.

It's best to moor here on the opposite bank and use the footbridge to visit the pub. Enjoy a game of darts or bar billiards and conversation with the locals along with the odd pint of Greene King's excellent draught beer (served here by fake handpuls). By the time of publication, the Green Dragon may be offering accommodation.

DENVER SLUICE
Jenyns Arms

Tel: (0366) 383366
Denver Sluice, Downham Market, Norfolk. By Denver Sluice on the River Great Ouse

✗ lunchtime and evening (not Thur or Sun)

🍴

🍺 Greene King IPA, Abbot Ale; Adnams Bitter

Few boats these days pass through Denver Sluice into the tidal Ouse. This historic structure is a natural place for holidaying boaters to stop for a bit of sightseeing and refreshment then to return from whence they came. In times past the lock here could only be negotiated when the water levels either side of the sluice were equal, and only with the assistance of the "berthsmen" or pilots for whom the Jenyns Arms provided lodgings. Hence the pub has historically served a great congregation of boats and continues to do so to this day

Painted in black and white the Jenyns Arms has a stately classical frontage. An attractive tree-decked garden leads down to the pub's own moorings. The interior has in recent times been knocked through to form a large eating and drinking area, partitioned in places by the skeletal beams of the original walls.

The Jenyns Arms is the sort of pub that packs them in but retains a friendly intimacy. Judging by the buffet display it could cater for a whole armada should one sail up the Ouse.

FOTHERINGHAY
Falcon

OFF THE TOWPATH
Tel: (08326) 254
Main Street, Fotheringhay, Northants. On River Nene, 250 yards north from bank via footpath

✗ lunchtime and evening (not Mon)

🍴

🍺 Adnams Bitter; Elgoods Bitter, Greyhound Special Bitter; Greene King IPA, Abbot Ale

It's impossible to imagine the country's waterways offering a more beautiful mooring place than here on the Nene at Fotheringhay. The river meanders on nature's chosen route past gently sloping tree-fringed meadows, free from the human interference elsewhere evident along its course. Crowning the valley's edge and dominating the horizon for many miles is the uplifting sight of the splendid 15th-century parish church of St Mary and All Saints. Nearby is the castle mound, all that now remains of the great fortress in which Mary Queen of Scots was imprisoned and beheaded.

It is a short walk from the riverbank, past the churchyard, to the doorway of the Falcon. This smart old stone-built country free house offers high-class service amid traditional surroundings.

A tiny public bar with separate entrance once segregated the sons of toil from the local gentry in the lounge. In today's more egalitarian times, with so many knock-through, lounge-only country pubs around, it is nice to be able to visit a pub like the Falcon and choose a bar according to one's mood (rather than station in life) especially if a bit shabby from energetic cruising.

ELY
Cutter Inn

Tel: (0353) 662713
River Great Ouse, West bank riverside by railway bridge

✕ lunchtime and evening

🍴 Adnams Bitter; Ruddles Best Bitter, County; Websters Yorkshire Bitter

The Cutter Inn was once part of the brewery and maltings of Hall, Cutlack and Harlock, only becoming a pub and thus the brewery tap in 1830 when the river was conveniently brought to the pub's front door by the construction of New Cut. Hence the name, which refers to a person with a trade similar to that of a navvy rather than to the sailing vessel illustrated on the pub's sign. Occupying a picture postcard setting with tall willows and the great cathedral looming in the background, the Cutter has been the subject of many a photograph and watercolour painting. Its steeply pitched roof is pleasingly pierced by chimney stacks of different periods and design but spoiled by characterless modern tiling.

The large, low-ceilinged public bar fronts the river. Two bay windows are surrounded by bench seating and provide congenial drinking areas with fine views. The attractiveness of this bar is enhanced by some exceptionally fine woodwork dating from the time of the pub's modernisation in the early 1960s. The bar counter is quite spectacular, fashioned as half of clinker-built boat hull in highly polished hardwood. At the back of the pub is a restaurant-cum-lounge bar with panelled walls of the same quality and period though of more conventional design.

Grand Metropolitan pubs in East Anglia tend either to be neglected or done up to the nines. The Cutter falls pleasantly between these two extremes. With the present landlord due to retire, one hopes this situation is maintained.

GREAT BARFORD
Anchor Inn

Tel: (0234) 870364
High Street, Great Barford, Beds.
North bank by bridge on the River
Great Ouse

✗ lunchtime and evening

🍽

📶

🍺 **Charles Wells Eagle Bitter,**
Bombardier

Apart from the little stiletto spire of All Saints church, the dominant landmark in Great Barford is the 17-arch span of the village's superb medieval bridge. There is a pleasing irregularity about this structure with a patchwork of masonry and brickwork resulting from widening and repair work over the centuries. Just across the road from the bridge's northern abutment and overlooking a grassy bank to the river's edge that provides attractive and convenient mooring stands the Anchor Inn, an imposing white-painted building of late Georgian vintage. This is a large and friendly pub which offers bar meals along with a popular restaurant. There is also accommodation consisting of three guest rooms.

Unsurprisingly the riverside theme is strong and reflected in the decor of the pub. The wooden panels about the bar show the mileage between locks on the Ouse Navigation, which is certainly of great interest, if not of some assistance, to the visiting boater.

HOLYWELL
Old Ferry Boat
Inn

Tel: (0480) 63227
*Holywell, Cambs. River Great
Ouse. On north bank*

✘ lunchtime, evening;
   restaurant weekends only

🛏

🍺 Adnams Bitter, Broadside;
   Draught Bass; Greene King
   IPA, Abbot Ale; Marstons
   Pedigree Bitter

Please note this isn't just the Ferry Boat Inn. It's the *Old* Ferry Boat Inn. In fact this ancient hostelry boasts of being the oldest inn in England, dating back to at least 560 AD.

It has other boasts as well – a superb riverside setting, a classy menu of freshly prepared traditional food, a range of fine English ales, luxury accommodation, wedding and conference facilities and – a ghost. Spurned in love, a young Saxon wench committed suicide and ended up buried under the bar-room floor. A particularly large flagstone marks the unconsecrated tomb of this tragic young lady whose apparition is said to return every March 17, the anniversary of her death, much to the benefit of trade in the Old Ferry Boat.

The pub can vaguely be described as rambling in its physical appearance. The outside is of white painted brick (with the odd black beam attached) and, appropriately to its age and location in a reed-growing area, pleasantly thatched. Inside there are beams and brasses galore, inglenooks and a multi-layer undulating stone floor. Unfortunately somebody in the 1960s decided that despite its thousand odd years, the place didn't look old enough. Every beam has been ruthlessly exposed and internal walls stripped or removed. A restaurant extension of similar vintage manages to dominate the older parts of the pub and to be totally characterless at the same time. Imagine if Anne Hathaway's cottage, for example, had been abused in this way. Doubtless, however, this interesting and well-run establishment is worthy of a visit. Motorists are well directed by signpost from Needingworth on the A1123, and there are handy moorings right by the pub.

MARCH
Red Lion

OFF THE TOWPATH
Tel: (0354) 54510
15 High Street, March, Cambs.
50 yards south of March Bridge
on the old course of the River
Nene

✖ bar snacks lunchtime and
evening

🍺 Elgoods Bitter

Room for children? "No." Any outdoor drinking area? "No." How about food – do you do meals lunchtime or evenings? "Well, we do rolls and the like." I don't expect you provide accommodation, then? "No, it's just good beer and good cheer," replied the landlord. And what else need a pub offer if it is done with enthusiasm and skill and in the sort of homely environment provided here at the Red Lion?

The core of this pub is probably early 19th century. The façade and the interior show evidence of refurbishment in the middle years of this century, but this cannot disguise a typical small town boozer very much of its period, with classic floor plan of side corridor running the whole length of the building to the backyard toilets, and doorways leading off to a central saloon bar and public bar overlooking the street. All in all a charming, friendly, basic boozer that has served generations of local people and visitors alike and will, I'm sure, continue in the same tradition for generations to come.

Ship Inn

Tel: (0354) 56999
Nene Parade, March, Cambs.
Riverside on the old course of the
Nene, 50 yards east of March
Bridge

✖ lunchtime and evening

🍴 riverside and back

🛏

🍺 Greene King XX Mild, IPA,
Abbot Ale

Since the late Middle Ages, the Ship has stood at the bank of the Old River Nene as it slides sluggishly through this attractive Fenland town. Then known as the Travellers' Rest, it also served as the local lock-up.

Today, its thatched roof and picturesque riverside location create every temptation to make further enquiries. Once inside, the appeal is heightened by the fine range of Greene King beers – including the rare XX Mild – and by the carved beams above. The middle one, especially ornate, is said to have fallen off the back of a barge en route to Ely cathedral where it was destined to form part of the extensions. Nobody is really sure whether the story has any truth in it, but they keep telling it anyway. My own theory, more mundane perhaps, but giving credit where credit may well be due, is that the whole ornate structure is the work of the same local craftsman who built the magnificent double-hammerbeam roof in the parish church of St Wendreda.

The Ship offers home-cooked meals at all times and value-for-money accommodation, provided you don't mind sharing with the almost obligatory ghost. In one room in particular it sometimes got so cold that a previous landlady used to keep the cheese in it — a close encounter of the curd kind?

The Ship has one large, comfortable, pleasantly appointed bar/lounge and a separate dining room. Everything from bar snacks to a three-course meal is offered. It still has a regular boat trade, with much-improved moorings outside, though more would be able to negotiate this stretch of river and enjoy the pub and the town if Stanground Lock were lengthened. At the moment, length is restricted to about 49 ft. A wide selection of odd vessels does take to the unsuspecting waters during the annual Raft Race, and odder ones still at carnival time. It's all part of tranquil country life in the Fens.

NORTH SIDE
Dog-in-a-Doublet

Tel: Peterborough 202256
North Side, Whittlesey, Cambs.
On the River Nene 200 yards
below the lock

✗ lunchtime and evening,
  restaurant all day Sunday

🛏

☺

🍺 Adnams Bitter, Broadside;
  Greene King IPA, Abbot Ale

I would have thought that a pub known as the Dog-in-a-Doublet was unique in this respect but there is, apparently, a small pack of them somewhere. This is certainly the first that I have come across. Knowing the peculiar origins of English pub names, it seems unlikely that an actual historical dog, literally thus attired, could have inspired this dedication. Whatever the case, there on the expertly painted sign stands a fetching little mongrel clad in a yellow waistcoat with red spots and trimmed round the neck with a lace ruff (surely no pun intended here).

Once the isolated haunt of navvies and wildfowlers and others on society's fringes, the

Dog-in-a-Doublet is now a pleasant and respectable free house. It is still very much on its own, though, set apart even from the tiny hamlet of North Side. A vast expanse of sky, huge riverbanks, the gaunt superstructure of the lock and an eerie silence set a typical Fenland scene.

The eponymous Dog-in-a-Doublet lock marks the limit of pleasure cruising for most craft on the Nene. Mooring just above it leaves one a walk of some 200 yards to the pub. For drivers, the nearby river bridge carries the B104 between Whittlesey and Thorney.

STANGROUND
Woolpack

Tel: (0733) 54417
29 North Street, Stanground,
Peterborough, Cambs. Half mile
west of Stanground Sluice on the
River Nene

✘ lunchtime, Saturday evening

🍴

☺

🍺 Whitbread Castle Eden Ale,
Boddingtons Bitter, Flowers
Original; guest beer

Like many of man's habitations on this once-rogue river, the Woolpack gets as close as it dare to the water's edge; dipping its toes gingerly in at the bottom of a very long and narrow back garden. Attracted by the pub's waterside sign and ample willow-shaded moorings, boaters have quite a trek before attaining the object of their desire, but they will pass much of interest on the way. The garden itself is a horticultural work of art and it would need somebody with greener fingers than I to describe the varieties of display. Beyond an arch of roses a barn-like outbuilding comes in to view. This houses a little museum dedicated to the landlord's collection of militaria and historic agricultural equipment. Get here on a weekend if you want to see it open.

A little further and the odyssey is complete. The well-appointed bar of this small pub shows the same enthusiastic stewardship as is evident outside. The Woolpack is owned by Whitbread but their policy of operating some pubs as "free" houses, with a wide range of beers on tap is here exploited to the full.

The visitor by river has a far more dramatic introduction to the Woolpack than the visitor by land. The front of the pub is pleasantly under-stated, sandwiched as it is between its neighbours in a workaday village street. The nearby boatyard entrance gives the only clue to the Nene's close proximity. The Woolpack is an unexpected riverside gem with surprises aplenty.

ST. IVES
Oliver Cromwell

Tel: (0480) 65601
13 Wellington Street, St Ives, Cambs. North bank, east of town bridge, on the Great Ouse

✗ lunchtime snacks

🍴

🍺 Adnams Broadside; Greene King IPA

I'm sure that the Lord Protector of England (once a brewer himself, they say) would have been proud to give his name to this delightful little boozer. Typical of the ambivalence of the town of St Ives to its most famous son, the Oliver Cromwell is hard to find. A sign with a representation of the great man would help but the ornate wrought iron bracket that overhangs the road from the pub's upper floor is thus unburdened.

Wellington Street is a short continuation of the town's quayside that lies in the shadow of the famous medieval bridge and chapel and where good moorings and water are available. One is well placed here for more than just water as the Oliver Cromwell, though barely visible, is less than 50 yards distant. One is drawn to one's goal more by a great pubby smell than any visual evidence. And once entry is gained that classic atmosphere of pubbiness is overwhelming. The single bar is all in wood; panelling on the walls, boards on the ceiling. There is a real fireplace, flanked by alcoves with comfy chairs arranged before it. The hum of good-humoured conversation is punctuated by the occasional raucous laugh, while little eddies of smoke dance in beams of sunlight. No music, no din of fruit machines invade this scene. Every detail reflects a perfect harmony, right down to mine host's handlebar moustache.

ST. NEOTS
Old Falcon
Hotel

OFF THE TOWPATH
Tel : (0480) 72749
*Market Square, St Neots, Cambs.
River Great Ouse, East bank, 200
yards south of town bridge*

✗ no bar snacks Fri, Sat

🅱 in the coach entrance

☺

⨝

🍺 Adnams Broadside ; Charles
Wells Eagle Bitter,
Bombardier

The Georgian market square of St Neots is one of the most imposing in the country, sad as it is that it serves today merely as a car park. Sad also that the historic old Cross Keys Inn is now a shopping mall and the magnificent yellow brick and stone frontage of the recently closed brewery of Paine & Co. stands boarded up and neglected, the steam from its coppers and the smell of hops now just a memory.

You can begin to forget these calamities, however, in the bar of the Old Falcon. This venerable coaching inn has chosen to avoid the pomp and circumstances its pedigree may have imposed. A jovial, easy-going air prevails as full advantage is taken of liberal licensing hours.

With its fine 18th century frontage facing the square, the Falcon has its back turned to the river. The tiny waterside patio is available only to those hiring the function suite. Consequently a visit by boat entails a short walk from the many nearby mooring areas the town provides.

WADENHOE
King's Head

Tel : Clopton 222
*Church Street, Wadenhoe,
Northants. Riverside by
Wadenhoe Lock on the River
Nene*

✗ lunchtime and evening

🅱

🍺 Bateman's XXXB ; Marston
Pedigree Bitter ; Hook Norton
Old Hookey ; guest beer

The King's Head occupies the prettiest part of one of Northamptonshire's finest villages. Nearby among ancient earthworks stands the medieval church and at the bottom of the pub's steeply sloping garden flows the river Nene in an incomparable wooded setting. The pub is built of mellow local stone, its roof of Collyweston slate providing rich contrast in materials with the little thatched cottage adjoining on one side and the pub's old pantiled stable block on the other.

Inside, the striking feature is the huge inglenook fireplace in the public bar, capacious enough to hold a Northants skittle table and seating for two or three customers (who would nevertheless be advised to sit elsewhere once the cheeses start to fly).

The wood-panelled lounge bar has a little perspex panel that shows the wattle construction of the internal walls laid bare, and a discrete notice to explain how fine an example of the craft this is. This reverence to the pub's antiquity is in sharp contrast to those establishments where original surface materials are torn away to reveal gnarled, naked beams and rough stone walls that the original builders intended to remain unseen.

We are also spared here a superabundance of horse brasses and the like, for this is a genuine, unspoilt old world (very much opposed to "olde worlde") country inn.

To reach Wadenhoe by road you turn off the A605 between Thrapston and Oundle.

WELNEY
Lamb and Flag

OFF THE TOWPATH
Tel : (035 471) 242
Wisbech Road, Welney, Norfolk.
Old Bedford River, 200 yards west of Delph bridge

✗ lunchtime and evening

🏠

🛏

🍺 **Elgoods Bitter, Greyhound Special Bitter**

The simplicity of the nearby Three Tuns is in sharp contrast to the ivy-clad opulence of the Lamb and Flag. They have in common, however, the same excellently kept and eminently quaffable local beer along with a cheerful and friendly ambience.

Should you feel hungry eyes upon you as you enjoy a meal and a pint in the saloon bar, these most likely belong to the very plump stuffed pike displayed above the fireplace.

Boaters with neglected coiffure and thoughts of souvenirs for the folks back home will find this a mecca. The Lamb and Flag has on its premises both a hairdressers and a gift shop.

Three Tuns

Tel: (035 471) 254
*Bedford Bank East, Welney,
Norfolk. West bank by Delph
Bridge on the Old Bedford River*

🕿

☺ in snug

🍺 **Elgoods Bitter**

There must be something about the vast levels of open, wet Fenland, where roads and rivers run in straight lines under huge skies that encourages expansive conversation and gentle contemplation, and brings out the raconteur in people. At the Three Tuns it all begins behind the bar. Sheffield-born landlord John Waring, a dead ringer in looks and dialect for Seth Armstrong from TV's *Emmerdale Farm*, calls his pub "the College of Further Education".

"There ain't 'alf some clever folks get in 'ere," he explains with a perpetual twinkle in the eye. "Most debates start with politics and end up wi' sex. Or *vice versa*." John and wife Mabs have run this simple, classic rural house since they "retired" 22 years ago. There are no machines, unless you count the old and rarely-used Wurlitzer juke-box, and no food.

"We have to talk in here," said Mabs. "Do you think it'll catch on?" With the regulars it already has.

The pub is very old, though no one seems really sure how old. The bar and lounge are small and almost identical, rendering any distinction superfluous. They are both homely, furnished with wooden stools and floral-pattern armchairs and settees, dotted haphazardly around wooden tables. The bar contains a small coke fire and its answer to the Wurlitzer, an often-used piano. An awesome punt gun fills almost the entire end wall.

When I asked whether the river outside gets very busy with boating traffic, John nodded solemnly towards the pub door. "You can get anywhere in't world by water from this front door. Probably."

The last word rests with one of the locals. "I drive as many miles around here as anybody, and I tell you this is the best pub left on the Fens – the only one. You can have a bloody good argument and still part as friends, and there's no small of food hanging around and spoiling the beer."

For character and characters, simply do not miss it. Catch it before it becomes extinct.

WEST ROW
Judes' Ferry
House Inn

Tel: Mildenhall 712277
*West Row, Mildenhall, Suffolk.
On the River Lark by Jude's Ferry
Bridge*

✗ lunchtime and evening (not Mon)

🍽

🍺 **Greene King IPA, Abbot Ale**

I know not if West Row has a village hall, but as a centre for communal activity there could be no more suitable a venue than Jude's Ferry House Inn. Built in the early nineteenth century in Regency style, the pub's sober symmetrical façade has an almost demure appearance, suitable as a backdrop for those old photographs of Victorian families picnicking on the front lawn.

Much of the front lawn here has become a car park, while what remains forms a large and attractive beer garden leading to the water's edge.

You enter the front door directly into an open plan bar of generous proportions. This takes up the whole ground floor of the main building with a rectangular archway leading to another bar in a large single storey back extension. No attempt is made to distinguish these two connecting bars one from another as either saloon or public. The dartboard and sports club noticeboard are in the larger bar, while the pool table is in the back, with a happy mix of comfortable and utility seating throughout.

The Jude's Ferry is a well known landmark and natural stopping point on the River Lark, as much for the quality of its welcome as for its position marking the limit of navigation for larger craft.

WHITTLESEY
Boat Inn

Tel: (0733) 202488
*2 Ramsey Road, Whittlesey,
Cambs. By bridge near Briggate
bend on King's Dyke*

✖ lunchtime and evening

🕮

☺

🛏

🍺 Elgood's Bitter

King's Dyke approaches Whittlesey as a broadish tree-lined waterway. Through the town itself, however, it is forced through a channel little wider than a ditch, set deep within sheer concrete walls and squeezed around the acutest ninety degree bend in the whole inland navigation system. Overlooking this aquatic bottle-neck, pantiled and pink-painted, is the attractive Boat Inn.

How long it has stood here is hard to say. The building is probably 17th century and it has certainly been a public house since the late 19th century when the typical Victorian bar-room windows would have been inserted. Through the main door is a small lobby, of similar style and vintage, leading on the right to a pretty lounge-cum-restaurant and on the left to the larger, more rugged public bar. This has a curious post-modern feature in the recently constructed fireplace surround. Built of yellow brick with sharply contrasting black pointing it cleverly incorporates a dartboard above the fire.

Those intrepid boaters charting this difficult course between the River Nene and the Great Ouse system via the Middle Level Navigations will find their efforts amply rewarded by mooring at the Boat Inn.

FOSSDYKE &
WITHAM
NAVIGATIONS

The Roman-built Fossdyke Navigation is the oldest artificially-constructed waterway in the country, designed to link the River Witham with the Trent which it meets at Torksey. It flows right through the centre of the fair city of Lincoln, becoming the Witham Navigation beyond the wide expanse of Brayford Pool in central Lincoln for the remaining thirty-two miles of its journey, culminating at Boston Grand Sluice.

BOSTON

OFF THE TOWPATH

The centre of this fine Lincolnshire town is just a short walk from the moorings at the end of the non-tidal Witham Navigation at the Grand Sluice, and also close to the end of the Maud Foster Drain. At its heart is the immense 272-foot tall tower of St Botolph's church, better known as the "Boston Stump". It is visible from miles around the flat fenlands surrounding the town, and on a clear day Lincoln can be seen from the top, 32 miles away.

There are several notable pubs in Boston for the real ale drinker. Virtually opposite the railway station is **The Eagle** in West Street, a CAMRA favourite, host to beer festivals and meeting place for local folk clubs and other organisations. It has Adnams, Everards, Batemans, Timothy Taylor's and numerous guest beers, good value lunches and a separate Sunday menu.

The Carpenters Arms, a Bateman's pub in Witham Street, is a busy back-street local with an interesting menu including vegetarian options. It offers accommodation. **The Britannia** is a tiny basic street corner local in the shadows of the Stump, with a rear terrace overlooking the Witham near to the handsome ornate town bridge. Batemans XB Bitter and wonderful Dark Mild are served on handpump. Spick and span it certainly ain't, but it's got character.

Roper's Arms

Tel: (0205) 362881
Horncastle Road (B1183), Boston, Lincs. RIverside on the Maud Foster Drain

---

✗ lunchtime

🍺 **Batemans Mild, XB Bitter**

The Witham navigable drains (of which the Maud Foster Drain is one) are a remarkable network of waterways to the north and east of Boston. Unfortunately, the Witham Navigation and the Maud Foster Drain do not connect in central Boston, but the Roper's can be reached via Anton's Gowt lock and then (for craft of up to 62 feet) Cowbridge lock, where there is a great waterways junction.

It's a journey worth making, for here is your opportunity to stand on the very soil trodden by guru Michael Jackson and the Channel 4 team during filming of the Batemans episode of The Beer Hunter. Apparently the brewery is prone to despatch people to this cheerful, down-to-earth street corner pub when they ask to see a proper traditional Bateman's pub. It's a wise choice, for the Roper's is a real locals' local, lively and full of character. People come here to talk, laugh, play pub games and drink good traditional beer (it's been a Good Beer Guide regular for eight years), and a friendly lot they are too, always ready to share a laugh with a stranger. It's predominantly (though by no means exclusively) a man's pub, and very popular with anglers, despite the algae infestation affecting the water during 1990. Food is confined to lunchtime rolls, made to order, but there is a good traditional fish and chip shop next door.

About 100 years old, the pub's name derives from a former ropery which used to stand on the opposite bank, making rope for the barges and horses to be tethered at night, and whose workers used to cross the bridge to refresh themselves at the pub. It has been extended into the cottage next door – though you'd hardly notice – and sports an unusual skirt or canopy around its ground floor as though it's wearing plus fours. The traditional bar has a quarry-tiled floor and a pool table, and the decor throughout is cheap and cheerful, with a haphazard mix of styles. But it's people and excellent ale which makes the Roper's a star pub.

There are some other pubs close at hand worth investigation, two other Batemans pubs nearer the town, the **King William** and the **Kings Arms**, and further east, the **Cowbridge Inn**, a large brick built suburban Home Ales pub which looks post-war.

DOGDYKE
Packet Inn

Tel: (0526) 42294
Belle Isle, Dogdyke, Lincs.
Riverside, north bank

✗ lunchtime and evening

🍴

☺

🍺 **Batemans Mild, XB Bitter**

With the flat Lincolnshire wetlands of straight lines and big skies as its backdrop, the Packet Inn enjoys an enviable rural setting on the banks of the river, although in common with all the other pubs and houses in the area it is prone to having its peace regularly shattered by the circling jets from the nearby Conginsby air base. The Battle of Britain museum is also stationed there.

The front (riverside) part of the pub is at least 300 years old and was originally a cottage. It was extended when the railway was taken through, and passed into Bateman's capable hands before the start of the last war. As its name suggests, it used to be a regular stopping place for the old steamers or packet boats that plied their trade to and from the inland port of Boston.

Colourful hanging baskets do not completely disguise the pub's somewhat down-at-heel appearance, with chipped or crumbling brick-work and peeling paintwork. Inside it's rough and ready too, but friendly – a real locals' local – and that's how it's going to stay according to the affable Cheshire-born landlord and his wife who will not countenance its conversion into a fancy fake palace. A pool table and other pub games take up a good portion of the L-shaped interior, which has a part-tiled floor and lots of pictures of World War II aeroplanes like the Spitfire and Lancaster bomber. Plain but good value food such as steaks and grills, burgers and sausages, vegetarian lasagne, baps and sweets, is available every session apart from Monday evenings and Sunday lunchtimes. Special Sunday roasts have to be ordered ahead, enabling them to reduce waste and consequently offer the meals at astoundingly low prices.

Children are welcome at the Packet Inn, and outdoor drinking is limited to a couple of rickety old wooden tables overlooking the river.

LANGRICK
Ferry Boat

Tel: (020 573) 273
*on B1192, Langrick, Lincs. 50
yards north of Langrick Bridge,
Witham Navigation*

✗ lunchtime and evening

🍴

☺

🍺 **Home Bitter**

With its hanging baskets, leaded windows, tables and chairs and whitewashed frontage, the Ferry Boat's exterior looks delightful. Inside the pub is a bit of a curate's egg, a blend of the new and the old, the genuine and the replica. The original parts of the building date back over three hundred years but there have been many additions and alterations since then. The lounge is pleasant and interesting, despite another burgundy dralon attack. With its low beamed ceiling, dark wood settles, open fireplace and two leaded bay windows giving views of the side garden, it almost has the academic air of the cloistered study, although this is somewhat compromised by piped pop music and the smell of cooking. There are lots of brasses and plates, and a couple of tables with the unusual feature of large brass salvers as table tops. There are unused handpumps behind the bar, a concept I can't begin to understand. The traditional bitter is dispensed by electric pump, with mild sadly on keg only. There are no keg bitters.

In stark contrast the basic public bar is almost post-war working men's club in mood. The dark wood of the lounge is replaced by light pine panelling, the wooden settles by long tables with bench seating; DIY supplants craftsmanship. The good point is that at least there is a choice, so often denied by the current vogue for single-room anonymity. There is a pool table and a collection of plates.

Reasonably priced "safe" pub food in the something 'n' chips mould is available every lunchtime except Saturdays and every evening except Monday and Thursday. Children are allowed in but not too late in the evening.

LINCOLN

OFF THE TOWPATH

Lincoln is a splendid Roman and before that, Celtic city, watched over from on high by its magnificent cathedral. The Fossdyke Navigation which enters the city from the north is joined to the Witham by the dramatic expanse of Brayford Pool, and it is the Witham which then passes under the famous "Glory Hole", a half-timbered building arched across the navigation. The High Street is above the bridge.

Sadly the few pubs which are actually waterside are disappointingly kitsch, despite their quaint exteriors but there are plenty of good pubs in town. Two can be found on Broadgate, a couple of bridges east of the Glory Hole (look for the striking blue Royal British Legion building) and a couple of minutes walk from the bridge. North is the **Jolly Brewer** (26 Broadgate), a Thirties style art deco freehouse offering cask conditioned beers from Everards, Bass, Hardys & Hansons, Youngers and guest beers, as well as lunchtime food. It doesn't open Sunday lunchtimes. The same distance south is **Sippers**, with a nautical theme and every type of rum known to man, in addition to beers from Batemans, Tetley, Ind Coope and John Smith's.

For those straying further afield, the scope broadens dramatically, most notably in the area up the hill around the cathedral and castle. **The Victoria** in Union Street at the foot of the castle is a vibrant real ale institution, attracting a panoramic range of clientele – which used to be the whole point of pubs in pre-niche marketing days. Usually at least half a dozen different cask beers are on offer (including a mild), such as Batemans, Timothy Taylor's, Woods, Marstons, Nethergate, Fullers, Archers, Old Mill and others, along with excellent lunchtime food. Just around the corner in Westgate, **The Strugglers** is a small, lively basic boozer bursting with assorted life forms. Draught Bass, Bass XXXX Mild and lunchtime food are available.

TATTERSHALL BRIDGE
Royal Oak

Tel: (0526) 42413
Tattershall Bridge (A153), Lincs.
50 yards north of Tattershall Bridge

✖ lunchtime and evening

🍴

🍺 Home Mild, Theakstons XB

A pleasant, tastefully modernised pub with an excellent reputation for its interesting and imaginative food. The bar menu features the usual pub food items from chili/curry/lasagne land, grills, pizzas, salads, sandwiches and sweets, plus more unusual offerings like Mexican pancakes and a daily special. The full à la carte restaurant menu includes duckling, venison, veal, goulash, moussaka, curries and sweets. Sunday lunches are also served.

The Royal Oak has a light, spacious, part-carpeted bar with a TV in the corner and a pool table. The lounge is somewhat unusually put together, split level, long and narrow with a crescent shaped servery filling one end. It's pleasantly furnished and has beams, roughcast white walls, and patterned tapestry-effect fabric with matching curtains. Air Force stickers above the bar and photos and drawings on the walls proclaim the strong influence of the numerous air bases in the area. The roar of exercising jets constantly interrupts the tranquillity of the flat, open Lincolnshire countryside.

Having once been a Wards house, beer supply has fallen into the hands of Scottish & Newcastle. The traditional beers are well kept, the house well run.

The Black Horse, Greenford

GRAND UNION CANAL

GRAND UNION CANAL

The Grand Union is the spine of the Southern English canal system, an amalgamation of formerly separate canals, branches, arms, sections and junctions, only integrated as the Grand Union Canal Company as recently as 1929.

Its main line stretches from Brentford in London right up to Birmingham, picking a route northwards through Watford, Milton Keynes and Leamington Spa. The Regent's Canal and Paddington Arm connect it with the docklands, West End and heart of the capital, while various arms open up the towns of Slough, Aylesbury, Northampton and Warwick.

Apart from its two access points with the Thames in London – at Brentford via the River Brent, and at Limehouse Basin where the Regent's Canal and River Lee join the Thames – the Grand Union is linked with the River Lee via the short Hertford Union Canal in East London, the Oxford Canal twice (at Napton and Braunston), the Stratford Canal at Kingswood and the Birmingham Canal Navigations in Central Birmingham.

At Norton Junction the Leicester section leaves the main line and links the cities of Leicester and Loughborough into the system, sharing much of its course with the River Soar and finally expiring at its junction with the mighty River Trent. A short arm reaches the town of Market Harborough, and a shorter one still the attractive village of Welford.

APSLEY
Albion

Tel: (0442) 235116
Durrants Hill Road, Apsley,
Herts. Canalside by bridge 152

✕ lunchtime (not Sun)

🍴

☺

🍺 **Benskins Best Bitter**

The Albion signals itself in quite different ways to the land and water borne traveller. From the road its attractive yellow brick and flint, two-storey, flower bedecked frontage modestly beckons. From the canal, however, the pub is a dominant landmark, white-painted and towering three storeys over the waterway like the cliffs its name celebrates.

The interior consists of two comfortable bars. Both are tastefully decorated and adorned with many interesting pictures and ornaments, including a fine collection of beautifully embellished porcelain plates. Seating around the small bay window offers pleasant views over the canal.

There is a happy, cheerful mood about this pub, such as has been rare on my travels, and typified by the landlady's endearingly infectious giggle. There is evident glee when she points out that if you want moorings here your best bet is to tie up by the pub's attractive canalside garden. This is, of course, for patrons of the pub only. The shallow water on the towpath side provides the Albion with a captive clientele who will not be leaving disappointed.

BARROW-UPON-SOAR
Navigation

Tel: (0509) 412842
Mill Lane, Barrow-upon-Soar,
Leics. Canalside at Mill Lane
Bridge (No. 28)

✕ lunchtime

🍴

🍺 **Marstons Pedigree Bitter;**
Courage Directors; Greenalls
Shipstones Mild, Bitter

The Navigation's extensive facelift in spring 1988 muted some of the pub's traditional character and replaced it with a single room, split-level interior, fabric-covered stools, brass-topped tables and chintzy Austrian blinds. However, some important traditional features remain – a low-beamed ceiling, pub games like darts, dominoes, cards and long-alley skittles (the pub has its own league team) and a firm emphasis on good beer. And it still retains a homely, comfortable feel and mass popularity, especially in summer when visitors flock to the canalside beer garden. Pub food such as lasagne, ploughman's and filled jacket potatoes is served at lunchtimes except Sundays, and barbecues sometimes break out during hot weather.

The pub has long historical links with the canal. Built in the nineteenth century to house merchants visiting the nearby gravel pit, it was bought by the Leicester Navigation Company in 1861 (for £20, reputedly). The thirsts of the navvies who cut the canal and the bargees who worked it were slaked here, and the barge horses were stabled in part of what is now the bar.

The Navigation now hosts several annual events connected with the water, including a visit by the Mikron Theatre and a traditional Whitsun barrel race, usually starring a cast of thousands. Its traditional appeal may have been compromised, but for busy, bustling good humour and well kept beers, it still warrants a visit.

BERKHAMSTED
Boat

Tel : (0442) 877152
Gravel Path, Berkhamsted, Herts

✗ lunchtime and evening

🍴

🍺 **Fullers Chiswick Bitter, London Pride, ESB**

Like many of our more ambitious regional brewers, Fullers are busy expanding their estate by acquiring pubs that others, especially the national companies, are unable or unwilling to make a go of. From their riverside brewery in Chiswick they seem to have a special penchant for pubs situated on the waterways radiating out from the capital. Thus, when Benskins put the run-down Boat on the market some four years ago, Fullers were eager and successful bidders.

There followed an epic battle as the company tried to get their renovation proposals through the planning procedure. The whole story would be long in the telling, but the upshot was the demolition of the old (and, from what I gather, little-loved) pub and the construction in traditional materials and in the classic English vernacular style of an impressive brand-new Boat, very grand but wholly in keeping with its modest but attractive surroundings.

The site has been skilfully used to provide a

delightful canalside patio. There are flowers and shrubs all over with even a bed of marigolds flanking the towpath. Inside the decoration is traditional neo-Victorian with old mirrors, fireplaces and potted plants and with original bric-à-brac and dried flower arrangements displayed on a magnificent carved wood bar. The use of space, however, and the way natural sunlight is deployed to create light and airiness is wholly modern.

There is a healthy competition between Berkhamsted's canalside pubs to make a positive contribution to the community. It can do the Boat no harm to involve, as it does, local people in special theme nights accompanied by raffles and regular barbecues and (always with respect for the neighbours) the occasional evening of live music. This is a town where Britain's publicans are really doing their job.

Crystal Palace

Tel: (0442) 862998
Station Road, Berkhamsted, Herts. Canalside 200 yards east of bridge 141

✕ lunchtime and evening

🍴

☺

🍺 **Adnams Bitter; Benskins Best Bitter; Tetley Bitter**

The Crystal Palace was built in 1854, three years after the Great Exhibition and, like one or two pubs in this area, inspired in name and appearance by Joseph Paxton's great Victorian greenhouse.

There is not as much glass on the pub's façade as when it was first built. The elaborately barge-boarded gable end, once wholly glazed, is now tile-hung. Only the ground-floor windows to the saloon bar remain to give some echo of its architectural antecedents.

The pub shares an attractive canalside setting with an ivy-clad bridge and, on the opposite bank, the Berkhamsted totem pole. Other than that this exotically carved and brightly painted teak monolith advertises the presence of a woodyard, I know nothing of its history.

The licensees of the Crystal Palace are Chris and her husband Tad, a self-confessed eccentric who eschews any lengthier appellation. After years cruising the Thames, a necessity to base themselves on dry land (but as close as possible to the watery environment they love) brought them to the Crystal Palace. From a run-down state on their arrival, they have transformed the pub into a lively, boisterous community boozer with an exceptional welcome for the boater.

The recently refurbished interior consists of an attractive saloon and a large panelled public bar where weekend singalongs are accompanied by the Hammond organ.

The beer is well cared for and the food excellent, with much pride expressed in the authentic jumbo-size Cornish pasties.

If you have trouble with your boat, Tad will happily provide "the odd bit of mains power" to effect a repair, and he'll fill your water tank for a small fee. If you need to leave your boat for a couple of days at the pub's moorings, Tad will guard it with his life. This is a canal user-friendly pub, run by people whose great love and enthusiasm for what they do is manifestly evident.

Rising Sun

Tel: (0442) 864913
Canalside (off George Street), Berkhamsted, Herts by bottom lock

✗ lunchtime and evening (not weekends)

🍴

🍺 **Benskins Best Bitter**

This is the third pub in Berkhamsted's holy trinity. It's the smallest and the most basic, but arguably enjoying the best canalside setting.

Despite its size it has majestic proportions. It seems to tower above you as you stand by the lock; only two storeys but boosted in height by the cellar ceiling being two or three feet above ground level. Two bays run the height of the front of the building, with on one side an attractive doorway with hooded lintel approached by a short flight of steps.

Inside, the two bars are quite tiny. Apparently it gets very crowded here, but there is much to attract people and on my visit, with just one other customer, it was already beginning to feel that way. There are lots of pictures and ornaments around the place, including an interesting modernistic painting showing scenes of the pub and portraying Mr & Mrs Wilkins, who have been tenants here for many years. A small fortune in pennies is stuck to the low ceiling, using what I assume to be Guinness as glue.

There is much more I could say if space would allow. I have a letter from one of the locals positively raving about the place. I've considered plagiarising it word for eloquent word but will limit myself merely to quoting its conclusions, which give an idea of the pub's human qualities. "All in all," writes Ray Flanigan, "it's a really good place to hang around in, just chatting and having a laugh. Mind you, nobody minds if you stand there quietly keeping yourself to yourself. Give it a try if you're ever down this way." These are sentiments with which I heartily concur, but get there soon because there are people in the brewing industry who believe pubs like this have no place in the 20th century.

BOURNE END
Three Horseshoes

Tel : (0442) 862585
Winkwell, Bourne End, Herts. By Winkwell swing bridge, no. 147

✕ lunchtime

🍴

🍺 **Benskins Best Bitter, Ind Coope Burton Ale, Tetley Bitter; Greene King IPA (H)**

It is strange how often this sign appears over our public houses when common sense dictates the usual numerical requirement for horseshoes as being four. Perhaps it commemorates some dreadful pre-motor car road traffic accident.

The date boldly proclaimed in gothic script on the front of the Three Horseshoes is 1536. Thus it predates by some 300 years the canal that passes within inches alongside. The scene here must have already had picture book quality before it became reflected in the Grand Junction Canal's limpid waters. The roof sags and heaves in characterful fashion, pierced by a great clustered chimney stack. There's a big ivy creeper, hanging baskets, a fine old lamp over the sign and a very nice wooden porch with fixed benches, some 200 years old. Needless to say this is a popular pub for outside eating and drinking, with charming rural views and the swing bridge to provide entertainment.

Inside, there's a huge inglenook, old settles, exposed beams and lots of horse brasses, unsurprising but very attractive. The pub runs a nice line in positive discrimination for the elderly in the form of an over-30s bar. So quiet and peaceful!

The food here is good, if somewhat pricey and – being freshly prepared – can take time to arrive on a busy lunchtime. Sandwiches such as crab and hot salt beef should be worth the wait, though.

Like many of those pubs that time seems largely to have forgotten, the Three Horseshoes is off the beaten track, which is in this case the A41 between Hemel Hempstead and Tring. Once in Bourne End look out for the steep narrow lane going east, and get there early because others know how to get there too.

BRAUNSTON

OFF THE TOWPATH

At Braunston Turn the Oxford Canal bears north, while the Grand Union passes through the canal centre of Braunston, which has all the facilities a boater needs, including pubs. Close to the marina in the High Street is the **Old Plough** ((0788) 890000), an imposing seventeenth-century coaching inn of character, with Ansells and Ind Coope real ales and good value food lunchtimes and evenings. It has a family room with table skittles and a long narrow garden.

COSGROVE
Navigation

Tel: (0908) 543156
*Castlethorpe Road, Cosgrove,
Milton Keynes, Northants.
Canalside at Castlethorpe wharf,
bridge 64*

✗ lunchtime and evening

🍺

☺

🍺 **Draught Bass; Hook Norton
Best Bitter; Morlands Bitter,
Old Masters; guest beers**

Castlethorpe wharf has been a popular stopping point on the canal ever since the days when the produce of local farms and industry was shipped from here on its way to Birmingham or London. The Navigation, a fine stone-built country free house, may well than have been home to the wharfinger and remains today a highly canal-orientated establishment. It even has its own slipway, which doubles as a winding-hole for any boater skilful enough to take advantage.

The Navigation's rural setting provides a delightful contrast to the designer-sprawl of Milton Keynes just a few miles to the south, and the pub is fully deserving of the cliché "catering for all tastes." The beer enthusiast will find it a shrine to traditional beers, of which it regularly stocks a minimum of six, and frequently more. This list changes endlessly and each beer that has appeared is represented by its own pump-clip, over 100 of which frame the bar, while a collection of canned beers from around the world lines the shelves. These are the dominant decorative theme in a pub whose simple white painted interior eschews an excess of worthless bric-à-brac in favour of the occasional genuine antique.

The large open fire and the absence of noisy machines, obtrusive music and infernal electronic bleepings will please those who favour traditional values, while the food won't disappoint anyone either; apart from being very good value, a wide range is available from bar meals and snacks to the full sit-down three-course binge. Barbecues are held in summertime in the large canalside garden, which is overlooked by a pleasant separate family room in which children are welcome. Below this, a summer-only canal-level cellar bar provides yet another alternative – the plan here is to serve the draught beers by gravity straight from the cask.

The wharf is about a mile north of the village of Cosgrove and car owners will have a frustrating time seeking out the Navigation if they arrive in the village itself. Bisected by the canal and bridgeless, it is a succession of dead-end roads.

It's more straightforward for the boater. With plenty of moorings on hand for patrons, the only trick is to time your visit to coincide with opening hours.

COWLEY PEACHEY
Paddington
Packet Boat

OFF THE TOWPATH
Tel : (0895) 442392
High Road, Cowley Peachey, Middx. Bridge 190, then 200 yards east on Packet Boat Lane

✗ lunchtime (snacks only evening)

🍴

🍺 **Fullers London Pride, ESB**

This pub is a reminder of the fact, extraordinary to us today, that in the first half of the nineteenth century, before the railways took hold, there were scheduled passenger services on Britain's canals. This particular service was renowned for its speed over fifteen lock-free miles. The journey was never bridge-free, however, so I question the accuracy of the boat's depiction on the pub sign with folk sitting high on the roof, rather as on a stagecoach.

The pub itself is of Victorian design, probably built in its present form after the undertaking it celebrates had ceased. Recent refurbishment has emphasised heavy dark beams and exposed brickwork which might seem out of place, but somehow do not. There's a lovely garden and friendly, efficient service in this genuine and attractive boozer.

CRICK

OFF THE TOWPATH
A ten minute walk from Bridge 12 in the village of Crick will take you to the **Royal Oak** in Church Street, a lovely traditional village pub with a good atmosphere and featuring an unusual high bar, oak settles, an open fire, a small cosy lounge and separate restaurant. Landlord enthusiastic about his real ales – Marston's Pedigree and Burton Bitter, and Websters Yorkshire Bitter. Food is available lunchtimes and evenings.

GREAT LINFORD
Black Horse

Tel : (0908) 605939
Wolverton Road, Great Linford,
Milton Keynes, Bucks. Canalside
at bridge 76

✘ lunchtime and evening

🕮

☺

🍺 **Ind Coope Burton Ale**

The Black Horse can best be described as a collection of disparate buildings that somehow combine together as a whole. There are four different roof lines including the modern single storey toilet block, with fine old roof tiles the unifying material of construction. Below this there are old bricks, new bricks, rustic stonework and white-painted pebbledash thrown together in jaunty confusion.

Once inside, and there is a choice of three entrances, you are immediately disorientated. Much of the pub predates the canal. Those parts built subsequently have had to cope with the topographical change caused by the embankment and bridge approach. There are three bars, the two oldest of which have brush-grained panelling and settle-ended benches round the walls and lots of old features and atmosphere.

A door and passageway lead to more modern bar on two levels from which a flight of stairs gives access to a room where the pub's speciality salads are displayed and dispensed. Beneath this is the restaurant, not open every night, so it is best to book.

The Aylesbury Brewery Company, a non-brewing subsidiary of Allied-Lyons, have a good reputation for their stewardship of country pubs. They've even won awards for it. For this reason I am confident that the wholesale refurbishment of the Black Horse that will have been completed by the time of publication will enhance rather than destroy its considerable charm.

GREENFORD
Black Horse

Tel: (081) 578 1384
*425 Oldfield Lane North,
Greenford, Middx. Canalside at
Black Horse Bridge (number 15)
on the Paddington Arm*

✗ lunchtime (not Sun). Evening
snacks on request

🏠

🍺 Fullers London Pride, ESB

Hemmed in by the factories, offices and works of the ceaseless outer London sprawl, the Black Horse brings a real piece of the country to the unrelenting urban setting and presents a picturesque and welcome contrast with its old black and white frontage, shuttered windows, flowers and hanging baskets.

The pub leans against the southern approach to the eponymous Black Horse Bridge, a characterless modern concrete structure in stark contrast to its namesake. Internally the pub is straightforward enough and quite large and roomy, with a barn-like and boisterous public bar and comfortable lounge, where pub grub is served lunchtimes – salads, burgers, anything with chips – and where constant live entertainment comes courtesy of a chirpy, talkative, highly extrovert parrot by the name of Tobin.

There is a good-sized and surprisingly rural garden which shields the industry but allows a pleasant view of the canal. A new canalside pub sign has been erected to attract canal-users, whose attention will as likely be flagged down by the rather curious multi-purpose hollowed-out plastic tree, bedecked with swings and slides and nameless devilish devices to lure the kids.

This is very much the gateway to London's canal system, an environment for the enthusiast rather than the casual boater. These intrepid souls will find a warm welcome and superb beer here at the Black Horse, whose eleven consecutive years in the Good Beer Guide are richly deserved.

HAREFIELD
Fisheries Inn

Tel: (0895) 823180
Coppermill Lane, Harefield,
Middx. Canalside at bridge 177

✖ lunchtime and evening

🅱

🍺 **Benskins Best Bitter, Ind**
Coope Burton Ale

Sandwiched between the canal and the willow-bedecked River Colne, the Fisheries Inn enjoys a setting which is both pleasantly rural on one side and greatly of interest for its old but still active industrial buildings, the original copper mill, on the other.

The pub itself is of late Georgian vintage and notable for its bold dormer windows and the unusual cut away corners of its canal frontage. These are three-sided on ground floor level and project out to the more conventional two-sided arrangement on the upper floor.

Inside, the pub has been recently well renovated. There is one large single bar which is partitioned by low walls with wooden pillars supporting shelves upon which potted plants are displayed. There is much decorative canalania and the wallpaper has impressionistic fish swimming by at eye level. This may inspire a floating sensation unconnected with the effects of alcohol.

There is a large, well-lit patio beer garden overlooking the river with purpose-built play area for children. A large converted stable bar can be hired for functions and also hosts a blues club on Sunday lunchtimes.

The boater is lucky to see this part of the Middlesex suburban divide at its interesting best and has a warm welcome in store at the Fisheries Inn.

HAYES
Blue Anchor

Tel: (081) 573 0714
Printing House Lane, Hayes,
Middx. Canalside at bridge 199

✗ lunchtime; evening Thu, Fri, Sat

🍺

🍺 **Fullers London Pride; Ruddles Best Bitter, Websters Yorkshire Bitter**

It is always a great joy to find a pub owned by certain of our national "brewery" companies which is neither neglected and depressing, nor showy and tarted up in boring corporate style.

The Blue Anchor has an excellent situation; a little oasis among the featureless industrial sprawl. It has a very grand half-timbered and tile-hung Edwardian façade with decorative gable ends, and a lovely tree-shaded garden over-looking the canal.

The high-ceilinged interior has long been stripped of any substantial original features, but recent renovation has very successfully created a friendly and atmospheric environment. The walls are painted pristine white, with carpets, drapes and furnishings all in attractive fabrics. There is a new carved wood bar with coloured glass inserts, nothing flash but very effective. Unlike many of its sister pubs in the Grand Metropolitan empire, the Blue Anchor displays the human touch.

Nice also to see a genuine guest beer on the bar, one that has maintained over many years a reputation for character and flavour as well as for mere consistency.

Printing House Lane is a narrow highway that links the southern part of this conurbation with the town centre of Hayes, via the premises of EMI. Outside of working hours the factory gate is closed on the far side of the bridge and the Blue Anchor enjoys relative, if popular, isolation.

KEGWORTH
OFF THE TOWPATH

Although Kegworth is close to the river, access is only easy from Kegworth Shallow Lock. Do not be deterred – nestling in an inconspicuous back street called Borough Street is a classic and famous pub, one of the finest in the country. The **Cap & Stocking** ((0509) 674814) serves Draught Bass, M&B Mild and a guest beer from jugs filled in the cellar, and is everything a good pub should be.

Excellent value food is available lunchtimes and early evenings till 7.45. It has a beer garden and its own Flat Earth Society, and is now the local of What's Brewing cartoonist Bill Tidy. An essential visit.

KILBY BRIDGE
Navigation

Tel: (0533) 882280
Kilby Bridge (A50), Leics.
Canalside at Kilby Bridge (Bridge 87)

✘   lunchtime and evening

🏠

☺

🍺   **Ansells Bitter, Ind Coope Burton Ale; Marston Pedigree Bitter**

The Navigation is a long-standing canal favourite, very popular in summer with its small garden overlooking the canal. It is quite possibly older than the canal itself, though its name and much of its history are canal-linked. There was once a coal wharf outside, and a company house occupied in the mid–late nineteenth century by one George Foxton, who later became chairman of the Leicestershire & Northamptonshire Union Canal Company.

Today this atmospheric, low-beamed pub has a very broad appeal, with something always going on (due in no small part to the eccentricities and character of the landlord, armed with his water pistol). The latest venture is the attempt to form a petanque club. People with children can use the large and well-appointed family room, while diners can concentrate on the Bridge Lounge, where curries, moussaka, trout, Barnsley chop, various salads and other bar meals are available, complemented by a wine list. The pine-panelled room is a touch contrived but perfectly acceptable. Traditionalists, however, will head straight for the tiny snug bar – if they can get in, that is, for it can only seat fifteen or so in as much comfort as the wooden bench seating lining the walls will allow. It has an open fire in an inglenook, brasses and some nice old glass-framed advertisements. It's a lovely cosy bar in which to sit, talk and linger over some well-kept real ales, for which the Navigation has earned regular Good Beer Guide inclusion.

LAPWORTH
Navigation

Tel: (0564) 783337
*Old Warwick Road, (B4439)
Lapworth, nr Solihull, Canalside
at Bridge 65 near Kingswood
Junction*

✗ lunchtime and evening

🍴

🍺 **Draught Bass, M&B Mild, Brew
XI; guest beers**

Despite being perilously close to Birmingham and the West Midlands sprawl, the Navigation enjoys a lovely tranquil rural setting next to the canal. Tranquil, that is, except for the hordes of families who descend upon its large, enclosed weeping willow-lined canalside garden in search of their own slice of the country. Sanctuary can be found in the superb unspoilt bar. It's small, cool, quiet, everything you'd want from a classic traditional bar with its stone-slabbed floor, black oak cross beams, large inglenook fireplace, high-backed wooden settles, whitewashed brick-work and cosy corners. Its low ceiling groans under an assortment of old lamps, gleaming copper jugs and roses 'n' castles buckets. Further embellishment comes courtesy of a collection of glasses and tankards, and stuffed mounted fish in glass display cases. Some steps lead up from the bar to a carpeted lounge with a nice solid fuel stove.

Of course a bar as traditional as this without a good range of traditional beers would be horribly incomplete. Fortunately the landlord feels the same way, and has turned the pub into something of a feast for traditional ale-lovers. A nicely balanced selection is dispensed from a fine array of handpumps – a branded premium beer, an ordinary bitter, a mild and a regular and changing guest beer, which so far had included star names like Batemans, Greene King, Hook Norton, Wadworths and Adnams as well as the beers of more recent small breweries like Clarks, Moles and Titanic.

The comprehensive menu changes daily but tends to confine itself largely to safe pub food like steaks, grills, chili, curry and lasagne. It's reasonably priced though, and available lunch-time and evening till 9 pm. With shops five minutes away and full boating facilities on the Stratford canal at nearby Kingswood Junction, the area makes a most agreeable stop.

LONDON – HANWELL
Fox

OFF THE TOWPATH
Tel: (081) 567 3912
Green Lane (off A3002), Hanwell,
London W7. 100 yards east of
Hanwell bottom lock

✗ lunchtime; bar snacks only
   evening

🍺

☺

🍺 **Courage Best Bitter, Directors**

Moor up below Hanwell locks where tug-power was once provided by miniature tractors, cross the bridge over the weir stream, follow the footpath until you come to the bottom of Green Lane and on the right hand side you'll see the back of this impressive turn of the century public house. Turning the corner your eyes will light on its grand frontage of decorative ceramic tiles and half-timbered gables.

Inside there are high ceilings and some excellent original brush-grained woodwork. While gazing in awe at the skill of our Edwardian forebears you can enjoy some very well-kept draught beer, and, if it's sustenance you require, the Fox enjoys the Egon Ronay seal of approval.

HARLESDEN
Grand Junction Arms

Tel: (081) 965 5670
Acton Lane (B4492), Harlesden,
London NW10

✗ lunchtime and evening

🍺

🍺 **Youngs Bitter, Special Bitter, Winter Warmer**

For any canal-boater making his or her way through the frenetic suburbs of north-west London, the Grand Junction is a popular and welcome stopping place. Built at the end of the last century, the pub has a large, L-shaped public bar, which was converted into a single room during the summer of 1988. The saloon and lounge bars, the latter of which has a roof supported by a complex structure of massive beams, have also undergone facelifts, as has the superb art nouveau-influenced façade with its deep green decorative tiling on the ground floor and white painted stucco above.

Despite the alterations, the pub still keeps an attractive face for anyone arriving by boat, who will be greeted by a delightful two-tier beer garden and terrace, including chairs and tables right next to the canal. In summer, canalside barbecues add to the attraction, and good quality hot bar food and snacks are available at lunchtimes (except Sundays, when prior arrangement should be made).

Hardly surprisingly, the Grand Junction gets very busy, especially at lunchtimes in the week when it needs every bit of its vast space to cater for the workers who flood in to escape for an hour from the nearby offices and factories and enjoy the charms of a canalside break. It all makes for a lively, friendly and cosmopolitan atmosphere which still manages to retain something of a canal flavour. And the place is sure to suit anyone who likes the idea of sitting in the sun with a delicious pint of Youngs Special Bitter, idly watching the boats chug past while the other London thunders across the bridge above you. It's hard to escape a feeling of smug satisfaction that on this occasion you're the one who got it right.

ISLINGTON
Island Queen

OFF THE TOWPATH
Tel: (071) 226 5507
87 Noel Road, Islington, London N1. 100 yards north west of Wharf Road bridge on the Regent's Canal

✗ lunchtime and evening

🕮

☺

🍺 **Draught Bass, Charrington IPA; Young's Special Bitter (H)**

If the Island Queen had a ghost it would probably be that of Joe Orton who lived nearby in Noel Road. A famous, perhaps notorious, bohemian hangout, it is best known for the larger-than-life puppets suspended from the high Victorian ceiling. A feature of the pub for some 20 years and very much in Spitting Image tradition, they are changed from time to time to keep them topical. Thus I assume that Nigel Lawson won't be up there with Mrs Thatcher very much longer.

If I used the word "trendy" to describe the Island Queen it might betray my age. After all, this was one of my youthful haunts. But the beer is just as good as it always was and some imaginative bar meals are augmented by a superb restaurant upstairs.

Narrow Boat

Tel: (071) 226 3906
*119 St Peters Street, Islington,
London N1. At Wharf Road bridge
between Wenlock Basin and City
Road Basin on the Regent's Canal*

✗ lunchtime

🍴

☺

🍺 **Draught Bass, Charrington IPA**

The Regent's Canal offers few places for moored craft to be safely left unattended; and what with towpath gates closing at dusk crews face acrobatic contortions on returning to vandalised boats after exploration of nearby drinking establishments.

All this makes the Narrow Boat a particularly welcoming sight for the imbiber afloat. A doorway directly on the towpath gives access via a metal latticed stairway to a very pleasant little canalside patio, from which vantage point a weather eye can be kept on one's boat, with private moorings on the far bank making for safety in numbers.

The pub has a two-storey decorative stucco façade on street level and directly abuts the yellow-brick bridge. The signs are in the proper tradition of the waterways and include two models in shallow relief of brightly-painted working boats. A corner doorway provides access to a large and quite plain bar brightened up with pictures of canal scenes and a clever working model of a narrow boat descending a lock. The back bar carries this theme even further. Both inside and from outside on the terrace it resembles the cross-section of a canal boat, if rather wider than the widest of Grand Union wide boats.

The Narrow Boat is in some state of flux at the time of writing, with a new manager taking the helm and the pub in need of a lick of paint and a bit of a refit. We must hope that its interesting and intimate character survives this period.

Prince of Wales

Tel: (071) 837 6173
*1a Sudeley Street, Islington,
London N1. South bank of
Regent's Canal 100 yards from
east portal of Islington tunnel*

✖ lunchtime (evening if
requested)

☺

🍺 **Ind Coope Burton Ale, Tetley
Bitter**

In the melting pot that is this part of Islington, council blocks stand proudly in the midst of terraces of fine Georgian houses that underwent "gentrification" 30 years ago. Here you can find typical Cockney street corner boozers such as this next door to properties that would set you back five hundred grand or more. "It's a proper pub", commented one of my companions, not an accolade she would have bestowed upon the nearby Island Queen, for all its qualities.

The Prince of Wales was built some time in the 1930s. In plan and elevation it takes traditional form but the detail and decoration have echoes of the Art Deco style so popular at the time. There are some excellent etched windows and the pub is panelled from floor to ceiling in very fine wood veneer. There are two walk-through bars, a tiny public with dartboard and a larger comfortable lounge. The pub acknowledges its waterside status, though separated from the towpath by a road, with tasteful prints of canal scenes set around the walls.

Traditional London hospitality is cheerfully dispensed along with foaming pints of good traditional beer in this attractive, well-run and unassuming little pub.

LITTLE VENICE
Bridge House

*13 Westbourne Terrace, Little
Venice, London W2. Across road
from Westbourne Terrace bridge
on the Regent's canal*

✖ lunchtime and evening (not
Mon)

🍴

🍺 **Draught Bass, Charington IPA**

To describe the Bridge House's position as end-of-terrace is somewhat to understate its architectural splendour. The terrace in question is part of the superb Regency and early Victorian development that flanks the canal at Little Venice and is hardly less impressive than the world-famous Nash terraces on nearby Regent's Park. The façade has a grand entrance and fine bay window but is somewhat overshadowed by a giant tree on the pavement. The side elevation, overlooking the canal, is visible in its full glory, with fine classical stucco-work in a perfect state of preservation. There are decorative quoins and tall, heavily pedimented windows on the first floor, and a central balcony sufficient to hold the Royal Family or a returning officer with a host of fringe election candidates.

The interior is also rich in 19th century plasterwork and decorated in sombre shades of green. Heavy velvet drapes, old pictures and huge Victorian mirrors advertising Bass's ale and Rawlings mineral waters complete a very evocative scene. The theatricality of this decor is most appropriate because upstairs the pub has its own stage, well known in London for the quality of its repertoire.

The Bridge House, as its name implies, guards one of Little Venice's exuberantly designed iron canal bridges, right next to the BWB office, and is popular with both the residential and just-passing-through floating population that this historic, colourful and most famous canalside setting attracts. It is also convenient for the terminus of the London Waterbus Company and other similar undertakings.

Warwick Castle

OFF THE TOWPATH
Tel : (071) 286 6868
6 Warwick Place (off Blomfield Road), Little Venice, London W9.
200 yards north of Westbourne Terrace bridge on the Regent's Canal

---

✗ lunchtime and evening

🗟

🍺 Draught Bass Charrington IPA ; Morrell's Varsity ; guest beer

This smart Victorian pub has enjoyed an excellent reputation over many years for the quality of its beer, and was an early standard-bearer of the guest ale policy with the only Morrells regularly on tap in London. It is also noted for its food, with a tempting array of buffet meals on display at lunchtimes and doorstep sandwiches available in the evening.

The wood-panelled interior is darkly atmospheric and there are plenty of interesting and historic items on display including brewery mirrors and canalania.

Tucked away at the back of Little Venice in one of London's more exclusive villages, the Windsor Castle nevertheless attracts a large, cheerful, socially diverse and cosmopolitan clientele.

PRIMROSE HILL
Engineer

OFF THE TOWPATH
Tel : (071) 722 4083
65 Gloucester Avenue, Primrose Hill, London NW1. 300 yards north of Cumberland Basin on the Regent's Canal, then 100 yards west of Gloucester Avenue bridge

---

✗ lunchtime and evening
  (sandwiches only Sat)

🍴

🍺 **Draught Bass, Charrington IPA**

There cannot be many historical associations with I. K. Brunel east of Paddington station, but as the Victorian engineer most prominent in the public mind it is not wholly inappropriate that his stern countenance should grace the sign of the Engineer.

One of London's better street-corner locals, the pub has a grand classical 19th century exterior and two very well refurbished bars within. There are plenty of interesting and historic working drawings, plans and memorabilia on the walls to celebrate the work of the civil engineer. It makes a change to find an attractive and truly educational theme pub.

VICTORIA PARK
Royal Cricketers

Tel : (081) 980 4681
211 Old Ford Road, Victoria Park, London E2. Bridge side between Old Ford lock and the junction with the Hertford Union on the Regent's Canal

---

✗ lunchtime

🍴

🍺 **Whitbread Wethered Bitter;
Green King Abbot Ale**

After Limehouse Basin the Regent's Canal begins a strictly urban and industrial but very private journey through the East End of London. It is not until Victoria Park (where I have myself played cricket, but never in the company of royalty) that the canal opens up and the environs could in any way be described as scenic. Old Ford Lock is pleasantly accompanied by old canal offices and stables, with the park's massed ranks of London plane trees creating an attractive tableau. Just below the lock stands the Royal Cricketers, a typical canal bridgeside pub but very much in the grand manner.

The exterior is of yellow brick and stucco and early Victorian. The inside retains much of its original subdivisions and there are two open staircases of interesting modern design leading to the cellar bar and canalside patio, where limited moorings are available. The ceilings are of interspersed strips of mirrored glass, a surprising effect but quite restrained by normal East End standards of pub embellishment.

Sadly there is evidence of recent neglect here and there was no permanent manager at the time of my visit. I expect that Whitbread are soon to embark on major refurbishment which, if done well, could properly exploit the Royal Cricketers' considerable potential. It is a listed building, so let us hope we don't see another case of vandalism and wasted opportunity.

LOUGHBOROUGH Albion

Tel: (0509) 213952
Canal Bank, Loughborough, Leics.
Canalside just south of A6004
Belton Road Bridge

✕ lunchtime

🍴

🍺 Banks's Mild, Bitter; Batemans Mild; Samuel Smith's Old Brewery Bitter; Hoskins & Oldfield Old Navigation Ale, Xmas Noggin (winter only); Mansfield Old Baily; guest beers

From the Albion's front door to your moored boat is just a short stumble across the towpath, but beware! Look left, right and left again. Fresh tarmac and those bright yellow stripes bear witness to the unlikely fact that the towpath here is part of Loughborough's highway system.

Nevertheless it is principally to the canal that this flourishing free house addresses itself. Its architecture is of the classic style associated with lock-keepers' cottages and the humble, utilitarian waterside warehouses of the canal age. Modern pebbledash, replacement windows and a haphazard collection of brewery adverts fail to disguise the pub's essential character. Cream-painted plasterwork and pleasantly mellow half-timbering with original and reclaimed beams in their natural colour play their part in creating a warm, friendly atmosphere. The interior with its two small drinking areas and games room is dominated by bank upon bank of handpumps, providing a bewildering selection of interesting and well kept ales, none of which seem to be advertised outside.

Tasty pub food is available at lunchtimes. Evening meals for large groups are on an ad hoc basis. There are some tables and chairs for outdoor drinking.

Boat

Tel: (0509) 214578
*Meadow Lane, Loughborough,
Leics. Canalside at Bridge 39
(Meadow Lane Bridge)*

✗ lunchtime

🏚

🍺 Marston Pedigree Bitter

Historically a classic, the Boat will now be unrecognisable to those who last visited it more than two years ago. The three plain rooms have made way for a single multi-level bar with stripped pine, floral patterns, old canal prints and shelves sagging under bric-à-brac. In place of the tiny bay window is a vast glazed extension running the full length of the pub and echoing the canal theme with its bright green, red and yellow panels. Some will mourn even more the passing of the chip butty, to be replaced by more standard pub fare.

The Boat was the property of the canal company in the late eighteenth century, becoming part of the brewery's estate in 1909. It once had its own brewhouse, piggeries and skittle alley. Many will miss the old, uncompromising boozer it once was, but the quality and craftsmanship of the new work is beyond dispute. With its front door opening directly onto the towpath, full advantage has been taken of its superb position, with canal, towpath and pub combining to form a most pleasing architectural tableau. All-day opening and catering for families has served to broaden the pub's appeal.

OFF THE TOWPATH

The Grand Union skirts the old heart of Loughborough, and many of the town's fine pubs are within easy reach. A hundred yards south of the canal basin is the **Swan in the Rushes** [(0509) 217014], a superb free house serving Marston's Pedigree, Tetley Bitter, guest bitters and a regular guest mild. It also has an imaginative menu including vegetarian, available every session except Sunday evenings. High standard and reasonably priced accommodation is available. **The Gate**, one hundred yards south of Bridge 39, near the Boat, is a down-to-earth red brick nineteenth century terraced boozer, recently refurbished rather less dramatically than its neighbour. It offers excellent handpumped Marston's Pedigree and Mercian Mild.

MARSWORTH
Red Lion

OFF THE TOWPATH
Tel: Cheddington 668366
*Vicarage Road (off B489),
Marsworth, Herts. 50 yards east
of bridge 130*

✗ lunchtime and evening

🅱

ⓖ

🍺 **Draught Bass; Wadworth's
6X; guest beers**

I sat in a comfortable little low-ceilinged lounge bar with antique plates displayed in the Georgian corner dresser. Before me was a pint of Bass I couldn't have faulted and a bowl of chicken Provençal. It was delicious, and swimming in the rich sauce were carrots which were demonstrably home-grown. All misshapen and crinkly, unrecognisable to those used to the squidgy tinned variety, and tasting exactly as carrots should.

The Red Lion is an idyllically attractive pub. From my upper level vantage point over the cellar I could look down to another little carpeted bar to my right by the entrance, and through the bar hatch, past the lines of fine whiskies and carefully selected wines, to the large jolly quarry-tiled bar with its ancient settles, open fireplace and bar billiard table. Character veritably oozes from every corner.

The exterior, eighteenth century I suppose, is of mellow brick, partly roofed in old tiles and partly thatched. There is a constantly changing menu so my chicken Provençal will not always be available. But you'll find equally appetising alternatives and the pub is renowned for its curries. Arrive in good time if you want to eat. Despite being part of the Aylesbury Brewery estate, the Red Lion is run very much as a free house with a guest beer policy of long-standing. On my visit the landlord was bemoaning his inability to shift more Banks & Taylor Shefford Bitter as he liked the stuff so much himself. The popular Marston's Pedigree was on its way as a replacement. Just like the oddly-shaped carrots, the quality that is the watchword of this fine pub is not the sort that comes in a standardised package.

NEW BRADWELL
New Inn

Tel: (0908) 312094
*2 Bradwell Road, New Bradwell,
Milton Keynes, Bucks. Canalside
near bridge 72*

✕ lunchtime and evening

🍴

🍺 **Charles Wells Eagle Bitter,
Bombardier**

The New Inn is a very well-proportioned stone-built pub of the last century. Two-storeyed, it has a nice original doorway flanked on either side by well-designed modern bay windows. There are window boxes and hanging baskets and on one corner a large creeper clings to the wall like a giant green hand. In the near distance, behind trees at the back of the pub is the recently restored new Bradwell post mill. Hard to believe you're in the middle of a city of millions of people, but Milton Keynes is like that.

The pub is large and well demonstrates the wisdom of having separate bars of contrasting character. The public bar is plain but quite smart and is itself subdivided to create a separate area for darts. The saloon bar is impressively wood-panelled and dignified. Upstairs there is a huge restaurant with a high ceiling supported by wooden posts. This is very pleasantly decorated and offers good value set price lunch and dinner with a dinner dance taking place on Saturday evenings. Boaters who avail themselves of this are advised to book beforehand and not to arrive dressed in wellington boots and carrying torches.

The landlord and landlady seem to employ an army to run this thriving enterprise and obviously work pretty hard themselves. Despite its size and popularity the New Inn is notable for the friendliness and courtesy extended to each and every one of its customers.

NORMANTON-ON-SOAR
Plough

Tel: (0509) 842228
Main Street, Normanton-on-Soar, Leics. Riverside at Normanton

✗ lunchtime and evening

🍴

☺

🍺 Ansells Mild, Tetley Bitter, Ind Coope Burton Ale

This lovely, rambling old pub has, in common with the rest of the village of Normanton-on-Soar, an identity crisis. It has a Leicestershire postal address, but comes under Nottinghamshire's licensing laws – the actual boundary is in Zouch, the next village. Despite this, and the fact that it is a managed house, the Plough manages to cater for all tastes, especially for families.

Dating back to the mid-eighteenth century, it has always been a pub or coaching inn. Its charming exterior features a black and cream frontage and a half-timbered rear. The interior is large and irregular-shaped, with a large rather plain bar with a pool table, a better-than-average lounge and a popular small family room, all leading off a central entrance hall which contains fruit machines and a gong on a stand.

The picturesque riverside garden is a real treat, its neat lawns dotted with wooden tables among the trees, bushes and shrubs. There are slides, swings and a herby tree for the children, and another drinking patio nearer the pub. The outbuildings to the side of the gardens used to be a restaurant and, in earlier times, a mortuary where they used to keep the dead bodies fished out of the river – a problem which seems to have diminished somewhat in recent times. The plan is to turn this into a family room, releasing the existing one in the pub itself for use as a cosy additional bar and/or function room.

Pub food consists of hot and cold lunches every session except Sunday evenings. Steaks are on the menu on Fridays and Saturdays.

Mooring is not easy at Normanton, and even the pub's own limited moorings are restricted to pub licensing hours.

NORTH KILWORTH

OFF THE TOWPATH
Further north, ten minutes walk west of Bridge 45 at North Kilworth, the **White Lion** on the Lutterworth Road (A427) is a large coaching in catering for all tastes. It offers Marston's Pedigree, Burton Bitter and Border Mild and excellent food without being a foodie place. Cheese skittles is played. There is a pleasant beer garden.

SIMPSON
Plough

Tel: (0908) 670015
Simpson Road, Simpson, Milton Keynes, Bucks. East bank, just north of the aqueduct

✕ lunchtime and evening

🛏

☺

🍺 **Charles Wells Eagle Bitter, Bombardier**

The village of Simpson may well be one of the most attractively named in the country but, surrounded as it is by the weird semi-rural city of Milton Keynes, arguably not the most attractively situated. The city planners, however, have undeniably made a very pleasant feature – in the linear park mode – of the Grand Union Canal and this is greatly to the benefit of the properties that lie beside it.

The Plough has little to be said for it architecturally. In plan and elevation and in the pitch of its roof it takes a pleasantly traditional form, but otherwise, like a house bombed by the Luftwaffe and rebuilt in utilitarian style with minimal government grants, its outward appearance is rectangular and modern. The makings of a pub are not bricks and mortar alone, however. Much can be achieved with enthusiastic stewardship, which is certainly the case here.

The pub's great natural (if man-made) asset is its garden, sweeping up the steep canal embankment to a little wooden gate on to the towpath. Within, the bars are as architecturally plain as the outside, but the judicious placing of ornaments and pictures has transformed them into a pleasant and friendly drinking and eating environment.

Few country pubs find themselves host to both office workers and canal boaters. The Plough caters for all with steaks, quiches, curries and vegetarian dishes for consumption either in the bar or the separate restaurant, and it does an excellent pint of beer as well.

SOUTHALL
Old Oak Tree

Tel : (081) 574 1714
The Common, Southall, Middx.
Canalside at bridge 202

✖ lunchtime bar snacks

🏨

◎

🍺 **Courage Best Bitter, Directors**

For much of the canal's course through Southall the towpath runs beside pleasant tree-lined avenues of suburban terraced housing. At the corner of one of these terraces is the Old Oak Tree, a friendly Victorian tavern just across the road from a little green open space where children and their mothers while away the long summer days.

Inside the pub a handful of customers while away those afternoon hours when once no licensed premises was permitted to be open. The arrival of a stranger excites no comment, with an exception in my case, having been mistaken for John Entwistle of The Who. Before I took my leave, the bar was gradually, soul by soul, beginning to fill with a cosmopolitan and good-natured band of regulars.

The pretty white-painted stucco exterior leads into two rather plain bars with uninspiring wallpaper and a smattering of canalania. A bit of woodwork would help here, but this is the sort of pub whose ambience is supplied by the people who use it rather than the physical surroundings. Add to this the excellently main-tained beer and safe convenient moorings, and you have a highly recommended stopping place on this interesting, if not always scenic, stretch of urban canal.

STOKE BRUERNE
Boat Inn

Tel: (0604) 862428
Bridge Road, Stoke Bruerne,
Northants. Canalside by top lock

✗ lunchtime and evening

🍽

☺

🍺 Everards Old Original;
Marston Burton Bitter,
Pedigree Bitter; Samuel
Smiths Old Brewery Bitter

I well remember visiting the Waterways Museum at Stoke Bruerne as a teenager in the company of my mother. An abiding interest in inland navigation was here awoken at a time when the last regular commercial narrowboat traffic had still some years to run. The awakening of my interest in public houses was yet to come, however, so it was not before my second visit to Stoke Bruerne, some 25 years on, that I found myself in the bar of the Boat.

The setting of this pub, its outside appearance and its history are so well known from countless guide books, calendars and postcards that there is little that can be added here. Suffice to say that this beautiful stone-built, thatched pub, run by the same family for over 100 years, is a star contributor to one of the most picturesque scenes on the waterways.

Inside, two rustic low-ceilinged bars overlooking the canal are wholly original, little about them having changed for very many years. There are open fires, flagstone floors and wooden benches around the walls. There are some interesting murals of canal scenes and a large area set aside for Northamptonshire skittles.

Less pleasing is a new bar at the back of the pub; a worthy effort of its time, the 1960s, to blend with the old building without creating a pastiche but very much the victim of changes in architectural fashion.

The pub provides bar meals and also has, quite separately, a restaurant and a little tea shop, the latter much appreciated by the coach loads of senior citizens that descend upon Stoke Bruerne in the summer months.

UXBRIDGE
General Elliott

Tel : (0895) 37385
St Johns Road, Uxbridge, Middx.
Canalside at bridge 186

✘ lunchtime and evening

🍽

☺

🍺 Benskins Best Bitter, Ind
Coope Burton Ale, Tetley
Bitter

To one quiet, traditional pub in London's outer suburbs add a pinch of history and one landlord from Baltimore, USA, stand back and wait for two and a half years. That's how long it took Mike Rutowski and his English wife, Trisha, to fashion a pub of immense character and good humour, spicing its appeal with some typical American virtues sympathetically and gently.

The General Elliott's name derives from the British military man who defended the Rock of Gibraltar, except his name only had one "l". His portrait hangs in the bar. The listed building dates from 1824, and was first licensed between 1825 and 1831. The interior consists of a large U-shaped room with central bar and has recently undergone thorough renovation with many original features retained. The style is of the chintzy, stripped pine, old adverts and book-lined variety and works very well here.

There is a colourful fenced canalside garden, all hanging baskets and parasols in summertime. Apparently it can accommodate one hundred and fifty.

The American influence of the generous, softly-spoken landlord is clearly reflected in the cleanliness, the friendly efficient service in which the customer comes first and surliness is out, and emphatically in the home-cooked food. The humble sandwich is transformed into a North American feast, stuffed with inches of filling and great value for money. As Mike says about these doorsteps, "the butter doesn't get too close together". There are proper barbecues and pig roasts at weekends if the weather's good, and a real speciality will be hot seafood buffets, steamed crab and prawns Baltimore-style, dripping with butter and herbs and eaten with messy fingers, all washed down with jugs of ale, which is, of course, traditionally English.

The relaxed atmosphere seems to entice characters both local and floating to the General

Elliott, adding an endearing hint of eccentricity to the affable mix. As a result, it can get as congested as the canal outside, and, as mooring can prove difficult, be prepared for a towpath hike.

WEEDON
Narrow Boat

Tel: (0327) 40536
Stone Hill, Weedon, Northants.
At bridge 26

✘ lunchtime and evening

🍴

☺

🛏

🍺 **Charles Wells Eagle Bitter, Bombardier**

It may not have escaped the reader that the authors of this modest work are both staunch defenders of the traditional English pub. This is not to neglect, however, that this tradition has enjoyed organic (as against imposed) development over the years and manifests itself in all manner of shapes, sizes and in sometimes surprising forms.

Here we have, on first sight as its name implies, a typical Victorian bridge and canalside pub. Substantial gardens sweep down the water's edge. There's a large barbecue and the perfectly acceptable modern innovation of motel chalets set apart from the main building (there are seven of these, and rather than numbered they are identified as Dopey, Grumpy etc., after … yes, you've guessed it).

The outside of the Narrow Boat is of white-painted brick – always shows the dirt. I think – with a rather untidy profusion of signs, but it looks an eminently pleasant and welcoming establishment, which indeed it is.

Inside, there is a large bar with walls decorated with canal scenes and other related memorabilia and some nice all-brass beer-pumps handles. The rest of the pub, probably half of it, is partitioned to form a restaurant area. For the hurried, the usual bar snacks are also available.

When visiting the Narrow Boat it is worth remembering that the pub is about a mile south of the village, both by canal and the main A5 trunk road.

Wheatsheaf

OFF THE TOWPATH
Tel: (0327) 40670
*34 High Street, Weedon,
Northants. 100 yards east of
bridge 24*

✗ lunchtime and evening

🍴

☺

🍺 **Banks's Mild, Bitter**

Weedon is an important victualling base for explorers on the Grand Union. There are three boatyards, and the High Street shops, including a good wholefood grocery, offer most of the boater's requirements.

Also in the High Street is this very attractive little pub. Modest but well-proportioned outside, its single bar is an Aladdin's cave of brass and copper.

The Wheatsheaf, part of the Watney's empire until three years ago, is now an outlet for Wolverhampton and Dudley Breweries. While they continue to expand from their Midlands base it's still a surprise to see a Banks's pub so far south.

This provides the unusual feature of a regularly available draught mild, not seen in these parts for many a year. Equally unusual, in a W&D house, is to find their beers on handpump. Us southerners must still need an obvious outward sign to indicate real bear – in this case, as they say in the Black Country, bostin good real beer at that.

WELFORD

OFF THE TOWPATH

The best pub on the short Welford Arm is **The Swan** in Welford village itself, a quarter mile from the basin in the High Street. It's a good, spacious, one-room pub with good beer (Marston's Pedigree, Burton Bitter), good food lunchtimes and evenings and a beer garden.

THE KENNET AND AVON CANAL

Completed in 1810 the Kennet & Avon consists of the two river navigations joined together by a canal to provide an unbroken link of some 87 miles between Bristol and Reading and thence, via the Thames, to London. Derelict over much of its length since the early 1950s the Kennet & Avon became the subject of a massive restoration effort and was officially re-opened by the Queen in August 1990.

AVONCLIFF
Cross Guns

Tel: (02216) 2335
*Avoncliff, Wilts. South side of
Avoncliff aqueduct*

✗ lunchtime and evening

🕮

◎

ᕤ

◁ **Hall & Woodhouse**
Tanglefoot; Ruddles Best
Bitter, County; Smiles Bitter;
Ushers Best Bitter

Nestling in the beautiful Avon valley, the Cross Guns justly claims the most spectacular location of any waterside pub, its terraced gardens cascading three levels down through tall trees towards the river's fast-flowing waters.

The Kennet & Avon canal enters the scene from behind the pub to stride across the valley over the great Georgian stone arch of John Rennie's Avoncliff aqueduct. It is worth remembering that this dramatic rural idyll was once, with its mills, its quarries and with the canal itself, the scene of frantic industrial activity, while the Cross Guns slaked the thirst of those who made their living here.

The pub is basically of the 17th and 18th centuries. Behind the fine gabled façade, painted boldly in black and white, is a beamy atmospheric bar with pottery and brass ornaments in abundance. Recent times having seen dividing walls knocked through and plasterwork stripped away to reveal rough stonework. The effect of this could better be described as "olde worlde" than old world.

While remaining very much a pub the Cross Guns lays great emphasis on food. A large menu holds no great culinary surprises but the proud boast is that it is all home-made and that the portions are guaranteed to satisfy any appetite.

BATH
Dolphin Inn

Tel: Bath 445048
Lockbrook Road, Bath, Avon.
River Avon, north bank by
Dolphin Bridge on Weston Cut

✗ lunchtime and evening (not
Tue or Sun eve)

⊠

☺

🍺 **Whitbread Flowers IPA,**
Original; Marston's Pedigree
Bitter

For those more used to navigating canals than rivers, a brief respite from the perils of the Avon is afforded by Weston Cut as you leave the city of Bath to head west. This friendly little channel offers trouble-free moorings and a perfect stopover for the night, which will inevitably entail a visit to the Dolphin. The pub was built in 1728, the year after the cut was completed and, in classic canalside tradition, the side that faces the water is as imposing as that facing the road; it has no "back".

The river frontage is certainly prettier. Nearby is the delightful stone footbridge which is, again in canalside tradition, eponymous with the pub. The garden is large and well cared for with flowers and shrubs and some discreet paraphernalia for the amusement of the young. In recent redecoration the brewery has been wise to leave the upper areas of wall unpainted. The effect is far mellower than the pastel shades so often employed.

Recent works inside has been far more comprehensive. The large drinking area that results is comfortable and atmospheric.

In the choice of materials and the treatment of space, however, there is an echo of Whitbread pubs from the Weald to the Wirral, and one is nostalgically inclined to miss the old interiors of pubs thus refurbished, even if one has never seen them. I have since learned that the Dolphin was previously somewhat dossy.

I did enjoy, though, the barn-like family room. The dramatic use of deliberate holes in the plasterwork to reveal heavily varnished stonework was reminiscent of the set of a Vincent Price horror movie. This should either delight the kiddies or scare the life out of them.

BATH

OFF THE TOWPATH

Bath has no pubs apart from the Dolphin that can be called waterside. The many fine beer houses in the city are accessible for the boater after a healthy stroll but these are beyond this guide's remit. The following three are conveniently placed within easy reach of good moorings.

The Royal Oak, known also as Rossiters, is on Pulteney Road, 200 yards north of lock 12 as the canal enters the city, and thus an excellent place to visit before or after the rigours of Widcome flight. A comfortable, lounge-barish hostelry, it serves the full range of Gibbs Mew's distinctive ales along with good food, and is a haven for professional spoof players.

The Hop Pole Inn is in Upper Bristol Road at the end of an insalubrious alleyway that joins the towpath between the suspension bridge and the city's old gasworks, from which three barges carrying tar to Bristol were the Avon's last commercial users. This is a comfortable, friendly pub, very much a local whose regulars involve themselves in every form of sport including skittles on the premises. There is live entertainment some evenings and beer from Ushers with Butcombe Bitter guesting.

The New Westhall is a Marston's pub 200 yards further west on the same road. A plain, congenial boozer, offering excellent Pedigree and Border Bitter.

BATHAMPTON
George Inn

Tel: Bath 425079
Mill Lane, Bathampton, Bath, Avon. On towpath by Bathampton Bridge

✗ lunchtime and evening

🍴

☺

🍺 **Courage Best Bitter, Directors John Smiths Bitter**

As the canal approaches the suburbs of the city of Bath the closely manicured sward of Bathampton cricket club reaches right to the water's edge. Speculating as to how many lofted drives have deposited cherry-red projectiles into these dark waters, you pass under Bathampton Bridge to be greeted by a sight strikingly familiar perhaps even to those who have never been here before. For this is the most attractive, superbly situated and thus much-photographed George Inn.

The pub's origins are lost in history, possibly monastic and as far back as the fourteenth century, but certainly they long predate the canal which veers sharply to the left as if to avoid so venerable an establishment.

There are three distinct drinking areas inside on ground level with low heavy-beamed ceilings and separated by massively thick stone walls. On a higher level, accessible by a spiral stairway, is a bright, airy room with a doorway opening directly on to the canal towpath. The furniture and decor is either antique or in period style throughout.

Attracted by the fine menu and good beer, the besuited expense-accountant up from Bath, with German engineering in the car park, is as likely a customer as the ragged unshaved flotsam from the narrowboat on the canal. The George, in a centuries-old tradition, gives welcome and succour to all.

BRADFORD-ON-AVON
Barge Inn

Tel: (02216) 3402
17 Frome Road, Bradford-on-Avon, Wilts. Backing on to the wharf, by the lock

✕ lunchtime and evening

🍴

🛏

🍺 **Ushers Best Bitter; Ruddles Best Bitter**

As its name implies, the Barge has long seen its fortunes linked to that of the Kennet & Avon canal. It once provided stabling for horses of the Midland Railway fleet that plied these Great Western-owned waters and has more recently been at the hub of the successful campaign for restoration of the waterway. The delightful dry dock nearby in the wharf is headquarters of the Wiltshire branch of the Canal Trust.

The Barge is an imposing three-storey Georgian building of Bath stone, with an airy high-ceilinged interior decorated with canal artefacts. There is a particularly fine beer garden with a large and exotic evergreen tree at its centre and a barbecue inventively housed in an eighteenth-century baroque stone grotto.

Canal Tavern

Tel: (02216) 5232
Bradford Wharf, Frome Road, Bradford-on-Avon, Wilts. Town side of Bradford lock and bridge

✕ barmeals (not Wed); à la carte (not Wed & Sun)

🍴

☺

🍺 **Wadworth IPA, 6X**

The original Canal Tavern, forlorn and empty, can be seen just across the towpath from the building that now bears the title. The licence was transferred many years ago when the old site proved too constricting, but advantage only recently seems to have been taken of this opportunity to expand – and to good effect.

The pub has two friendly and rustic bars facing the street, decorated with model boats and canal memorabilia. At the back, facing the canal, is a brand new glazed extension, built in neo-Victorian style with the usual tasteful bric-à-brac in evidence. This functions as a saloon bar-cum-restaurant. The landlord explained that service here was 'à la carte'. Although this little French phrase is employed to avoid some clumsiness in English, its use also implies certain standards of catering. I was keen to check this out and my crew and I duly seated ourselves at an enormous circular table, made our orders and waited. And waited.

Our mistake was that we hadn't booked and the food at the Canal Tavern is cooked to order.

But when it did arrive it more than justified that little French tag. In fact it was outstanding. The starters lived up to their mouth-watering descriptions and the main courses (monkfish and scampi with bacon and cream sauce, hazelnut roast for our vegetarian, chicken breast with smoked ham and wild mushroom sauce, venison steak with port and orange sauce) were absolute works of art. Alas we left no room for sweets such as chocolate roulade with raspberries. The prices looked a little daunting but the superb fresh vegetables were inclusive so the great surprise was the smallness of the final bill. And, washing it down with Wadworth's fine beer, we had no need of the extensive wine list. There is also a tempting bars menu with such delights as deep fried Brie and chicken korma.

Here you have what is surely one of the best restaurants in Wiltshire tacked on to a traditional boozer, itself with few equals.

BRISTOL
Nova Scotia Hotel

Tel: (0272) 262751
Nova Scotia Place, Cumberland Basin, Bristol. South side of Cumberland Basin on the River Avon

✗ lunchtime snacks

🍴

🍺 **Courage Best Bitter, Directors; Smiles Bitter**

In great shipbuilding towns the art of the shipwright is sometimes seen in the architecture of buildings on land. The craftsmen who fitted out ocean liners in Victorian times were often much in demand by the brewers, notably in some fine public houses in the city of Liverpool. Here in Bristol the practice was either less widespread or much of its physical manifestation has been destroyed. The Nova Scotia exhibits certainly the best, if not the only surviving example of this kind of work in its superb mahogany bar and back bar fittings. This is one of the finest pieces of Victorian furniture you're likely to see. The style suggests possibly a later date than that of the pub's opening in 1811 but it is in any case of great antiquity and value. Of a similar date is the elegant baroque cast-iron lampholder projecting five feet over the pavement above the doorway.

Apart from this architectural splendour the Nova Scotia is a modest, unpretentious and friendly little boozer. The exterior is three-storeyed and nicely proportioned although in latter years painted by Courage a rather inappropriate shocking blue. Benches and tables for outside refreshment overlook an old lock chamber now used for moorings at this westernmost point of the navigation before sea-going conditions prevail. The low-ceilinged interior provides a suitably changeless setting for that glorious bar and there is a tiny screened-off snug for those requiring privacy.

Hopefully this pleasant scene survives the publication of this book. The landlord is retiring and grandiose and destructive plans are rumoured. A petition is circulating urging conservation, for which here is an exciting opportunity. I cannot believe that the brewery would wish, or be allowed, to act in any other way.

Ostrich Inn

Tel: (0272) 273774
*Lower Guinea Street, Redcliffe,
Bristol. At entrance to Bathurst
Basin on the River Avon*

✗ lunchtime

🅱

🍺 **Courage Best Bitter, Directors**

Some pubs seem to attract celebrities. You know the kind of place – walls festooned with signed publicity snaps, landlord looking down his nose at lesser mortals. The Ostrich is getting a little like that. First it was Allison Holloway who reads the news on HTV, then it was Billy Boswell from Bread spending his spare time there, far from his Liverpool home, on an acting engagement down south. The way pubs get a reputation, the stars will soon be flocking here. Unlike some other celebrity traps, however, people from all classes and callings are attracted to the Ostrich by its friendliness and the warmth of its welcome. If you're waiting here at the bar in front of Joan Collins and Paul McCartney you'll still be served first, be ye ever so humble.

With its fine Georgian façade boldly painted in black and white, the pub has an imposing location with the Redcliffe cliffs and the high rusticated stone walls of Bristol General Hospital in the background. The broad cobbled pavement in front is embellished with newly planed trees and rows of benches and tables, and directly overlooks the old lock chamber that once guarded the entrance to Bathurst basin. A strikingly modern bright red swing bridge completes this attractive scene.

The Ostrich was by all accounts once something of a rough dive. A cider house in the days when Bristol docks teemed with hard-drinking matelots and stevedores, it hardly surprisingly witnessed a certain amount of mayhem. Today's customers are more likely to be office workers enjoying the highly recommended lunchtime snacks and the draught beer, rubbing shoulders, of course, with the odd celebrity.

Pump House

Tel: (0272) 279557
8 Merchants Road, Hotwells, Bristol. North end of Cumberland Basin on the River Avon

✗ lunchtime and evening

🍴

🍺 **Draught Bass**

After the great engines that pumped water into Bristol's Floating Harbour and powered the huge gates of the tidal locks were replaced by little electric motors, the building that had housed them needed a new purpose in life lest it fall to the demolisher's ball and chain. Happily, in the late 1970s, the decision was made to transform it into licensed premises – hence this highly successful conversion.

As befits its former function the Pump House is massively built of brick, with decorative stonework employed on cornices and door and window arches. The architecture is of the Italianate style favoured by Brunel and the founding fathers of Victorian industrial Bristol. As if to turn the theory of form following function on its head, the high empty space within has become as comfortable and atmospheric an environment for bibulous relaxation as can be imagined.

Buffet meals are available in the bar and there is a separate restaurant for more elaborate sustenance. There is only the one real ale on offer, but when Draught Bass is at its best, as it is here, the need for an alternative seems superfluous.

DEVIZES
Black Horse

Tel: (0380) 723930
Bath Road, Dunkirk, Devizes, Wilts. Between locks 48 and 49, north bank

✗ lunchtime and evening

🍴 Wadworth IPA, 6X

The Black Horse is superbly placed to receive thirsty boat crews completing their descent of the newly restored Caen Hill flight of locks. They can reasonably be expected to consume large quantities of the products of the town's renowned local brewer. The pub has been pleasantly refurbished with many an old photograph and artists' impression of the canal system in its heyday. Weeping willows whisper in the breeze by the new canalside patio, competing with brash umbrellas to shade the drinker.

There are plans to keep the Black Horse open all afternoon if trade allows. In view of the difficulty in estimating the time taken descending a flight such as Caen Hill, this is to be heartily welcomed.

HONEY STREET
Barge Inn

Tel: (067285) 238
Honey Street, Wilts. Canalside 150 yards west of Honey Street bridge

✗ lunchtime and evening

🍴 Courage Best Bitter, Directors; Wadworth 6X

On my visit to this famous canalside pub the usual lunchtime throng had been augmented by sightseers and media folk investigating the phenomena of crop circles, which have a habit of appearing in this locality from time to time. My interview with the landlord was cut short by Arthur C. Clarke demanding a pint of bitter. Or should I say the thirsty customer had at least a passing resemblance to the famous science fiction author, whose presence would certainly not have been unexpected.

Honey Street is a remote settlement near the village of Alton Priors. It grew up around the canal bridge early in the last century and consists of a well-preserved wharf, a few cottages and the Barge itself, this being approached by a dead-end lane from the northern approach to the bridge. Outside it is of unusual design, mostly dating from 1858, the year the original building was gutted by fire. The slate-covered roof has heavily overhanging eaves beneath which, canalside, double wooden doors provide access to the third floor loft. Aided by a hoist this must have allowed the unloading and storage of considerable cargoes and gives the Barge a warehouse-like appearance. Since its history as a public house is unbroken this facility must relate to the need at one time for grain and other materials for its brewhouse and bakery.

Inside much has changed, the sole reminders of the past being old photographs of the pub displayed on the walls. The main entrance leads into a comfortable lounge bar. The hatch-served public bar lies beyond and contains a pool table. Both rooms are cheerfully decorated. The bar food menu offers some tempting and imaginative dishes, and Courage's two mainstream draught bitters are joined on the bar by a welcome guest from Devizes.

HORTON
Bridge Inn

Tel : (0380 86) 273
Horton, Devizes, Wilts. By
Horton Bridge canalside

✗ snacks lunchtime and evening

🏠

🍺 Wadworth IPA, 6X

To say that the Bridge Inn includes "outside pool" among its facilities may imply the provision of a back garden lido for these hot summer days, a healthy alternative to swimming in the dubious waters of the Kennet and Avon. This, though, is a little ambitious even for a pub that not only facilitates the canal user with a water-point and rubbish and Elsan disposal but also hires out a fleet of rowing boats and is the base for sight-seeing trips by wide-beam canal cruiser. The pool in question is of the long stick, bakelite balls and green baize variety. The weather-bleached table in the garden is a surprising sight.

The Bridge Inn is a classic canal bridge-side

pub. Some three centuries old, stone built with steeply pitched tiled roofs, its welcoming three-roomed interior maintains a solid workaday country feel.

HUNGERFORD
John o'Gaunt

OFF THE TOWPATH
Tel : (0488) 683535
11 Bridge Street, Hungerford, Berks. 100 yards north of Hungerford Bridge

---

✗ lunchtime and evening

🍴

🍺 **Morland Bitter, Old Masters**

Those who associate urban canals with satanic mills, dead cats and supermarket trolleys will have their prejudices confounded by the Kennet and Avon as it winds through Hungerford. The John o'Gaunt forms part of the pleasant townscape around the old Town bridge.

Should you venture into this attractive sixteenth century inn on the second Tuesday after Easter, beware of the Tuttimen. These characters play a part in the Hocktide Ceremonies, Hungerford's annual excuse for pleasurable overindulgence. Like many seasonal celebrations around the country, their origins remain obscure but responsibility for their inception is attributed to the third son of Edward III of England, after whom the John o'Gaunt is named. The pub is today owned by the town and by his successors as Lords of the Manor of Hungerford.

Run as a Whitbread free house until a couple of years ago, the John o'Gaunt is now part of the tied estate of Morlands of Abingdon, who have overseen a most successful and sympathetic refurbishment, and who, most importantly, produce an excellent pint of beer.

KEYNSHAM
Lock Keeper

Tel: (0272) 862383
Bitton Road, Keynsham, Bristol.
By Keynsham lock on the River
Avon

✗ lunchtime and evening

🍴

☺

🍺 **Courage Best Bitter;**
Wadworth 6X

Keynsham lock is approached by a short cut of canal-like dimensions. Looming over the waterside by the bridge is what appears to be a small Scottish baronial castle. A sign on the stonework proclaiming the availability of Simmonds' Beers attests that this is in fact a public house. Simmonds beers, sadly, are no longer available in the Lock Keeper or anywhere else, though the products that can be had here make adequate compensation.

This is a comfortable pub with a strong emphasis on food. Very much family-orientated its facilities include an enormous children's room with toys and boldly executed murals of all their favourite cartoon characters.

The lock cut affords good moorings and nearby there is a marina with well-stocked chandlery. Nearby also, unfortunately, is the concrete viaduct that now carries the A4 over the river, blighting an otherwise pleasing and tranquil scene.

KINTBURY
Dundas Arms

Tel: (0488) 58559/58263
Station Road, Kintbury, Berks.

✗ lunchtime and evening

🍴

🛏

🍺 **Adnams Bitter; Eldridge Pope**
Thomas Hardy Country Bitter;
Morland Bitter

Lord Charles Dundas, Baron Amesbury in the county of Wiltshire, first chairman of the Kennet & Avon Canal Company, was modest enough a man only to allow his name to grace two of the many edifices along the canal's route. Sharing this honour with the great aqueduct at Limpley Stoke is this pleasant little country hotel.

Overlooking Kintbury lock and situated by the old road bridge on a small island between river and canal, the white-painted late Georgian Dundas Arms is a picture of rural tranquillity framed by willow trees. Hard to imagine that when it first opened it played host to roistering navvies who "never drank water but whisky by pints". The atmosphere today tends to discourage anti-social behaviour but the bar is genuinely pubby and welcoming to all. It contains some sturdy old furniture and the surface of the bar top is made up of highly polished pennies (the old copper ones, if you remember them). Three handpumps dispensing a well-chosen range of traditional ales also decorate the bar.

If you fancy a little more than a pleasant drink and a snack, the restaurant at the Dundas Arms is reputed to be the best around.

LITTLE BEDWYN
Harrow Inn

OFF THE TOWPATH
Tel: (0672) 870871
High Street, Little Bedwyn, Wilts.
250 yards SE of Little Bedwyn footbridge

✘ evening

🍽

☺ under 10s allowed in bar

🍺 **Marstons Pedigree Bitter and regular guest beers**

The village of Little Bedwyn is in two distinct halves, bisected by the canal and the main line railway which runs alongside. On the north side is a collection of Victorian estate cottages and the pretty bespired medieval church, screened by ancient yew trees until the recent storms did their work. South of the transport corridor the village has a Georgian character – fine red brick mansions with walled gardens, summer houses and gazebos.

Amid this classic English village scene resides the Harrow Inn, a finely proportioned building totally in harmony with its surroundings. The interior has the feel of simple sophistication – furnishings and floor are of plain wood and the cream painted walls are hung with the work of local artists. The Harrow is not a games and music pub. It is dedicated to providing fine beer and excellent food.

It is as well that there is much to discover in the village itself because on an ill-timed visit chances are that you will find the business of pulling pints superseded by the selling of stamps. The shutters are down weekday lunchtimes when the pub takes on its secondary role as the village post office. Handy for those postcards you keep meaning to send!

READING
Fisherman's
Cottage

Tel: (0734) 571553
224 Kennetside, Reading Berks.
Riverside on the Kennet, just W of
Blake's Lock

✖ lunchtime and evening

🍺

🍺 **Fullers London Pride, ESB**

Sitting squarely on the riverbank, the Fisherman's Cottage is isolated from the hubbub of the nearby town centre. Visitors by boat, bicycle or foot need only follow the towpath, but to approach by car you need to negotiate a winding maze of little streets that forms the adjoining modern housing estate.

This charming building of the early nineteenth century Gothic revival was daringly extended seven years ago by virtually opening up the whole of one side into an enormous Victorian-style conservatory. This may sound like desecration but in fact the extension merges well in scale and style with the pub's façade, and the result inside provides some pleasant contrasts. The old bar area has been left intact, with just a lick of nicotine-coloured paint, simple furniture, some of it original, and with a delightful little alcoved drinking space retained. You step directly from here blinking into a spacious vista of light and greenery. Plants abound in pots and hanging baskets. There is a ceiling fan, tiled floors and white cast-iron garden furniture. The next step from here is into the garden itself. This has been beautifully landscaped and furnished, well-maintained and attractively lit at night time. At the front, of course, is the river and the immaculately maintained Blake's Lock. There can be few more attractive places for al fresco drinking of a summer's eve.

Not forgetting a pub's most basic and important provision, the Fisherman's Cottage experienced its transformation when it was acquired by Fullers, down river on the Thames at Chiswick, whose superb beers are not commonly available this far west. Here they are to be enjoyed absolutely at their best.

Jolly Anglers

Tel: (0734) 61666
Kennetside, Reading, Berks.
Riverside on the Kennet, 150
yards east of Blakes Lock

✗ lunchtime

☏

🍺 **Courage Best Bitter, Directors**

"Best pub in Reading", interrupted the callow youth from the university as I quizzed the landlady of the Jolly Anglers. If his student days are as dedicated to study as mine were, he probably knows every pub in town and is well qualified for such an opinion. The similarly dedicated pub some 200 yards up the towpath would probably run the Jolly Anglers a close race in my view, but the two hostelries are so different that they can hardly be compared. If you're looking for a good honest down-to-earth boozer this is the place for you.

The feature that distinguishes the Jolly Anglers from its neighbouring buildings in a row of modest two-storey boatmen's cottages is the broad central arch, containing the entrance doorways to both saloon and public bars, upon which the pub's name is boldly lettered.

The interior is circa 1920 with panelled walls and moulded wood fire surrounds typical of the period. The two rooms are mirror images of each other served by a central servery. The public bar has the dart board while the saloon caters for more sedentary drinkers. The beer, trunked up the M4 as it is from Courage's brewery at the other end of the navigation in Bristol, is quite superb.

To describe the Jolly Anglers as a basic pub is by no means a detraction. The basics that make a good pub are frequently forgotten or submerged under a flood of gimmickry. Here, however, they are reverently observed.

SALTFORD
Jolly Sailor

Tel: Bath 873002
*Mead Lane, Saltford, Avon. By
Saltford Lock*

✕ lunchtime and evening

🍴

◎

🍺 **Courage Bitter Ale, Best Bitter,
Directors; John Smith's Bitter;
Butcombe Bitter**

It was on the night of Sunday May 6 1990. As the household slept a stray spark from the dormant barbecue set light to a small shed in the waterfront garden of the Jolly Sailor. Flames leapt high into the air and the pub itself seemed threatened. Moored nearby, as luck would have it, was the NB Wessex Defender. Alerted to the danger, and reasoning that the loss of so fine an alehouse would inconvenience the return journey, the plucky crew wasted no time. Raising the alarm with wild shrieks, they set about fighting the inferno with pint glasses and plastic dustbins filled with canal water until the fire brigade arrived.

At few pubs have I enjoyed free ale at 1 am on a Monday morning, but on that occasion in the Jolly Sailor, as captain of the Wessex Defender that glorious May weekend, it felt richly deserved.

Thus saved for posterity was a very fine hostelry of the early 18th century. The stately lines of its ivy-clad façade betray its origins as home to a wealthy miller. It has an unusually close association with the river and lock which is literally in the front garden. The lock island, furnished with wooden tables and benches, is part of the outdoor drinking area, so that locking up or down can attract not always helpful attention from those using this facility.

Tall trees complete an attractive and timeless scene, as can be appreciated by studying the fascinating contemporary painting of the Jolly Sailor that hangs above the fireplace. Executed in "naive" style, it shows the place shortly after the opening of the Avon navigation in 1727. All that has since changed is the addition of car park, boules court and a stylish conservatory.

The fireplace also bears witness to an odd custom of the bargemen once frequenting this tavern, who liberally punctured the wooden surround with a red-hot poker. Save for this little shrine to the past and the flagstone floors, the interior is predominantly modern. This in no way detracts from the sense of history, the bar counter itself being a superb example of today's craftsmanship in wood.

Complimentary to all this ambience, the food here is excellent and, for a brewery tied house, a welcoming selection of draught beers is on offer.

When you moor here, as moor you must, be sure to do so above the lock. The piled stagings at the lock mouth are an ideal place where, in the neighbourliness of the waterways, boats can double or even triple up. There is also the weirside of the lock island (check your knots here) and a short stretch of public mooring beyond the next door boatyard. The Jolly Sailor will also happily water your boat and receive your refuse for disposal.

SEEND CLEEVE
Barge Inn

Tel: (0380) 828230
Seend Cleeve, Wilts. South bank by Lock 19 and Seend Wharf Bridge

✗ lunchtime and evening

🍴

◎

🍺 **Wadworth IPA, 6X, Old Timer (Winter); Adnams Bitter**

Canalside pubs are frequently situated at either end of lock flights for reason of the oft observed phenomenon that these are places where boats naturally congregate. The Barge is exceptional in being positioned beside the pound between locks, where fluctuating water levels can make mooring hazardous, especially on the Kennet & Avon where water has always been at a premium. At one time the Barge was a farmhouse (and incidentally home to an 8 ft 4 ins individual known appropriately as the Wiltshire Giant) and had its own wharf here. What made all this possible is the presence of a feeder from a nearby brook entering the canal at this point.

Wadworth have taken the opportunity of the canal's recent reopening as a through route to invest heavily in the Barge as a tourist asset. This has been done with praiseworthy exuberance. A new conservatory overlooks the canal and reproduction gas lamps bathe the pub and car park in a brilliant glow of light. Inside, ornaments and canal-related ephemera are everywhere to be seen, while Victorian-style rose patterned wallpaper of the brightest hues covers both walls and ceilings.

With its excellent food and fine beer the Barge is an experience not to be missed.

WOOLHAMPTON
Rowbarge

Tel: (0734) 712213
Station Road, Woolhampton,
Berks. Riverside by swing bridge
on the Kennet

✕ lunchtime and evening

🏠

🍺 **Courage Best Bitter, Directors;**
John Smith's Bitter

Passing this way in the 1940s during his pioneering voyages on the narrowboat Cressy, the author and transport historian L. T. C. Rolt was confronted by the swingbridge at Wool-hampton. Unequal to the task of opening this stubborn obstacle alone, he and his wife were obliged to call upon the local population to see them through. Prominent among their helpers was the then landlord of the nearby Rowbarge, his motives no doubt being purely charitable. The pub, however, must have enjoyed con-siderable trade when success was achieved after three hours of concentrated toil.

The old bridge now has a brand-new hi-tech replacement. Without falling victim to excessive optimism (having experience of the reliability and simplicity of operation of these structures) I am sure that we can now enjoy a pint of the Rowbarge's excellent ale uninterrupted by pleas for assistance from thwarted boat crews.

The pub itself is a fine old building which can have changed little since it first occupied this site some 300 years ago. The only structural addition of any scale is the pleasant restaurant at the back. The first room entered has a low ceiling and wood panelled walls surrounded by settle-ended benches, all dark brown brush-grained in traditional manner. This opens into the bar itself, of modern construction but much in keeping and a comfortable lounge that was once no doubt the bar parlour or a private family room.

This friendly, welcoming and attractive pub is one of few on this stretch with a genuine riverside location. Forced to stop at the bridge, the boater is offered a not-to-be-resisted temptation.

LANCASTER CANAL

The Lancaster is isolated from any other waterway, its only diversion and direct outlet to the sea being the Glasson Arm into the port of Glasson Dock. The main line runs north from Preston through Garstang and the fine university city of Lancaster, terminating just past Carnforth.

BILSBORROW
Owd Nell's
Tavern

Tel: (0995) 40010
St Michael's Road (off A6),
Bilsborrow, Lancs. Canalside,
Bridge 44

✗ lunchtime and evenings

⋈

🍺 **Whitbread Castle Eden Ale,**
Owd Nell's Bitter, Chesters
Best Mild, Boddingtons Bitter,
Fremlins Bitter

As you draw alongside the mock gas-lamps, wishing well and fake stocks outside this recently built thatched tavern, you could be forgiven for thinking you are on the brink of a terminal outbreak of OTT tastelessness. Not so. Brash, contrived, high-profile and unashamedly commercial it might be, but you have to concede it has been done well – almost irritatingly so – with great attention to detail, so that it falls comfortably short of outrageous.

"A Country Tavern" proclaims the sign on the door, a claim supported by the flagstoned floor, beams and wooden tables, chairs and stools. The farmhouse-style interior consists of one large, elongated barn-like room divided into several distinct areas, including at the canal end a conservatory-style extension in which children are welcome, and at the other TV and gaming machines. Good "Food of the Country" is available all day every day. The main menu, including starters, main courses (like steak and kidney pudding, fish, chips and mushy peas, steak and chicken), salads, sandwiches, desserts, coffees and hot mulled wine, is supplemented by afternoon snacks between 3 and 6 pm and imaginative "Tasty Finger Snacks" between 8 and 10.30 pm. There is also an "informal" restaurant called Guy's next door, part of the same complex. A range of traditional ales is offered, although it is not hard to detect the face of Whitbread behind the "free from brewery" mask. They even brew the house bitter.

A traditional pub it's not, and it won't be to everyone's taste, but Owd Nell's is one of the better examples of the numerous licensed canalside barn conversions springing up around the country. In avoiding, albeit narrowly, the tackiness into which it could so easily have descended, it succeeds where many would fail. The food and drink are of a high standard, there's plenty of interest for adults and children alike and it's open all day.

White Bull

Tel: (0995) 40324
Off A6, Bilsborrow, Lancs.
Canalside past Bridge 44

Theakston Best Bitter,
Matthew Brown Mild,
Younger No. 3

There could not be a more complete contrast to Owd Nell's than this compact, simply modernised village local, which will probably please all those people likely to be deterred by the big brash tavern on the opposite bank. The White Bull has a tiny serving area at one end, dispensing its traditional ales in fine condition. The decor and open fire give the impression of being in someone's drawing room. Traditional pub games are played, dominoes in particular, for which several trophies are dotted around on mantelpieces and shelves. A comparatively unobtrusive juke box plays things like "Spanish Eyes" a lot, which (for me at least) places the pub quite precisely. The place is almost plush but that would create a misleading picture if you regard "plush" as being next to "impersonal".

It's the kind of pub where you can sit and sup and blend into the fabric of everyday life of the exceptionally friendly regulars, who provide a warm Lancashire welcome. An hour or two in their company will have you convinced that there's not much wrong with the world that a beer or two wouldn't cure.

GALGATE
Plough Inn

Tel: (0524) 751337
Main Road, Galgate, Lancs. Near
Bridge 86

✗ lunchtime and evening
(Sunday evenings by request)

Whitbread Boddingtons Bitter

The unassuming village of Galgate is just round the corner from the canal's junction with the Glasson Branch. The sedate canal stands as a stark contrast to the roar of the A6 trunk road and the main railway to Scotland which also pass through the village, and the nearby M6 motorway. The village contains a boatyard, supermarket and shops, Post Office and three pubs. Close to Bridge 86 (where there are good moorings) stands the most enterprising of them. The Plough is low-key but professionally run by tenants who won Boddingtons' coveted Tenants of the Year Award for 1989/90. To capitalise on its convenient location for road and canal users, it declares, unequivocally, its policy on opening hours (11 am–11 pm) and food availability.

The food covers daily specials, sandwiches and hot snacks, main course salads, sweets and coffee. Vegetarians are not overlooked either, and there is a special "Boddies Children's Menu". Indeed, the Plough caters well for the family: children are welcome and the beer garden hosts a bouncing castle on holidays and special occasions.

The pub's interior is straightforward enough, one room with a central bar and separate areas off, one of which is more of a diners' area. It's comfortable and carpeted throughout, with a real fire, small TV and juke box. The main bar area has button-backed seating, beaton copper-effect tables, tie-back curtains, old printed mirrors and horse brasses. High stools are dotted haphazardly around.

Sadly, real mild is no longer available as demand was insufficient to guarantee quality. The bitter, however, sells in vast quantities and is well kept.

GLASSON DOCK
Caribou Hotel

Tel: (0524) 751356
Victoria Terrace, Glasson Dock, Lancs. Opposite Glasson basin canal terminus

✘ lunchtime and evening

🛏

🍺 **Thwaites Best Mild, Bitter**

The Glasson arm of the Lancaster canal terminates at Glasson, a tiny but intriguing working port which handles trade from coastal and continental ships entering the port from the River Lune estuary through a huge sea-lock. Water-borne visitors can moor in the vast basin into which the canal leads and explore the port and harbour area and its three pubs.

The Caribou Hotel is said to be the oldest building in Glasson, dating back over 200 years. Originally the "Pier Hall", it later became "The Grapes", remaining in the same family for many years until a former sea captain, one Captain Hayward, took over and named the hotel after one of the ships he skippered.

Today it has an unhurried, distinctively local

flavour and some depth of quirky character, due in no small part to the gentle, unassuming, laconic Lancastrian who runs it. There is a large airy bar with plenty of cosy corners and stained glass, an adjoining room for pub games including pool, and a day-time family room which is used in summer. The selection of bar food, always available, includes locally caught rainbow trout. The traditional beers from Thwaites' Blackburn brewery are in supreme condition, as the unsteady-legged crews of many a visiting vessel could testify (the Caribou is the first licensed premises from the harbour).

Should you wish to stay and explore the area more fully, the hotel has eight bedrooms.

HEST BANK
Hest Bank Hotel

Tel: (0524) 822226
Hest Bank Lane, Hest Bank,
Lancs. Canalside at Bridge 118

✖ lunchtime and evening

🍴

◎

🛏

🍺 **Whitbread Boddingtons Mild, Bitter**

Just a few miles north of Lancaster, Hest Bank used to be the Lancaster canal's nearest point to the sea before the Glasson Arm was cut. The sea shore is only a few hundred yards from the canal, with miles of sandy beach uncovered at low tide. The area still has a seaside air, with a faint whiff of holiday resort when the sun shines.

The picturesquely situated Hest Bank Hotel must be one of the most historic hostelries on the waterways of England. It dates back to 1554 when it was the "Sands Inn". Over the subsequent centuries it has been frequented by abbots and monks from Cartmel Priory and Furness Abbey, Cromwell's officers and the King's men during the Civil War (a double booking, presumably!), highwaymen and footpads, gangs of Irish navvies digging the canal, the Duke of Devonshire and Prince Frederick of Prussia. As local graphic artist Travis Jackson quotes in his potted history of the establishment: "Those who linger here are in the company of many happy ghosts".

In coaching days the Hest Bank was the first or last call for travellers crossing the sands, and the window for the guiding light which showed the way across the sands can still be seen. From the privacy of the fine canalside gardens are splendid views across the sands and Morecambe Bay towards the Cumbrian slopes.

The hotel's interior is an impressively random assortment of rooms, including a wonderful, atmospheric basement cellar bar, all low ceilings and oak beams, and a glass conservatory overlooking the garden and the moored boats of the canal. Behind the main bar is an unusual collection of antique serving bells. A good range of hot meals and snacks is available at this fine pub on weekdays only.

LEE AND STORT NAVIGATIONS

The River Lee (equally correctly spelt Lea) leaves the Thames via Limehouse Basin and the tidal Bow Creek and connects with the Regent's Canal via the short Hertford Union Canal. Having left London it passes through progressively more rural scenery until it reaches its navigational limit at the county town of Hertford, $27\frac{3}{4}$ miles from the river's mouth.

Branching off the Lee at Hoddesdon, the River Stort can be navigated for $13\frac{3}{4}$ miles as far as Bishop's Stortford.

BISHOP'S STORTFORD
Tanners Arms

Tel: (0279) 651837
93 London Road, Bishop's Stortford, Herts. East bank of the Stort by main road bridge on southern edge of town

✕ lunchtime and evening (not Tue or Sun evenings)

🍴

🍺 **McMullen Original AK, Country Bitter**

There are no pretensions about the Tanners Arms, it's just a good, honest, well-run and well cared for pub. Built in Victorian times, it has an attractive white-painted façade and two spacious bars within – a comfortable, homely saloon and a down-to earth, recently extended, public bar with pool and darts. It is all that a pub should be.

The regular occurrence of what seem like small earthquakes rattling your beer slowly across the formica table will cause no alarm when you remember that the Tanners backs directly on to the Liverpool Street to Cambridge main line railway.

CHESHUNT
Red Cow

OFF THE TOWPATH
Tel: (0992) 23701
198 Windmill Lane, Cheshunt, Herts. ¾ mile north of Waltham Common lock then 300 yards east, by station

✕ lunchtime snacks

🍺 **Draught Bass, Charrington IPA**

The Red Cow alludes in its name to an agricultural environment that cannot long have survived the pub's arrival within it. It is Victorian, small but distinctly urban in appearance and most likely had its origin at the same time as the railway came here. Nowadays it serves both the nearby light industrial estate and the home-bound commuter.

There is a traditional public bar at the front of the pub and an interesting saloon with a side entrance containing some good fixed furnishings from the 1950s. The interior has very much the feel of a beer drinker's venue.

Major refurbishment is due here soon, but the landlord assured me that the bar arrangement and pleasant atmosphere will be preserved. In fact the appeal would be to the 'middle-aged' drinker. Whether this entails barmaids with nursing qualifications and resuscitation equipment I know not.

To reach the Red Cow by boat, the only obvious landmark to moor by is a clump of poplar trees that hides a car park. Walk through this, across the railway level crossing and the pub is on your left. Please note that Windmill

Lane bridge just up river does not provide access.

ENFIELD LOCK
Greyhound

Tel: (0992) 764612
425 Ordnance Road, Enfield Lock, Middx. East bank across road from the lock

✘ lunchtime (Mon–Fri)

🍴

🍺 **McMullen Original AK, Country Bitter**

I well remember, from my cadet force days at school, shouldering the product of the Royal Small Arms factory at Enfield Lock. The Lee Enfield 303 rifle took its name both from the borough where its manufacture took place and the river that flows past it. Nowadays British Army rifles are made in Belgium or somewhere, and sadly no peaceful use has been found for the historic workshops across the river from the Greyhound. They stand empty and forlorn while the nearby Royal Small Arms public house, in another sign of the times, has tastefully been renamed Shooters.

Although this interesting and not unattractive stretch of urban industrial riverside no longer offers much employment it certainly offers scope for recreation – for boaters, fishermen, cyclists and for people just idly strolling along the towpath. Any beer drinkers among these (especially those over twelve) would be well advised to avoid Shooters and set their sights on a pub of real calibre.

The Greyhound is a straightforward boozer of World War One vintage and very likely built as part of the local state management scheme. Similar to the long-surviving nationalisation of pubs and brewing in Carlisle, this was imposed by Lloyd George to ensure the sobriety of armaments workers. While lacking frills it is strong on all the things that make a pub a pub. The L-shaped pebble-dash and brick exterior has a mellow air which promises a warm welcome. Inside, this is just what you find. There are two bars fulfilling their separate functions in traditional manner, dart-board and lino in the public, carpet and comfy chairs in the lounge. In summer you are well placed, pint of Mac's before you, to observe the world go by from the furnished terrace in front of the pub.

HERTFORD
Old Barge

Tel: (0992) 581871
2 The Folly, Hertford. Riverside by Mill Bridge

✘ lunchtime and evening (not Sun evening)

🛏

☺

🍺 **Adnams Bitter; Benskins Best Bitter; Greene King Abbot Ale; Ind Coope Burton Ale; Tetley Bitter; Youngs Special Bitter**

The River Lee winds a pleasant willow-lined course through Hertford towards its navigational limit in the town centre. The best views of this attractive townscape are to be enjoyed from the terrace of the Old Barge. There is the fine old Mill Bridge and on the opposite bank a large 17th century mansion backs directly on to the river. In the near distance, beyond the trees, is the grand Victorian tower of McMullen's brewery. It is a shame that their most palatable products haven't found an outlet in the Old Barge but there are plenty of Mac's pubs in town where they can be sampled.

The pub lies side on to the river. The main building has a discreet orange brick Victorian frontage with an attractive doorway flanked by two bay windows. Black weather-boarding covers various extensions (I call them this although they may well be older than the main building) to the side and back of the pub.

There is a cheerful, atmospheric interior with open fireplaces, old settles, lots of beams, and a variety of drinking and eating areas. Until recent renovation these areas would have been separate rooms. Much of the charm of the original arrangement has been preserved, however, with pre-renovation photographs on the walls providing testimony.

With its strong emphasis on food, the Old Barge is a popular lunchtime venue, especially in the summer months. The impressive range of beers must comprise practically the whole of Benskins' approved list of guest real ales.

**LONDON
LEA BRIDGE
Prince of Wales**

Tel: (081) 533 3463
*146 Lea Bridge Road, Lea Bridge,
London E5. By Lea Bridge*

✗ lunchtime and evening

☷

⊲ **Youngs Bitter, Special Bitter**

This is one of three north-east London pubs leased by Youngs from Whitbread in the 1960s. Two have sadly returned to their original owner but the Prince of Wales has now joined Youngs estate on a permanent basis. With its recent uncertain future the pub looks a little tatty due to lack of investment, but a thorough redecoration will have been effected by the time of publication.

This is a good solid building from around the first decades of this century with three fine contrasting elevations; facing the river, the road and the lane that runs alongside. The most interesting architectural feature is the heavy wooden canopy, of almost railway station design and proportions, that protects drinkers on the terrace and customers of the seafood stall from sun or rain.

Inside, there are three bars; a large separate public and a saloon linked with what may originally have been a snooker hall, now a high ceilinged lounge/restaurant. These are all finely panelled and furnished throughout.

The Prince of Wales is a popular and companionable hostelry, a mecca both for anglers fishing the river and nearby reservoirs and for boaters on their tranquil passage through the north-eastern suburbs of the capital city.

TOTTENHAM HALE
Narrow Boat

Tel: (081) 801 6499
Reedham Close (off Jarrow Road), Tottenham Hale, London E5.
West bank below Tottenham Lock

✖ lunchtime and evening

🍺

🍺 Greene King IPA, Abbot Ale; Marston Pedigree Bitter; Youngs Special Bitter; Guest Beers

The Narrow Boat was built in the early 1980s at the same time as the surrounding council estate it serves. Despite its recent date and less than totally endearing style of architecture it follows two distinct traditional public house genres, neither of which have many modern examples. Firstly it is a true back-street local. Well distanced from the Ferry Lane main road at the end of a cul-de-sac, it is sited as a community pub rather than to attract passing car-borne trade.

This no-through-road situation is also consistent with its other traditional role as a riverside hostelry. The towpath aspect with its sign, attractive garden and excellent moorings are all designed to draw the boater and angler, giving the Narrow Boat an interesting and untypical social mix.

The pub's exterior is brick-built and very much of its period. On the road side the dominant feature is the great sloping roof. One steps inside to a barn-like single bar with lots of canalania and some neo-Victorian detailing for relief. Then, through patio doors, to the bijou garden with its weeping willow and little pond which doubles as a wishing-well (all proceeds to charity).

The Narrow Boat is part of the admirable J. D. Wetherspoon chain of London free houses, most of whose pubs are elegantly converted car showrooms with imaginative names such as George Orwell's idealised Moon Under Water. Their policy of no recorded music and keenly priced beer has brought them much success and popularity.

UPPER CLAPTON
Anchor and
Hope

Tel: (081) 806 1730
*15 High Hill Ferry, Upper
Clapton, London E5. West bank, 1
mile north of Lee Bridge*

🏠

🍺 **Fullers London Pride, ESB**

On my most recent visit to the Anchor and Hope the tiny bar was heaving, and so also were some hundred yards of the towpath in either direction, with a cosmopolitan throng of bibulous characters. There were extended families with exotic dogs, a bearded youth playing his guitar, a giant of a man with a far-too-small T-shirt feeding the Canada geese on surplus Mother's Pride, gently ensuring that the greedy ones took no more than their share. Of the many cyclists, few passed the Anchor and Hope by. The only enforced spectators of this merry scene were the railway passengers flashing past on the nearby bridge.

A large section of humanity and its tame cousins in the animal kingdom had descended on this small piece of riverside in NE London, drawn by the simple delights of this basic little boozer.

This was not a good time to speak to the landlord so I rang some weeks later. The phone was answered by a customer. "You want to put this place in a guide book? (ironic laughter) You actually want *more* people to come here?" There was ill-concealed amazement that anyone could be so stupid. I took his point. Even in a pub this welcoming co-existence can be strained if the proportion of visitors to locals is tilted too far. Nevertheless, and the landlord happily agreed with me here, a book of this nature would hardly deserve its title if any of the cream of the best pubs was deliberately excluded.

Thus, as a compromise, I shall point out some of the pub's minus points. First of all, it is impossible to chat up the barmaid: she'll be far too busy serving the next customer. As for the beer, although there is nothing actually wrong with it, you'll feel quite strange and probably behave quite strangely if you drink too much. If your desire is for a plastic basket of aromatic scampi and chips you'll just have to forget it.

Finding the place by road is no joke either, but why bother? Once you're there, as Jim Dunk might say, you probably wouldn't like it anyway.

WALTHAM ABBEY
Old English Gentleman

Tel: (0992) 712714
85 Highbridge Street, Waltham Abbey, Essex. Bridge side 200 yards below Waltham Town Lock

✘ lunchtime

🍴

🍺 **McMullen Original AK, Country Bitter**

This fine old pub on the border of Hertfordshire and Essex, though modest in scale, is a delightfully situated architectural gem. The building is L-shaped and has a splendid tiled mansard roof with decorative barge-boarded gable ends. It shows two half-timbered and flower bedecked storeys to the road and three storeys of yellow brick to the river. A large vine, growing on trelliswork supported by rustic beams, shades the little towpath-level beer garden and endows it with something of a continental feel.

Inside, the pub comprises just two small rooms. The bar has low ceilings, busily adorned walls, high stools at the counter and a good pubby atmosphere. The lounge is a touch plusher but very similar. Snacks – sandwiches and rolls – are available and on Sunday lunchtimes cockles, prawns, and cheese and biscuits are placed on the bar for customers to dip into.

The Old English Gentleman is actually on the short stretch of road that links Waltham Abbey with Waltham Cross. Waltham Abbey is a charming old town, dominated by its ancient Abbey Church.

The Lee Valley here, despite the massive pylons striding purposefully on their way to power a million washing machines, vacuum cleaners and other essentials of twentieth century living, is beginning to lose some of its bleakness and enter the changeless rural charm of its upper reaches. A stop at the Old English Gentleman will give one a foretaste and allow contemplation of the joys to come.

WARE
Victoria

Tel : (0920) 462565
*2 Star Street, Ware, Herts. West
bank 250 yards north of town
bridge*

✕ lunchtime

🍴

⛵

🍺 **McMullen Original AK**

The Victoria is a building with a varied history, which is reflected in its charming mixture of English vernacular styles. As the name suggests, it probably first became a public house in the nineteenth century, and at one time it is even said to have functioned as a school for young ladies. The street frontage appears seventeenth century, or maybe earlier, with white painted pebbledash and some excellent carved Victorian barge-boarding on the roof gables. The back of the pub, in red brick, is pure Georgian and overlooks a spacious terrace and patrons-only moorings on the river.

There are two bars with their separate doorways on opposite corners of the building – a friendly tap room festooned with darts trophies, so you may think twice about taking on the locals; and an attractive panelled saloon with interesting pictures on the walls and plates and other antique bric-à-brac on the shelf above the wainscoting.

This is one of those Mac's houses that serves AK only on draught, Country Bitter still being regarded as a new-fangled oddity by some drinkers in these parts. This Hertford-brewed light mild is one of the country's classic beers, so even a confirmed bitter drinker should not be disappointed.

Reedham Ferry Inn

NORFOLK BROADS

LLANGOLLEN CANAL

Perhaps the single most popular cruising canal in the country, the Llangollen leaves the Shropshire Union at Hurleston Junction in Cheshire and makes its leafy (but not always tranquil) way through the north Shropshire towns of Whitchurch, Ellesmere and Chirk and into north Wales, passing high above the home of the Eisteddford to terminate at Horseshoe Falls.

ELLESMERE
White Hart Inn

OFF THE TOWPATH
Birch Road

A very old and interesting timbered pub in Shropshire's own Lake District. It serves a range of handpulled Marstons traditional beers and lunchtime food in season only (after Easter). There is a beer garden.

LLANGOLLEN

OFF THE TOWPATH

The canal runs on along a hillside to the north of the fair town of Llangollen, while most of the town is to the south of the bridge over the fast-flowing River Dee, wedged between the A539 and A5 roads. It's easily walkable from the canal. At the canal/river end of town, the seventeenth century **Wynnstay Arms Hotel** in Bridge Street is worth a visit for Ind Coope and Tetley beers, good food and a friendly welcome, whilst the **Cambrian Hotel** at the other end of town in Berwyn Street offers handpumped Younger's Scotch, good humour and plenty of character, especially in the tiny cosy bar.

RUABON
Duke of
Wellington

OFF THE TOWPATH
Tel: (0978) 820381
High Street, Ruabon, Clwyd

A handsome old pub with a bright and busy bar, comfortable extended lounge, Marstons traditional beers and food lunchtimes and evenings.

SUN BANK
Sun Trevor

Tel: (0978) 860651/860312
Sun Bank (A539), nr Llangollen, Clwyd

✘ lunchtime and evening

🛏

☺

🍺 **Ruddles County, Websters Yorkshire Bitter**

The Sun Trevor (not the Sun *at* Trevor as I had assumed, not unreasonably, since Trevor is in fact the next village along the A539), is not short on self-praise. The licensee and the publicity material wax lyrical, and the whole place exudes confidence. And not without justification, for if there's a more beautifully situated pub anywhere in the UK then I'm a XXXX drinker. From its patio or its raised terrace beer garden, or from its bay windows, you can feast your eyes on sumptuous views of the canal in the foreground, the River

Dee, a golf course and the dramatic backdrop of the wooded hills of Welsh border country.

Set back from the road at the foot of a hillside, the pub's attractive black and white exterior flags down road and canal travellers alike. The original parts of the building can be traced back to the fourteenth century, and some of the interior beams seemed original. There is a fine inglenook surrounded by partially enclosed seating — ideal for a cosy gathering — and big curved alcove windows offer more than fine views out across the valley. Curved settles and wooden pews, wood panelling, lots of brass and beaten copper and a display of Davy lamps foster a relaxed atmosphere, compromised somewhat by overbearing and incongruous pop music from the juke box and a preoccupation with food. Bar meals such as lasagne, chili, curry and steak and kidney are available at all times, complemented in the evenings by a restaurant menu in the adjoining dining room, which is used for buffet luncheons. There are also traditional Sunday lunches and a children's menu.

A games room at the back has pool, darts, TV and quiz machine. There is a telephone for customers' use, and a kiosk outside too, so there's no excuse for not phoning home.

LEEDS & LIVERPOOL CANAL

Britain's longest navigable waterway at 127 miles, the Leeds & Liverpool connects the two fine northern cities whose name it bears, passing through Lancashire towns like Wigan, Burnley and Blackburn before crossing the Pennines into Yorkshire. It passes through Skipton and skirts Keighley, Shipley and Bingley on its descent into Leeds, where the Aire & Calder can be joined. There are numerous arms and branches, and the Bridgewater canal connects with Leigh Arm, giving access to Manchester and the Cheshire canals.

ABRAM
Red Lion (Dover Lock)

Tel: (0942) 866300
Warrington Road, Abram, Gtr. Manchester. Canalside, Bridge 4 (Dover Bridge), Leigh Branch

✗ lunchtime and evening

🍴

🍺 **Greenalls Mild, Bitter**

There used to be two locks nearby – hence the pub's alternative name – but the mining subsidence which has affected much of the land in this area has rendered locks unnecessary.

This popular and friendly pub punctuates a fairly barren stretch of canal between Leigh and Wigan. It has retained much of its original structure and many original features, along with some of the unique atmosphere which hallmarks a typical canal pub. Much of its interesting collection of prints and artefacts have canal connections.

The large main bar is sub-divided into several distinct areas, with bar stools dotted haphazardly around the serving counter. (I have always regarded being perched on a bar stool at the bar as the definitive beer-drinking position.) A small cosy side snug is located off, pleasant if a little isolated, and at least offering the alternative which tunnel vision pub architects conspicuously fail to provide with their current crop of cavernous one-room wonders. There is also a games room with a pool table and a children's play area. A juke box lurks, ominous but relatively unobtrusive.

Available every lunchtime and evening, food at the Red Lion/Dover Locks is both varied and unusually thoughtful. Complementing the steak, grills, fish, chips, salads and sandwiches are pâté-filled mushrooms with garlic dip and a range of pasta dishes, reflecting the Mediterranean origins of the landlord. Lancashire Black Pudding and beefburger barmcake would seem to originate from a good deal closer to home, although opinions remain divided over whether black pudding is a speciality of the north-west or the Black Country in the West Midlands. There are also junior dishes.

I'm still unsure why Greenall Whitley – before they got out of brewing – opted for ornamental columns which look for all the world like handpumps but which conceal electric pumps. It smacks of obfuscation and the logic behind it seems blurred. If handpumps are regarded as an incentive to consumers, it's not difficult to have real ones. If they're not, what advantage can be perceived from the use of fakes? For all that, the beer here is good, as regular inclusion in the Good Beer Guide testifies.

BURSCOUGH
Lathom Slipway

Tel: (0704) 893312
Crabtree Lane, Burscough, Lancs
Canalside at Bridge 32
(Crabtree Swing Bridge)

✗ lunchtime and evening

🍴

🍺 **Thwaites Mild, Bitter**

This conversion of early nineteenth century canalside dwelling houses, was made as recently as 1982 when a pub licence was granted to make it one of the newest pubs in the area. From its black-beamed structure has been hewn a pub of no little character, compromised only by an unseemly illuminated refrigerated display of gateaux, cheesecakes and the like. The pub consists of a sort of side annexe and a multi-themed main L-shaped lounge bar with a mixture of styles. Its rough-cast cream plastered walls are home to a bewildering array of embellishments, including canal photos and paintings, posters for French wine, plates and vases, enough bric-à-brac to put the factories that produced it on overtime and other items as diverse as a ship's wheel, old muskets, ski sticks and a reindeer's head. Suspended above the bar is a selection of headwear – miners' helmets, firemens' helmets, soldiers' helmets. Many of the wooden tables are converted old sewing machines with foot treddles.

The Slipway is popular for food, which is available lunchtimes from 12–3 and evenings from 7–9.30, including Bank holidays. The wide range includes steaks, lasagne, vegetable samosas, sandwiches and salads, "Junior Meals" with chips, illuminated sweets and a choice of wines. In addition, daily specials are chalked on the blackboard.

Children are allowed in until 8.30 pm, and

there is a garden with play area. As the name suggests, the pub has its own slipway right in front and offers over half a mile of good private moorings. It has to be said that it hovers on the brink of twee-ness and, with many of its tables number-tagged, foodiness, but manages to stay on the right side of both – and the Thwaites beers are in fine form.

EAST MARTON
Cross Keys

Tel: (0282) 843485
Skipton Road, East Marton, N. Yorks. 50 yards up the hill from Bridge 161 (Double Bridge)

✗ lunchtime and evenings

🍽

☺

🍺 **Ruddles County, Websters Yorkshire Bitter**

The Pennine Way shares the towpath for a short distance at East Marton, supporting the impression that this is probably the most beautiful section of the entire Leeds–Liverpool canal.

Set back from the road, this large handsome pub stands among a cluster of mellow old stone buildings. Dating from the late seventeenth century, the Cross Keys developed out of a farmhouse and, as the only canalside pub for nine miles between Gargrave and Salterforth, has always been popular with boatmen. It offers fine views across the rolling hills, but must be very exposed in harsh weather.

Passing through the tables and chairs on the roadside forecourt, you enter through an entrance porch with leaded lights into a comfortable, spacious L-shaped interior, divided into three sections. Carpeted throughout, it has lots of polished wood and heavy old beams, a fine old stone fireplace and some creaky high-backed wooden settles, two of which are arranged back to back in the centre of the room with tables in front and rows of chairs facing, making an unusual feature. The faint but unmistakable aroma of woodsmoke permeates the room.

The bar menu is chalked on an expansive blackboard on the side wall, and consists of starters, sandwiches and salads and meals such as steaks, lasagne, fish, and steak and kidney. There are also a list of daily specials and a children's menu. A separate candlelit dining room/restaurant has its own full menu.

FOULRIDGE
Hole in the Wall

OFF THE TOWPATH
Foulridge, Lancs. 250 yards east of Foulridge tunnel, northern end

✖ lunchtime and evening

☺

🍺 Stones Best Bitter

You will have to visit the Hole in the Wall if you want documentary evidence of the curious tale of Buttercup, the cow who fell into the canal, decided for reasons of bovine illogic to swim the full length of the tunnel and had to be revived with brandy at the pub! (The earliest recorded incident of mad cow disease?) A nearby store sells good pies.

HASKAYNE
Kings Arms

OFF THE TOWPATH
Tel: (0704) 840245
Delf Lane, Haskayne, Merseyside.
100 yards north of Bridge 21A

✖ lunchtime and evening

🍺 Tetley Mild, Bitter

Built in 1823, it is now a managed house. It has two separate but adjoining lounge areas, public bar, games room and upstairs room. Straightforward, good quality catering, fresh and locally grown, available seven lunchtimes and four evenings (not Mon, Thur or Sun).

Ship

Tel: (0704) 840572
Rosemary Lane, Haskayne,
Merseyside. Canalside at Ship
Bridge, No 22

✖ lunchtime and evening

🛏

☺

🍺 Tetley Mild, Bitter

If the quality of canalside pubs in this area is unusually high, then this is probably the pick of an exceptional bunch. The Ship is a gem of a pub, from its attractive white frontage with hanging baskets and well-tended garden to the delightful atmospheric bar. Inside, the superbly done theme depicts the maritime history of the Mersey, the great days of Cunard and the tragically killed-off overhead railway (short sightedness is clearly not a new characteristic of our race). Ships' wheels, model ships, paintings and myriad nautical paraphernalia blend beautifully, and the subdued lighting from ship-style lanterns creates a cosy warm glow. The place has instant atmosphere, it doesn't need people. The well stocked three-sided service bar adds to it, with the imaginative use of mirror panels and more lanterns behind the optics. It's a pity that electric pumps are in operation: if ever a bar needed a fine set of gleaming traditional handpumps, this is it. There are two beamed and carpeted lounges either side of the bar, itself surrounded by tiled flooring, with lots of dark wood and brass. With an open fire blazing, it must be idyllic on a cold winter's evening. There is also a small TV and games room and, at the side of the building, an above-average family room and canalside beer garden.

Hot and cold food is available from 12–2 pm every lunchtime, and from opening time to 9.30 each evening. The food is good, wholesome and reasonably priced (although not devastatingly original) with lots of local fresh vegetables. Steak puddings, seafood platters and hot pot pies are among the favourites.

The Ship is well known among the boating fraternity and comes highly recommended.

LATHOM
Ring o'Bells

Tel: (0704) 893157
Lathom, nr. Burscough, Lancs.
Canalside at Bridge 34

✗ lunchtime and evenings

🏵

🍺 **Whitbread Higsons Bitter, Boddingtons Bitter**

Built in 1738, the Ring o'Bells became a familiar stopping place on the packet boat runs. Its square, ivy clad frontage with white shuttered windows houses a pub which, although modernised, still gives the impression of being homely and cottagey, with lots of cosy corners. It succeeds in achieving an amicable and at times tasteful co-existence of the old and the new. Authentic old beams and settles nestle comfortably alongside sections of recent brickwork, plush new carpet and more than a hint of Laura Ashley in the furnishing. There are several connected drinking areas including a non-carpeted low level bar with TV and dartboard, and a small separate dining area. Flickering electric powered gas lanterns hang from the ceiling along with an antique bird cage.

This old country pub is also a Henry's Table house, which means food is top priority. It is indeed popular for high quality eating, and deservedly so. Apart from the restaurant menu and the specials on the chalkboard, there is a bar menu every lunchtime and every evening except Monday, on which you'll find steak, kidney and mushroom pie, chicken dippers, fresh fish, sandwiches, Neptune's Choice (fresh salmon, prawns, salad, granary bread, seafood sauce), Henry's Wedge (a Lancashire cheese ploughman's), and Wedge 'n' Bite (a Henry's Wedge with added pâté).

The Ring o'Bells has two outdoor drinking areas, some canalside tables and chairs and an extensive children's play area next to the car park.

Ship

Tel: (0704) 893117
Wheat Lane, Latham, nr.
Burscough, Lancs. Canalside by
junction of Rufford branch and
Main Line, near second lock down

✕ lunchtime

🍴

🍺 **Theakstons Best Bitter, XB; Timothy Taylor's Landlord; Tetley Walker Bitter; guest beers**

I have to admit I have a soft spot for pubs with traditional beer menus chalked on blackboards: it suggests a common interest. This authentic old free house is indeed enthusiastic about its role as a drinker's pub and purveyor of good beers. In addition to those listed, the likes of Youngs, Batemans and several others are likely to make guest appearances. It was known formerly (and still locally) as the "Blood Tub" – black puddings were once made here, and a bucket of pig's blood could be traded in for a pint of beer. It's one of many apocryphal tales the pub seems to spawn, although this one seems plausible.

Following expansion into the cottage next door, the Ship nowadays has no less than four separate rooms, with at one end a games room with pool table and darts, and at the other a cosy lounge with a low beamed ceiling and lots of naval memorabilia and canal artefacts. The pub backs on to the canal and has tables and chairs there as well as outside its pretty whitewashed frontage, where two conflicting pub signs hang, one Theakstons, the other claiming somewhat ambiguously that it's a Whitbread Free House – as opposed to a Whitbread-free house, a consumation devoutly to be wished.

Home-made and freshly prepared food is available 12–2 Monday to Saturday, nothing fancy, pre-packed or frozen, and includes pies and quiches. Displaying a refreshing and increasingly isolated priority for drinkers, no food is served in the evenings. In an area well blessed with above average canalside pubs, the Ship is another fine example.

LYDIATE
Running Horses

Tel: (051) 526 3989
*Bells Lane (100 yards off A567),
Lydiate, Merseyside. Canalside at
Bridge 16*

✗ lunchtime and evening

🍺

☺

🍺 **Ind Coope Burton Ale, Walker Mild, Best Bitter, Winter Warmer**

Set in a semi-rural location, the Running Horses is a pub of great character and focal point for a panoramic range of interests and activities. It's a community pub in the true sense, serving the local community and travellers alike. Built in the eighteenth century, about the same time as the canal, it looks a picture from the water with its whitewashed frontage, window boxes and hanging baskets, wooden tables and chairs and nice old Walkers Warrington Brewery windows. Although extended and enlarged over the years, it remains an essentially traditional pub. The bar has some fine high backed settles, a line of domino tables end to end, a dartboard and a piano. Through a doorless doorway, the lounge is comfortable without being bland, with varnished dark wood panelling and assorted pictures on either nautical, canal or angling themes. Indeed it's a popular haunt for anglers, who can tuck into special early morning fishermen's breakfasts.

What the landlord describes as "predominantly farmhouse food" is sandwiches and rolls in the evenings, and the traditional beers are as well kept as you would hope for from a landlord who is a CAMRA member. Tuesday night is quiz night, Wednesday is for Irish music, Saturday for singalongs. Expensive trips on the Tetley Walker trip boat can also be booked from here.

The Running Horses is almost as busy as outside as in, with no less than three separate outdoor drinking areas; tables and chairs at the front and on a raised platform to the side, and a vast children's play area at the rear complete with slide, swings and pets including goats and chickens wandering inquisitively around. There is also a boules pitch. The pub caters exceptionally well for families, with an unusually cosy and well appointed family room which would serve as a perfectly acceptable snug or tap room. They also host children's parties and, on Bank Holidays, fun days where anything goes, with music all day, tug o'war, bouncy castle and eating and drinking competitions. The pub was the brewery's "Managed House of the Year" in 1990.

Scotch Piper

OFF THE TOWPATH
Southport Road, Lydiate,
Merseyside. *400 yards north of
Bridge 17A*

☎

◎

🍺 Burtonwood Mild, Bitter

Beautifully preserved, award winning pub dating from 1320, reputedly the oldest in Lancashire. Real ale straight from the cask.

NEW SPRINGS
Colliers Arms

Tel: (0942) 831171
*Wigan Road (B5238), New
Springs, Gtr. Manchester. 100
yards up the hill from Bridge 59A*

🍺 Burtonwood Mild, Best Bitter

From its picturesque black-and-white frontage to the delightful traditional interior with its central bar framed by a heavy arched beam, the Colliers possesses that unspoilt, timeless atmosphere that evades most pubs, and marks out this friendly eighteenth-century outlet as worthy of special merit.

The charming bar has beams, carpeted floor, wooden settles and fabric covered pews, lots of dark wood finish and an open fire. The walls are sparsely punctuated with photos and brasses. Unusually, the pub's dartboard and pool table are to be found in the lounge, along with a TV and fruit machine and, on Saturday nights, singers, for Saturday Night is Singers Night. Black and white canal prints and photos adorn the walls, while CAMRA posters and mirrors and a pile of old Good Beer Guides (most of which have a place for the Colliers) speak volumes for the pub's priorities. For this is a beer drinking pub, not merely because of the excellence of its beer or because it doesn't do food but because it has remained essentially true to its origins and traditions. It exudes a reassuring air of permanence in a business where change has become almost an end in itself.

The local sages, wits and philosophers can often be found, pint in hand, gazing solemnly from the bar window down across the rather forlorn (and usually rain and windswept) north-eastern outskirts of Wigan, before pronouncing "There'll be rain before long" or "Better inside than out today". Nobody could doubt the truth in either conclusion.

PARBOLD
Railway Hotel

OFF THE TOWPATH
Tel: (0257) 462917
Station Road, Parbold, Lancs. 100 yards north of Bridge 37

✗ lunchtime and evenings

@ children welcome until 8 pm

🍺 **Burtonwood Mild, Bitter**

Popular village local, bristling with railway paraphernalia.

SALTERFORTH
Anchor

Tel: (0282) 813186
Salterforth, Lancs. Canalside,
Bridge 51

✗ lunchtime and evening

🛏

🍺 **Stones Best Bitter, Bass XXXX**
Mild, Special Bitter

There are few pubs on this superb Pennine section of the canal – its summit level – but there is one with an unusual history. The Anchor is actually two pubs, one on top of the other. Dating from 1560, it stood for over a century as a small, two-storey roadside inn before the canal arrived. Then the road had to be raised to allow for the construction of the adjacent bridge, leaving the pub's bedrooms at road level. Consequently another storey was built on top and everything moved up one, as it were. Thus the bedrooms became the bar and the bar became the cellars, in one of which stalactites began to form. The longest is now more than four feet long and stalagmites are arising to meet them. The canal has also begun to seep into the cellars through the limestone. The regional TV news has featured the pub.

Sadly, the pub's character does not really reflect its long and fascinating history or fulfil the promise of its attractive stone exterior. Friendly and good humoured though it is, it's disappointingly ordinary inside, with its fully carpeted open plan lounge and stone fireplace. Twin arched entrances lead to a pool room, and a small bar area in the corner has a dartboard, TV and PVC seating.

Hot and cold bar meals are available lunchtime and evening seven days a week, and includes sandwiches, salads, a "Pie 'n' Peas" menu and the increasingly popular filled Yorkshire puddings. The beers were average, though none of them exactly set the pulses racing.

There is a small beer garden (not canalside) and good moorings close to the pub.

SCARISBRICK
Heatons Bridge

Tel: (0704) 840549
Heatons Bridge Road, (B5242)
Scarisbrick, Lancs. Canalside at
Bridge 28

✕   snacks and bar meals
     lunchtimes and evenings

🍴   Tetley Walker Mild, Bitter

After its construction in 1837, the Heatons Bridge spent 150 years in the hands of the same family before the current licensees took over in 1987. The lively, enthusiastic newcomers, thoroughly sympathetic to the pub's traditional values, have settled quickly in this tiny gem of a pub, wasting little time in adding to its facilities. The brewery classify it is as a "farmhouse pub" which, in their contorted way of thinking, means "hardly any facilities" or "one of those we haven't got round to modernising yet". (They won't while this landlord is in charge.)

The Heatons Bridge provides the simple things in an unobtrusive but effective way, without the need to impose some arbitrary standard of comfort, entertainment or organised fun on the many customers it attracts from the canal and from way beyond its immediate catchment area. Instead they pour in, in search of good beer, relaxed unpressurised surroundings in which to drink it, and conversation unhindered by juke box, electronic bandits, television or piped muzak. In short, they are considered capable and adult enough of making their own entertainment.

The basic but spotlessly clean interior consists of a cosy snug, a darts/games room and a comfortable, U-shaped public bar with bench seating, fabric covered chairs and highly polished wood. It survived refurbishment comparatively intact. The traditional beers are dispensed from an unusual set of gleaming, stainless steel handpumps, emerging in foaming fine fettle. A canalside beer garden has been established in the acres of land belonging to the pub.

Food at the Heatons Bridge is restricted to ploughman's and hotpot at lunchtimes, and rolls and sandwiches all day. its policy on opening hours is similarly straightforward – all day, every day, no nonsense.

There aren't many like this left and their

numbers are diminishing almost daily. Enjoy them while you can.

SKIPTON
Royal Shepherd

Tel: (0756) 793178
Canal Street, Skipton, N. Yorks

✗ lunchtime snacks

🍴

🍺 **Hartleys XB; Marston Pedigree; Bitter Whitbread Boddingtons Bitter, Trophy, Castle Eden Ale**

The Royal Shepherd owes a historical debt of gratitude to King George III. Its name is believed to be in recognition of his enthusiastic support of a late-eighteenth century plan to improve the quality of wool of our native sheep by breeding them with imported Merino sheep from Spain. And it was the same monarch who gave the royal seal of approval for the opening of the Springs branch by which the pub stands, to join the main Leeds-Liverpool canal a couple of hundreds yards away.

Today this splendid lively pub is popular with canal and beer enthusiasts alike, with both able to enjoy a good range of traditional beers. The Royal Shepherd has regularly featured in the Good Beer Guide. Situated at the end of a terrace of houses, its sandstone exterior overlooks the canal, with moorings on the opposite bank. Inside, its main lounge bar includes an old "Bentleys Yorkshire Brewery" mirror, some stained glass panels depicting canal scenes and many photos of old Skipton. A short side corridor leads to a small enclosed outdoor drinking area. There is a lovely small cosy snug, with fireplace, wooden settle and seating for seventeen. Photos of old Yorkshire and England cricket teams recall days when both were successful, which immediately dates them. "God must be a Yorkshireman" claims a sign on the wall, presumably based on the assumption that He is always right.

The Royal Shepherd is one of those pubs that exudes confidence, continuity and permanence. It's clear that the licensees care for and take pride in the place. It comes highly recommended, an essential stop if you're in the area.

SILSDEN
Bridge

Tel: (0535) 653144
Canalside, Bridge 191A (Silsden Bridge)

✗ bar meals lunchtimes; evenings on request

🍺

🍺 John Smith's Bitter

The cobbled area at the rear of the pub was once Silsden's main street. Then known as the Boot and Slipper (a nearby bridge is still known today as Clog Bridge, though I was unable to ascertain the precise reason for this mid-eighteenth century footwear fetish), the pub later became known as the Thanet Arms in recognition of the Earl of Thanet, owner of much local land. When the canal was built, an extra storey was added to the existing buildings to bring it up to canal level – a similar story to the Anchor at Salterforth.

It later became the Bridge in recognition of its new role as a canalside inn, and remains a popular three-roomed local today. Entering from Silsden's main through route, you are confronted by a short passageway which opens out into a small cosy tap room, with the serving counter facing and, somewhat unusually, a window behind it with views across the rear of the pub and the canal. There is also some unusual but effective mock dark wood panelling. A plush beamed lounge leads off the tap room, with green dralon and wooden tables and benches. There is a small, slightly remote snug off the entrance passageway.

Giant filled Yorkshire puddings – a dinner in a pudding – have been sighted here, with a choice of fillings such as chili, sausages and onion gravy. Snacks and bar meals like pizzas are also on the menu. The beer is well kept and gained the Bridge inclusion in the 1990 Good Beer Guide.

The land behind the pub and a small piece of wasteland by the towpath are earmarked for conversion into a beer garden. Outdoor drinking at the moment is confined to a few roadside chairs and tables.

WIGAN
Seven Stars

Tel: (0942) 43126
*262 Wallgate (A49), Wigan, Gtr.
Manchester. Canalside, Seven
Stars Bridge*

✗ lunchtime, evening on request

🍺 **Thwaites Best Mild, Bitter**

Just a five minute towpath stroll from the commercially but impressively redeveloped Wigan Pier complex, the Seven Stars is a typical Magee Marshalls turn of the century pub, large and friendly with a somewhat unusual layout.

At its heart is an irregular shaped, almost semi circular island bar, with individual snob screen-style serving windows. The bright, cheerful, strip-lit public bar runs along its straight edge, and has bright curtains, while the carpeted lounge area (lighting courtesy of upturned tulip bulbs with brass stems) has high ceilings and occasional live entertainment (mostly pub singers with their own backing tapes) which can tend to dominate proceedings. It's OK if you can handle "I love you just the way you are" and "Spanish Eyes" complete with obligatory vocal quaver, otherwise head for the bar. There is also a games room with pool tables and a corridor with a fruit machine and juke box. The whole place is spotlessly clean, with lots of highly polished woodwork.

Catering is safe and predictable – salads, sandwiches, everything with chips – but reasonably priced and the excellent Thwaites beers are in fine form. The Seven Stars is a Good Beer Guide stalwart, a popular and well regarded pub and the best choice for liquid refreshment in central Wigan or when visiting the Pier.

Swan & Railway

OFF THE TOWPATH
Tel : (0942) 495032
80 Wallgate (A49), Wigan, Gtr. Manchester. Opposite Wallgate railway station, 10 minutes walk towards the town centre from Bridge 51

✕   lunchtime and evening (not Sun)

◎

⋈

⅏   **Bass XXXX Mild, Special Bitter, Draught Bass, Stones Best Bitter; Courage Directors, John Smith's Bitter**

Superbly renovated traditional pub in Victorian style. Classic northern boozer. Don't miss it.

MACCLESFIELD CANAL

A typical Telford canal and part of the endlessly popular Cheshire Ring, the Macclesfield begins at Kidsgrove in north Staffordshire where it leaves the Trent & Mersey, passing through the Cheshire towns of Congleton and Macclesfield and hugging the western edge of the Pennines along its scenic and interesting journey to Marple Junction, where it meets the Peak Forest canal.

HIGHER POYNTON

OFF THE TOWPATH
Down the hill from Bridge 15, the **Boar's Head** at High Poynton is an unpretentious Boddingtons' pub with electric-pumped bitter and mild. It's close to Lyme Park and the Middlewood Way.

MACCLESFIELD

OFF THE TOWPATH
Macclesfield and its small neighbour to the north, Bollington, have been described as one of the seven wonders of the real ale drinkers' waterways, with a vast number of real ale outlets and a wide choice of different beers all within easy reach of the canal. In such circumstances it's difficult to single many out, but the **Britannia**, west of Bridge 34, is a lovely unspoilt terrace pub serving handpulled Greenalls real ales and bar meals, while the **Bridgewater Arms**, named after the Duke who built the canal, is a plain, basic friendly pub on Buxton Road close to Bridge 37, offering Wilsons & Websters cask beers.

MARPLE
Ring O'Bells

Tel: (061) 427 2300
Church Lane, Marple, Ches.
Canalside, Bridge 2, close to
Marple Junction

✘ lunchtime and evening

🍴

🍺 **Robinsons Best Mild, Best Bitter**

A canal junction and boating centre as popular and attractive as that at Marple deserves a pub to match. With the picturesque Marple locks and the dramatic hilly Goyt Valley scenery as its backdrop, the whole area is a magnet for the hordes from the Manchester and Stockport conurbations, and the pub itself a justifiably popular watering hole for users of the Macclesfield and Peak Forest canals.

The comfortable, spick and span main lounge bar has a stone pillar in the middle, a chiming grandfather clock and some words of wisdom above the corner table. Rise-and-fall lights hang above some of the tables as though a game of stud to the death is about to take place. There is some ornate glass partitioning and lots of dark wood finish. Two rooms lead off, both numbered and titled as if they are front doors to little cottages. "The Sportsmans" is a small bright comfortable smoke room, while the door marked "Waterways" opens to reveal a lovely canalified snug with prints, paintings and the odd Buckby can.

Leading from the main lounge is a small dining area, and food plays a major part in the pub's repertoire. Unusually, catering is franchised out and, equally unusually, available throughout Sunday afternoon, and can be accompanied by alcoholic drinks. The extensive and slightly expensive menu features starters, lunchtime bar snacks, main dishes (grills), vegetarian dishes, inter-continental (lots of goodies), home-made pies, salads, "From the Sea" and "From the Farm", daily specials chalked on a blackboard, Sunday lunches and an excellent Kiddies Corner menu. Food is available at all times.

There is an attractive canalside terrace with colourful window boxes, a telephone kiosk and a postbox. The pub has its own Golf Society, which makes it one of the better nineteenth holes in the country.

SUTTON
Fool's Nook

Tel: (02605) 2254
Leek Road, Sutton, Macclesfield, Ches. Canalside, Bridge 49

✕ lunchtime and evenings

🏠

🍺 Whitbread Boddingtons Bitter

An archetypal rural pub which dates from the eighteenth century and was until recently a Higsons house before Whitbread made their unwelcome entry. There are conflicting theories about the origin of the pub's name: the most likely is that the Nook refers to the corner or bend in the road near the pub, and the fool was the person who decided that it was a sensible place for the Nook.

Forming the front part of a large, whitewashed L-shaped building, the Fool's Nook looks very inviting from outside with leaded and shuttered windows and an attractive rear courtyard illuminated at night by a mock Victorian gas lamp. The two interior rooms are called the Fool's Paradise and the Anglers' Nook in a somewhat cumbersome and contrived division of the pub's name. There's nothing wrong with the rooms themselves though, with a typical country pub lounge made up of beams and wooden settles, lots of polished brass and copper, lamps and lanterns, an old grandfather clock in the corner by the fireplace, and subdued lighting to create a warm cosy glow. The bar is pleasant too, with nice wooden bench seating and a good atmosphere.

It's a family-run pub and there's an air of stability and continuity about the place. The new licensees have a ten-year lease and their son looks after the catering, producing a good range of reasonably priced food every lunchtime and evening. The home-made steak pies are a house speciality. Other items include home-roast ham, chicken, gammon, scampi and daily specials.

MONMOUTH & BRECON

For thirty-three miles between Pontypool and its northern terminal in the town of Brecon the Monmouthshire & Brecon Canal follows the beautiful valley of the river Usk and is a central feature of the Brecon Beacons national park. Once connecting with the Bristol Channel at Newport, it is now landlocked and remote from the main waterways system.

BRECON
Gremlin

OFF THE TOWPATH
Tel: (0874) 3829
*The Watton, Brecon, Powys. 250
yards north of canal terminus*

✗ lunchtime and evening meals

🍴

🛏

🍺 Draught Bass; Felinfoel
Double Dragon

Before the last war, when it was re-christened by visiting aircrews, the uniquely named Gremlin Hotel was just another Coach and Horses. The dictionary defines *gremlin* as RAF banter for a mischievous spirit that effects machinery. I don't know why this name was considered appropriate, but then again I often wonder how we managed to win the war from the stories I hear.

The Gremlin is a popular gabled Victorian inn with two lively bars presided over by an avuncular and dry-witted licensee. The catering and accommodation are both of good quality and value and the beer is lovingly kept. Very much the place to visit when moored at the canal's end, and an excellent base for discovering this scenic part of South Wales.

GILWERN
Bridgend

Tel: (0873) 830939
*Main Road, Gilwern, Gwent.
Canalside at bridge 103*

✗ lunchtime and evening

🛏

☺

🍺 Draught Bass; Brain's SA;
Felinfoel Double Dragon; Hall
& Woodhouse Tanglefoot;
guest beer

Progressing northward from its present-day terminus in Pontypool the "Mon and Brec" avoids practically any contact with civilisation as it charts a solitary rural course through what was once one of the most heavily farmed and industrialised landscapes in the Principality.

The pretty village of Gilwern provides the canal with a rare close encounter with the world beyond its banks and a welcome one it is too. Bounded on three sides by the village main street, the canal bridge and by the canal itself, this charming little family-run free house is a quiet haven magnetically attracting the boater but liable to be missed along with the whole village by the car driver thundering past on the A465 bypass.

The Bridgend is solidly built of stone with a little white-painted porch. There is a pleasant walled patio/beer garden with a grassy bank extending to the canal towpath. Look out for the sign advertising the now sadly defunct Rhymney brewery. The homely single-bar interior is decorated in the half-timbered style but not overdone.

A resident chef is on hand to provide nourishing victuals while a range of real ales to satisfy any tastebud completes an ambitious package in this friendly, unassuming tavern.

LLANGYNIDR
Coach and
Horses

Tel: (0874) 730245
*Cwm Crawnon, Llangynidr,
Powys. Canalside at bridge 133*

✕ lunchtime and evening

🍴

☺

⋈

🍺 **Ruddles Best Bitter, County;
Websters Yorkshire Bitter**

My image of the South Wales valleys was always one of coal mines and industry. The fact that the horse was of local significance was unknown to me. Although my two-day sojourn here failed to reveal a single member of the equine species in the flesh, evidence of its importance lay in the many Horseshoes, Horses and Groom, Horses and Jockey and other horsey names of public houses.

The Coach and Horses is yet another of this breed. A large and well appointed old inn, it has an impressive setting just above Llangynidr bottom lock and is thus a popular stopping point of boat crews. It has something of a farmhouse appearance, two-storeyed, white painted and slate roofed in traditional Welsh manner.

Misleadingly and, much to my subsequent disappointment, the outside signs advertise the availability of Usher's beers from Wiltshire. Is this a case for the Trade Descriptions Act? The open plan interior takes in the whole ground floor and comprises a large bar and larger restaurant. The walls are of rough-hewn stone and massive beams abound, some very low. If you are phobic about dogs and the pub's very large though very docile Great Dane alarms you, then mind your head as you flee.

There is a fine canalside beer garden which is, in fact, across the road from the pub. While gingerly crossing with a trayful of drinks, you can be reassured that such traffic as there is will be forced to a slow crawl by the narrow and acutely angled canal bridge.

TALYBONT-ON-USK
Star Inn

Tel: (087 487) 635
Canalside between bridges 143 and 144 on the B4558

✕ lunchtime and evening

🍴

☺

🍺 **Brains SA; Bullmastiff Best Bitter, Ebony Dark, Son of a Bitch; Felinfoel Double Dragon; Whitbread Flowers Original; Hook Norton Best Bitter; Marston Pedigree Bitter; Robinson's Best Bitter; Theakstons Best Bitter, Old Peculier; Wadworth 6X; Charles Wells Bombardier (not all available at one time)**

The canal skirts Talybont on its steep hillside embankment, with the attractively situated modern electric lift bridge providing novice crews with an interesting challenge. Nestling below the embankment, a small community has grown to serve both the canal and the needs of the holiday maker in this popular tourist area.

Here we find the Victorian Star Inn, attractively painted in black and white and flower-bedecked with window boxes and hanging baskets.

Pass through the front door into the characterful multi-roomed interior and there before you is a little island bar festooned with beer dispensers. Most of these are handpumps offering a bewildering variety of real ales. If panic sets in the bar staff will happily allow time for you to make your choice and offer sound and knowledgeable advice. And you are unlikely to catch them out with a bad pint, despite this challenge to any cellarman's skill. On the food side there is a similar cosmopolitan choice, including authentic, home-made Indian curries.

Much of the Star's internal fabric is original. The layout of the bars has been preserved and there are typical nineteenth-century padded benches around the walls and bays.

I much regret that my visit here was of necessity so short because this is one of those lively pubs where enjoyment is the order of the night. Try getting there on a Thursday night and sample the delights of live jazz.

Traveller's Rest

Tel: (087 487) 233
Taylbont-on-Usk, Powys.
Canalside 200 yards south of
bridge 142

✕ lunchtime and evening

🍴

☺

🛏

🍺 **Arkells BBB; Ind Coope
Burton Ale; Marston Pedigree
Bitter; Sam Powell Samson
Ale; Ringwood Old Thumper;
Smiles Bitter; Samuel Smith's
Old Brewery Bitter**

Approaching Talybont-on-Usk from the south east by road or canal, the first building you encounter, sandwiched between these two transport arteries, is the Traveller's Rest. You could do much worse than take the advice implied in the name of this comfortable and welcoming family-run inn. It's an ideal place to break your journey, to stretch your legs and take in some pure country air and a little refreshment or, as the evening draws in, to make a night of it. The pub itself inspires one to linger and there is much to see in this attractive and historic village.

The dominant feature here, looming high over the roof top of the Traveller's Rest, is the great canal embankment, atop of which is a charming beer garden with breathtaking views of the surrounding fields and distant mountains.

This is a traditional, enthusiastically run establishment with every modern facility. Outside it has been spruced up and decorated with considerable good taste and well-designed contemporary signs. There is a large back extension with floor steeply terraced on two levels as it climbs the embankment's sloping base. At the front is an atmospheric little bar with a Georgian feel and suitably decorated and furnished.

The food here comes highly recommended and for a genuine alternative to the fine range of well-kept real ales there is traditional German Warsteiner beer on offer. Please don't ask for "lager" as you are likely to be served with a less pleasing ersatz concoction.

Beauchamp
Arms
Caulton St. Peter

John Simpson

NORFOLK BROADS

NORFOLK BROADS

The Broads is a network of the rivers Yare, Bure, Ant, Thurne and Waveney, with their tributaries and a few artificial cuts, connecting a series of shallow lakes of obscure man-made origin after which the whole area takes its name. They occupy a large part of Norfolk and the tip of north Suffolk between the brash seaside town and port of Great Yarmouth and the fine medieval city of Norwich.

Though isolated from the main system of rivers and canals, the Broads, now a national park and the focus of an urgent environmental rescue campaign, are the most popular cruising waterways in the country.

ACLE
Reba's Riverside Inn

OFF THE TOWPATH
Tel: (0493) 750310
*Old Road (A1064 off A47) Acle,
Norfolk. 250 yards West of end of
Acle Dyke on the River Bure*

✗ lunchtime and evening

🍲

🍺 John Smith's Bitter;
Woodforde Wherry Best
Bitter

This pleasant little pub on the outskirts of Acle bears an intriguing name. *Reba* is a kind of anagram of Reg and Babs, the present incumbents. They bought the pub from Whitbread some four years ago and have personalised it in ways other than just the name. Outside there is fresh paint and attractive signs, while within a homely atmosphere prevails. Not a speck of dust can be detected on the host of ornaments that surround the bar. Here one feels a welcome guest, not just another punter.

As for Riverside Inn, well riverside it strictly ain't, but certainly closer to a river than its roadside aspect could suggest, and well worth the short walk from moorings on Acle Dyke.

BERNEY ARMS
Berney Arms

Tel: Gt. Yarmouth 700303
*Berney Arms, Norfolk. OS ref.
467 052. Closed end October to
mid-March. North bank of River
Yare near confluence with the
Waveney*

✗ lunchtime and evening

🍲

☺

🍺 Greene King IPA, Abbot Ale;
Courage Best Bitter, Directors;
John Smith's Bitter

Other than by water, this is the country's least accessible public house. Its remote location was a hive of industrial activity in the last century; a majestic windmill ground clinker for the nearby cement works while its massive scoop wheel drained millions of gallons of water from the surrounding marshes. The pub itself was an important stopping place for the wherries as they awaited the next tide to take them across Breydon Water and into Great Yarmouth. At the end of the century the cement works closed, the mill faced redundancy and dereliction, and an obscure incident involving the drowning of two drunken wherrymen lead to the closure of the Berney Arms for some 60 years.

Renaissance came with re-licensing in 1953 and (while the mill has become a well-preserved museum) the pub continues to capture trade from the river. It is as essential a haven for today's holiday maker as it was for the wherrymen of old, offering the only safe moorings between Great Yarmouth and Reedham (and extracting a small fee for this provision).

The visitor by land must let the train take the

strain. Reached from Yarmouth or points west, Berney Arms halt is a most desolate and lonely place to be left as your train splutters off into the far distance on a dead-straight single track. A further half-hour traipse across the marshes (head for the windmill) brings one to the pub and what seems like one of civilisation's last outposts. Police harassment is not known here, although the Chief Constable did happen to drop in on the eve of my visit.

The building itself is perhaps as featureless outside as are its surroundings. A squat two-storey edifice in the lee of the river's bank, there are no chimneys and the hatches are battened down further against the elements with airtight double glazing. The interior, however, despite its recent vintage, happily recreates a timeless pubbiness. Much of the furniture is revealed on close inspection to be made of old cask staves while fishing nets, glass buoys, and old prints and maps abound on walls and ceilings. The beer is excellent, surviving well its bumpy delivery by tractor across the marshes, and the bar meals are sufficient both in quantity and quality to tempt any boating family away from self-catering.

CARLTON ST. PETER
Beauchamp Arms

Tel: (050 843) 247
Buckenham Ferry, Carlton St. Peter, nr. Caxton, Norfolk. OS ref. 350 044. South bank of the River Yare

✘ lunchtime and evenings

🏮

☺

🍺 **Woodforde Wherry Best Bitter, Phoenix XXX; guest beer**

"We didn't want to make a barn of it", the landlord told me. I wish more owners of popular free-houses were as enlightened. Recent tasteful refurbishment has retained three distinct drinking areas – a genuine public bar, a large room for pool and darts players to flex their elbows undisturbed and a comfortable lounge and family room – plus a spaciously well-appointed restaurant in this impressive three-storeyed free house.

Built as an hotel after the turn of the century, the Beauchamp Arms is a welcoming landmark on this remote stretch of the Yare between Brundall, with its many boatyards, and the vast sugar-beet factory at Cantley. With plentiful moorings it is a boater's paradise which equally rewards discovery by the land-bound visitor in an area of generally uninspiring pubs.

Buckenham Ferry having long ceased to operate, the nearest river crossing is the toll ferry at Reedham or, to the west, Foundry bridge in Norwich. The hamlet of Carlton St. Peter is some miles to the south. Look out for the magnificent avenue of poplar trees that flank the private approach road.

GELDESTON
Locks Inn

Tel: Kirby Cane 414.
Locks Lane, Geldeston, Norfolk. OS ref. 390 909. At limit of navigation of the River Waveney

✘ lunchtime and evening

🏮

☺

🛏

🍺 **Woodforde Wherry Best Bitter, Baldric, Phoenix XXX, Norfolk Nog, Headcracker; James White's Suffolk Cider**

Twenty years ago the Locks was a very primitive place. Presided over by Miss Dorothy Ellis, an indomitable lady variously known as "Miss Susan" or "Boadicea of the Broads", it offered few of the facilities seen as compulsory in the modern public house. But it did offer shelter and warmth and good company – basics which today are oft forgotten.

Despite considerable change since Miss Susan passed away these basics remain, and the introduction of excellent draught beer (in Miss Susan's day it was bottles only) and imaginative bar meals are positively to be welcomed.

Sadly, the tiny lock-keeper's cottage of two decades past could never have supported the thriving enterprise we see today. Nevertheless, with its whitewashed brickwork and pantiled roof, the old frontage remains, easily recognisable from old photographs, flanked now by two recent extensions. These are large but built sensitively of matching materials and the old pub still has centre stage.

Inside, the original bar area has been preserved intact. The motley hued quarry tiled floor, the ancient settles and benches, the piano and venerable stove remain. That sweet odour of polish and wood preservative put me in mind of the smell of old churches. But perhaps this is also a place of worship.

The locks after which the pub is named lie derelict at the bottom of the garden. Not much remains that is recognisable. Nature, with willows and waterside plants and bushes, has totally reclaimed the site. The Waveney Navigation once extended from here to Bungay and there were great plans to link the Broads with the Midlands waterways by this route. These came to an end in 1934 when the last owners of the Waveney Navigation decided on closure. These owners went by the familiar name of Watney Combe Reid whose successors, beer lovers will tell you, have since attempted to close the whole of East Anglia.

Road access to the Locks is by the village and a well-signposted but interminably bone-shaking mile-long track. Mains electricity has yet to make this journey and the pub has its own generator, supplemented by candle power. The Locks has entered the modern world – just – but for the visitor the ghosts of a long and eventful past remain.

NORWICH
Rosary Tavern

OFF THE TOWPATH
Tel: (0603) 666287
Rosary Road, Norwich, Norfolk.
200 yards East of yacht station on
the River Wensum

✗ lunchtime and evening

🍴

☺

🍺 Adnams Bitter, Broadside;
Batemans XXXB; Marston
Pedigree Bitter; Woodforde
New Rosary Bitter, Phoenix
XXX, Wherry Best Bitter; guest
beers

This tiny one-room pub packs in a great deal, including a merry throng of locals of all ages and callings, and a fine selection of well-kept ales. There are no frills here and there is no need of them. The Rosary Tavern exudes an atmosphere of friendly warmth in which darts, cribbage and bar-room discussion are eagerly, yet civilly, contested.

The needs of the inner man/woman are also catered for. The pub began life as a farm smithy and today there is equally hot work afoot in the kitchen. All the bar meals here are home-made and freshly prepared and include unusual delicacies such as doner kebab and authentic pizzas from the landlady's own pizza oven.

The line-up of traditional ales is augmented by traditional cider from Inch's and traditional pure German beer from Bitburger.

REEDHAM
Reedham Ferry
Inn

Tel: Gt. Yarmouth 700429
Reedham, Norfolk. North bank of
the river Yare by the ferry

✗ lunchtime and evening

🍴

☺

🍺 Adnams Bitter; Woodforde
Wherry Best Bitter

Reedham chain ferry is the sole survivor of many such river crossings on the Broads, and also the only crossing of the Yare between Norwich and Great Yarmouth. Hence the Ferry Inn is strategically placed to offer sustenance to travellers both by road and river.

Facilities on offer in this whitewashed, flint-built seventeenth century inn include a vast family room (with rather too great a cacophony of electronic amusements for my taste), a caravan site, abundant moorings, showers in the hospital-clean toilets and even, in an outbuilding, a place to purchase hand-crafted wooden furniture.

An excellent menu, including local delicacies, is available in two attractive and comfortable bars with beamed ceilings, quarry-tiled floors and real fires.

ST. OLAVE'S
Bell

Tel: Gt. Yarmouth 488249
St. Olave's, Norfolk. By St.
Olave's bridge on the River
Waveney

✗ lunchtime and evening
(restaurant Wed–Sun eve)

☸

◎

🍺 **Whitbread Flowers Original,
Wethered Bitter, Winter
Royal; Marston Pedigree Bitter**

The Bell is a fine late medieval building of brick and timber frame standing near a large boatyard by the elegant iron span of St. Olave's bridge. There is a photograph in the bar, circa 1900, showing the innkeeper, in his best suit and high starched collar, standing proudly at the steps of his domain. A sign-board above his head offers his potential customer a vast array of services, including high tea and home-brewed beer. Next to this another photographs shows the pub as it is today from the same spot and with the present publican posed exactly as his predecessor. These pictures are evidence both of how little and how much has changed over nearly a century.

Today's signage denotes that the Bell is now part of the estate of Whitbread. Gone, sadly therefore, is the home-brewed beer, although the selection of brews now on offer is perfectly acceptable.

The brewers' architects, both Whitbread and Lacons before them, have not been idle here, but the new stuff is good and much of the old remains. The Bell has been somewhat prettified; it is more ordered and less robust than its turn of the century incarnation. The beamed, low-ceilinged interior is cosy with open fires and divided into two walk-through drinking areas and a small restaurant. There is still a big range of refreshments on offer with a bar menu of mouth-watering seafood dishes, three-course meals available in the restaurant and barbecues on fine summer evenings.

Pubs of the larger brewers tend to have a soullessness that results from a single-minded pursuit of maximum return. The Bell is a notable exception. My one complaint concerns a wireless tuned far too loudly to Radio One.

SOMERLEYTON
Duke's Head

OFF THE TOWPATH
Tel: (0502) 730281
Slugg's Lane, Somerleyton, Suffolk. 150 yards up footpath from old ferry crossing on the River Waveney

✕ lunchtime and evening

🅰

☺

🍺 **Whitbread Flowers Original, Wethered Bitter**

Aren't lounge bars supposed to have carpets? And don't you usually get them in the public bar these days as well, if indeed there is one? Well, not at the Duke's Head you don't. For the advice of those who, like myself, may miss the little sign on the door on entry, the lounge is the bigger of the two bars on the left-hand side in a large, friendly, people-orientated boozer.

While the public bar has its darts and dominoes, the lounge has pool and electronic amusement and a wonderful food counter. This latter, with its patterned formica, white-painted shelves and rows of sauce bottles, immaculately clean, has that heady feel of the best sort of street-corner cafe, serving such delicacies as fish and chips and tandoori pork slices.

There are too few genuine down-to-earth pubs of character in this part of the country, so get along to the Duke's Head before Whitbread decide to sanitise is to the normal standard of their estate.

STOKESBY
Ferry Inn

Tel: (0493) 751096
Stokesby, Norfolk. North bank ½ mile east of Acle Bridge on the River Bure

✕ lunchtime and evening

🅰

☺

🍺 **Adnams Extra; Wethered Bitter**

Whitbread ended centuries of proud brewing tradition in this part of Norfolk by the successive acquisition, closure and then the demolition of Lacon's Great Yarmouth brewery. The Ferry Inn is an ex-Lacon's pub which, some quarter of a century on, has yet to suffer any inept attempts at "improvement" and retains potent reminders of life before the big boys moved in. This solid eighteenth century building has a smart 1930s toilet and shower block extension, sporting the Lacon's ceramic plaque with its proud falcon unaware that its advertising efforts are in vain.

The bar interior, all beamed and panelled, exudes warmth and atmosphere. The food is good, and so, courtesy of a surviving East Anglian family brewer, is the beer.

Stokesby ferry was superseded by a new bridge upstream in 1910. Prior to this the Ferry

Inn held an important position in the social and commercial life of the village and surrounding farmlands. Its great days may be past but a warm welcome remains.

SUTTON STAITHE
Sutton Staithe
Hotel

Tel: Stalham 80244
Sutton Staithe (off the A149), Stalham, Norfolk. On the Staithe at the end of Sutton Broad off the River Ant

✕ lunchtime and evening

🍴

☺

⋈

🍺 **Adnams Bitter; Websters Yorkshire Bitter**

It is hard to believe that this most decorous and charming of the Broadland inns (known then as the Wherryman's Arms) should early in the last century have had a reputation akin to that enjoyed by the Jamaica Inn on Bodmin Moor. Such a haunt was it of smugglers and poachers that the authorities decreed that it should cease to trade as a public house. For some one hundred years it earned an honest living as a farmhouse until in 1928 it opened its doors again as the Sutton Staithe Hotel.

The building is basically L-shaped, two storeys of brick with paintiled roof. Inside the L is a delightful beer garden with lovingly tended floral borders and cherry and copper beech trees providing shade. Framed by wisteria creeper, two french windows lead from here into the two linked bar areas (one can imagine a dramatic entry here by a trouserless Brian Rix). The interior is simply furnished with old pews, windsor chairs and tables in natural wood with quarry-tiled floors and a highly polished copper stove in the inglenook fireplace.

Civilised relaxation and socialisation can here be enjoyed without intrusion from the sound of music or electronic games. The sole fruit machine lurks shamefully in the corridor to the gents. Behind the bar on wooden stillage of unusual and attractive design nest two barrels of Adnams Bitter, for which the Sutton Staithe has long been an outlet.

Too many pubs in the tranquil splendour of the Broads would be more suited to the sea front at Great Yarmouth. The Sutton Staithe is an honourable exception. As its name implies, accommodation is available and meals provided both in the bar and separate restaurant. In all these areas the same good taste prevails.

THURNE
Lion

OFF THE TOWPATH
Tel : Potter Heigham 670796
The Street, Thurne, Norfolk.
Across road at head of Thurne
Dyke off the River Thurne

✗ lunchtime and evening

🍴

☕

🍺 **Whitbread Flowers IPA;**
   Marston Pedigree Bitter;
   Wethered Bitter

This sober, grey-brick Victorian mansion, set in a large garden and surrounded by mature trees, somehow suggests itself as the dwelling of a prosperous nineteenth-century clergyman. The beer garden furniture and brewery insignia soon belie this impression, but it is evident that, vicarage or no, the Lion was originally built as a private residence and is far from the stereotype public house. Given the history of many of our pubs perhaps it is surprising that such a stereotype should exist in the mind, even though it seems far too often to exist in reality.

Inside the Lion is spacious and cool. There is a large bar distinctly nautical in its decoration and atmosphere. There is also a restaurant and small family room. Children are further catered for in the old coach house at the front of the pub which is also furnished for their amusement.

The Lion is another ex-Lacon's Whitbread house; one that has enjoyed benign (rather than suffered from uncaring) neglect. A fine boozer with every facility, it has not needed any insensitive tarting-up either. There is a boatyard and free moorings nearby and a selection of shops in the village catering for the boater.

OXFORD CANAL

Engineered by the famous James Brindley and bearing all of his
distinctive hallmarks of narrow gauge and winding contours, the
Oxford was one of the earliest and for many years one of the most
important waterways links between the south and the Midlands.
Beginning in Oxford, where the River Thames can be joined, it travels
through Banbury and the edge of Rugby on its way to Hawkesbury
Junction north of Coventry, where it meets the Coventry canal. Before
its junction with the Grand Union canal at Napton it is known as the
Southern Oxford. It then shares a short course with the Grand Union
until Braunston Turn, when the two canals go their separate ways and
the Oxford assumes the prefix "North" for the remainder of its
journey.

AYNHO
Great Western Arms

Tel: (0869) 38288
Station Road (B4031), Aynho, Northants. At Aynho Wharf by bridge 190

✗ lunchtime and evening (except Sundays and winter Mondays)

⊛

◎

⊲ **Hook Norton Best Bitter**

Travelling south from Banbury on the Oxford Canal, the tranquil rural course of the waterway does nothing to prepare you for the deafening aerial onslaught of the US Air Force, whose brave boys fly their extremely loud jets incessantly from their base at nearby Upper Heyford. But, as the name suggests, the Great Western Arms at Aynho is a shrine to a much older (and slightly quieter) form of transport – steam trains. It is situated between the canal and the main Birmingham-Oxford railway line, and is such a welcoming sight that one hireboat company established a boatyard right by it.

The Great Western has a most appealing exterior, while the bar is packed with prints, old newspaper cuttings, name-plates and a host of fascinating memorabilia devoted to the great days of steam.

The pub's steaks have a fine reputation, and the hand-pumped Hook Norton from that most traditional Oxfordshire brewery is delightful and most reasonably priced. If, like me, you discover the Great Western while on a canal holiday with a steam-railway nut whose favourite beer happens to be Hook Norton, you'll realise how much human happiness the place can create. It was easy to share his enthusiasm.

Just a note of caution – the pub is deservedly popular and so is the Oxford Canal, which means that both can be very busy at peak times. With a boatyard to contend with too, Aynho wharf can become quite congested and it may be necessary to moor a little way along the towpath. The visitor by road will find the pub a mile or so west of the village and quite isolated. Do not let any of this deter you from visiting the Great Western Arms.

NEWBOLD WHARF
Boat

Tel: (0788) 576995
*Main Street, Newbold-on-Avon,
Warwicks. 50 yards from
towpath by Bridge 50, near tunnel
mouth. Mooring space can be
very congested*

✗ lunchtime and evening

🅱

🍺 **Tetley Bitter, Thomas
    Greenalls Original Bitter**

There are two bustling pubs at Newbold Wharf, but if you're looking for authentic canal flavour and pub atmosphere, head for the one that's the further from the towpath. The Boat has been around over 200 years, and once had a wharf outside its doors (the term Newbold Wharf is still used). The lane on which it stands was once water, a short branch off the main line leading to the wharf.

The Boat's lovely white-painted frontage is festooned with colourful hanging baskets and its windows are reassuringly plastered with Good Beer Guide stickers. Its long single-room interior is split into three distinct areas. To the left, a relaxed lounge of some character, with beams, dark wood and a dartboard. Newbold Rugby Club's members have adopted the pub and some of their old archive photographs hang on the wall among the other old black-and-white aerial photos. There's a skittles table in the far corner. To the right, is a more recent lounge, used predominantly but not exclusively for dining. And, as you enter the pub and come face-to-face with the wood-panelled servery, there is a tiny low-ceilinged bar. The whole place is liberally sprinkled with canal relics and narrowboat regalia, right down to the scenes painted on the handpumps.

Food is a major attraction, drawing people from great distances to sample the renowned home-made curries, chilis and steak and kidney pies. Steaks, grills, snacks, vegetarian meals and special children's meals mean that nobody need go hungry, except perhaps on Sunday evenings when food is not served.

There is even a choice of outdoor drinking areas. Families can head for the raised children's play area at the top of the car park, others can sit in the pleasant beer garden behind the pub or on benches at the front.

The Boat plays host to diverse traditional

entertainers such as travelling theatre groups, mummers, minstrels and Morris dancers who help make this a fine, vibrant pub, full of atmosphere and vitality.

CROPREDY
Brasenose Inn

OFF THE TOWPATH
Tel: (0295) 750244
Cropredy, Oxon. 300 yards west of bridge 152

🍺 Draught Bass

The fine early eighteenth-century exterior of the Brasenose Inn will be familiar to devoted fans of Fairport Convention. The cult electronic folk group from the sixties reform for a well attended bash here in Cropredy every summer, and chose this pub as a backdrop for the band's photograph on the cover of Album Nine. This is quite naturally framed and proudly displayed on a wall in the public bar.

Regular attenders of the reunion gig, many of whom must surely journey here by the canal, will be aware that the vast beer tent is supplied by Wadworth of Devizes, who thus gain a temporary but very high barrelage outlet some way from their normal domain.

Red Lion

OFF THE TOWPATH
Tel: (0295) 50224
Red Lion Lane, Cropredy, Oxon. 50 yards west of Cropredy Lock and bridge 152

✗ lunchtime and evening

🛏

☺

🍺 Arkells BBB; Tetley Bitter; Wadworth 6X

The Red Lion is as close as you will find to the epitome of the English country pub. Set amid a terrace of rustic cottages and facing the parish church, it is built of mellow local sandstone and delightfully thatched. There is even a little thatched gabled hood over the doorway, which provides a halfway ledge for the giant ivy creeper on its long climb from beside the pavement steps to the apex of the roof.

The centrepiece within the pub is the splendid inglenook fireplace. One can get blasé about inglenooks – one sees so many on a quest such as this – but close examination reveals this particular example to be totally unrestored and original. Beneath the great blackened oak beam that supports the chimney breast are tiny settle-ended benches on either side which will have provided warm repose on those bleak Victorian midwinter nights, and there is much characterful old ironwork on display.

This fireplace enjoys a perfect setting in the low beamed and evocatively atmospheric public bar with its stone floor and venerable bench seating and tables in natural wood.

The saloon bar affords an elegant contrast. It is a large room with none of the old world features of its neighbour but it is light and airy, and tastefully and comfortably furnished.

I can pronounce from experience that the beer here is of the highest quality and an interesting selection from both far and near. The food I did not have time to sample, tempted as I was by the items chalked on the blackboard menu. I can pass on the fact that higher authorities, Les Routiers and Egon Ronay, have given the Red Lion's offerings their seal of approval, and I can also quote the unsolicited testimonial of a friend of mine who visited the pub by boat recently with his wife and baby daughter. The leek and potato soup he opined, licking his lips at the memory, was "a meal in itself".

FENNY COMPTON
George and
Dragon

Tel : (029 577) 332
The Wharf, Fenny Compton, Warwicks. Canalside at bridge 136

✗ lunchtime and evening

🍴

☺

🍺 **Draught Bass, Mitchells & Butlers Brew XI**

I have but one criticism of the George and Dragon which I trust causes no offence. Stone cladding may well enhance some nondescript buildings, especially if the stone is real, but to put this demonstrably fake stuff on an early nineteenth-century edifice of no little distinction is like using a compo ball in a Test match. I would urge whosoever decides these things at M&B to strip the lot off and see how nice the place looks without it.

Excepting its fine canalside location and attractive garden with swings and exotic birds the George and Dragon is seen at its best from within. A community boozer with extra trimmings, it has at its heart the large cheerful public bar where the game of pool seems to be the chief diversion. On the other side of a short central corridor is a small lounge and a smaller restaurant. These are recently refurbished and cosily smart. The decor includes a well carved and brightly painted little wooden relief of the legendary saint inflicting the *coup de grace* on his fire-breathing opponent.

Whatever its single architectural shortcoming, this is one of those unpretentious pubs that cherishes its locals while offering sustenance to the traveller in the form of good honest food and beer of the highest quality.

LOWER HEYFORD
Bell

OFF THE TOWPATH
Tel: (0869) 47176
21 Market Square, Lower Heyford, Oxon. 300 yards south west of Mill lift bridge (number 206)

✘ lunchtime

🍴

☺

🍺 **Tetley Bitter, Ind Coope Burton Ale**

This strikingly attractive sandstone and thatch seventeenth-century tavern is only a few short yards from the water's edge. Being separated from it by private dwellings on the side opposite the towpath, it can only be reached from the canal by crossing one of Lower Heyford's two bridges which lie at either end of the village. From here there is a short walk to the tiny central square where the Bell is located. Access from Heyford Mill lift bridge is probably the easiest, and quieter moorings can in any case be found here away from the busy main line railway.

The pub is family-run and unspoilt. What refurbishment there has been is of the homely brass and beamy variety with open fires, comfortable seating and subdued lighting. There is in addition to the two main bars a little partitioned snug where children are welcome and smoking is forbidden. For the friendly warmth of its welcome the Bell is well worth the short trek required to reach it.

NAPTON ON THE HILL
Napton Bridge Inn

Tel: (0926) 812466
Southam Road, Napton on the Hill, Warwicks. 1 mile south of Napton junction by bridge 111

✗ lunchtime and evening

🍴

🍺 **Davenports Bitter**

This well-known watering hole, having seen little to disrupt its quiet pursuit of excellence in the last twenty years or so, now faces a threshold of uncertainty. Davenport's Brewery, under whose name the pub operates, was closed by Greenall Whitley when they took the company over in 1989. The beer is now brewed by Allied Breweries, Burton-on-Trent. It is sad that Greenalls have not seen fit to invest in the maintenance of one of their more deserving houses. As the white paint peels from the outer walls, the roof of the family room remains holed the previous winter's gales, robbing the pub of a most useful amenity.

For the time being the Napton Bridge Inn soldiers on. It maintains its well-deserved reputation for good beer and there is strong demand for its imaginative bar snacks and restaurant meals which have an emphasis towards Italian cuisine.

Though the three bars have seen much modern refurbishment there remains in one corner of the restaurant an interesting and attractive nineteenth-century fireplace, a sort of inglenook with one end open and supported by a cast iron column. Behind the bar is a large collection of foreign bank notes which would probably purchase much Davenports Bitter if converted into sterling.

THRUPP
Jolly Boatman

Tel: (08675) 3775
Banbury Road, Thrupp, Kidlington, Oxon. Canalside by bridge 223

✗ lunchtime and evening

🍴

☺

🍺 **Morrells Bitter, Varsity**

In the early seventies Morrells decided to place greater emphasis on this pub's close association with the canal by changing its name from that of the Britannia. The Jolly Bargeman was considered to have the correct ring to it and, demonstrating the kind of obstinacy that can afflict brewers both small as well as big, it took a lot of lobbying to persuade them of their heresy.

As any inland waterway buff will tirelessly remind you a canal like the Oxford, with its seven foot wide locks, could never accommodate a vessel such as a barge whose width is traditionally twice that of a narrow boat.

Happily the cause of historical accuracy prevailed although this may result in no little confusion with the similarly named Boat just upstream.

The Jolly Boatman is tightly sandwiched between two highly contrasting transport arteries – on one side the tranquil meandering eighteenth-century cut and on the other a dead straight Formula Ford Sierra race-track known as the A423. Only yards separate the two physically but they are worlds apart in practice. The pub might be the link between these worlds but the visiting boater can nevertheless remain oblivious to the road and the driver totally unaware of the nearby canal. The effect may be partly due to the pub's brand new extension. This barn-like structure on the towpath edge is attractive in itself but nevertheless blocks the view of the old pub from the water.

Despite these identity problems the Jolly Boatman is a highly recommended pub to visit. It is pleasingly stone-built and has a smart, comfortable wood-panelled interior. The draught beer is excellent and the popular meals and bar snacks include hamburgers that have the same relationship to McDonalds as foie gras has to liver sausage, except the price. There is no booking for food, so it's first come first served.

The pub also has full facilities for the disabled – a thoughtful addition now that several narrowboats ply the canals on therapeutic cruises for disabled people.

Boat Inn

Tel: (08675) 4279
Thrupp, Kidlington, Oxon. West bank between bridges 221 and 223

✖ lunchtime and evening

🍴

☺ (dogs also welcome)

🍺 **Morrells Bitter, Varsity**

"This is the Canal Pub of the Year 1990," insisted my respondent on the telephone, "I've just done 1,000 miles on the waterways and ended up here helping Mrs Pryse-Davies run the place. You must print her name; she's been here for 19 years, you know."

I suspect that the Boat receives the above accolade at the discretion of its peripatetic bar cellarman alone, but I have no doubt it would certainly be in the running should ever such an award by objectively judged.

The onomatopoeic village of Thrupp is very much canal-orientated with its bridges and boatyard, while the Boat lies just across a narrow lane – the main thoroughfare in fact – from the towpath with its amenable moorings. It is built from Cotswold stone and slated, and a low wall of the same material delineates the car park and a convivial lawned and rose-bordered beer garden. These are overlooked by a colourful traditional painted sign that depicts a winsome water gypsy at a narrowboat's helm.

The interior of the pub is divided into two rooms; a large smart public bar and, across a central passageway, an intimate and comfortably furnished lounge dubbed the Captain's Cabin.

The Boat combines all the facets of a traditional village pub with the sort of amenities to be appreciated by lunchtime visitors from the city of Oxford (plenty had evidently braved the Kidlington bottleneck on the A423 to get here on my visit) as well as by hungry boaters on the canal. Morrell's distinctive traditional local beers are served beside a tempting selection of home-cooked food which includes several imaginative items of vegetarian cuisine.

The Isis Tavern, Oxford

RIVER THAMES

PEAK FOREST AND ASHTON CANALS

The Peak Forest canal is divided into two, the Upper and Lower. From Marple Junction where the Macclesfield canal joins, the Upper Peak heads south-eastwards through New Mills and the Goyt Valley down to Whaley Bridge in north Derbyshire, while the short Lower Peak Forest sets off for its junction with the Ashton canal at Dukinfield. The Ashton then continues into central Manchester through the unrelieved oppression of its endless suburbs.

BUXWORTH
Navigation

Tel: (0663) 732072
*Bugsworth Basin, Buxworth,
Derbys. By the Peak Forest canal
terminus at Bugsworth Basin*

✖ lunchtime and evening

🕭

☺

⋈

🍺 **Wilsons Original Bitter,
Websters Yorkshire Bitter**

In our moments of smugness we city dwellers can be deluded into seriously believing that the city is where it all happens. But few city pubs could match the startling focus of community life and scope of activity centred around this one stone-built pub, out in the wilds on the edge of the Peak District. It offers real ales in good condition, and serves a fine choice of food at all times. If you want bar meals, choose from sandwiches to gammon and mixed grills or, if you want something more formal, go for the cosy, intimate restaurant area, partly curtained-off from the rest of the pub and offering fresh salmon, local trout, Aberdeen Angus beef, the best of everything. The Navigation caters for anglers, walkers, boaters, motorists, morning drives, families and villagers. It hosts events as diverse as car boot sales and a poets' corner (it even has its own resident poet). It raises money for charities and the Inland Waterways Protection Society – it was a focus for efforts to restore the Bugsworth Basin complex and terminal, just outside the pub's front door and patio beer garden. It instigated an annual Vintage Transport Rally. It has a games room with pool, bar-top skittles, darts and cards, a coffee lounge doubling as a family room and containing a piano, a small snug bar and a main lounge bar, all with subdued lighting, dark wood panelling, stone floor, real fires and real atmosphere. It offers accommodation, use of which was once made by Pat Phoenix of Elsie Tanner fame. It even attracts toads – the Bugsworth Navi Toads phenomenon can be witnessed from time to time, if you're in the right place at the right time in the right weather ... scores of toads descend from the surrounding hills towards the river and canal in the valley. With a level of intelligence rarely found in amphibians, they head straight for the Navigation, presumably driven by ancestral instinct or lured by the static Pied Piper behind the bar, and refuse to budge until they are carried through the pub and out the back. There are signs around protecting the toads.

The re-opening of navigable waterway will doubtless boost the level of trade. If you're amongst it, and are stuck for something to do, chances are the Navigation could entertain you for a while. One way or another.

CLAYTON
Strawberry Duck

Tel: (061) 223 4415
Crabtree Lane (off Ashton New Road), Clayton, Manchester. Canalside at Lock 13 and Bridge 12, Clayton Junction, Ashton Canal

✗ lunchtime

☎

🍺 Holts Bitter; Whitbread Boddingtons Bitter; Websters Green Label; guest beers

It's the unlikeliest place to find a Strawberry Duck. Isolated in a dead-end street blocked by the canal bridge and lock, hemmed in by industrial units both working and derelict, it's a real surprise to find this real ale oasis for the canal travellers making the bleak passage towards Manchester. The pub's reputation has grown quickly since its rescue from Wilson's obscurity in the mid 80s, not only among locals and canal folk but among beer-hunters, too, and the reason isn't hard to fathom. Over sixty guest beers have already appeared, and the pump clips of some of them are displayed in rows behind the bar. It would be quicker to list the ones they've missed. Inclusion in the latest Good Beer Guide and Pub of the Month certificates from the Stockport & South Manchester CAMRA branch further highlight the pub's fast rising stock.

When the manager mentioned plans for further extensions and refurbishments to the 150 years old local to accommodate a large games room and fenced beer garden and patio, I hastily enquired whether this meant they were trying to gain entry into the record books as the oddest setting for a fun pub. The reply was in forthright Mancunian. I think he meant no. It's a friendly down-to-earth family local with a good mix of ages among the clientele and set to stay that way. Traditional beers and traditional pub games like crib and darts will remain the core of the pub's trade. Decent and extremely reasonably priced pub grub is available on weekday lunchtimes, from snacks to full sit-down meals like curries and rib of beef or chicken and stuffing with roast mash and two veg. The pub's one-room L-shaped interior consists of red vinyl button-backed seating, floral curtains, newish dark wood beams and wood finish, artexed walls, leaded lights, brick fireplaces. It's comfortable but nothing special – but that doesn't really matter, because this sort of pub works for different reasons.

MANCHESTER
Jolly Angler

OFF THE TOWPATH
47 Ducie Street, Manchester

✕ lunchtime (Mon–Fri)

⊕ **Hydes Anvil Bitter**

Right in the heart of the city near the canal's junction with the Rochdale canal, this unbelievably basic one-room boozer can be found near Paradise Wharf, just across the road behind "La Peniche", a floating barge that specialises in authentic Breton crêpes (you can't miss it). The pub positively throbs with vitality, with spontaneous outbreaks of song and a strong Irish influence – there are live folk/Irish music nights on Mondays and Thursdays. It proves real pub enjoyment has absolutely nothing to do with amenities or furnishings. Don't go in your best clothes, you'll feel out of place. A recommended stop and handy for moorings at Piccadilly Village.

NEW MILLS
North Western

OFF THE TOWPATH
Albion Road, New Mills.

A stone-built pub which doubles as a waiting room for New Mills Newtown station. It offers Robinsons Best Mild and Best Bitter and an outdoor drinking area. Access is via bridge 28, then head south towards the railway station.

WHALEY BRIDGE

Two interesting and worthwhile pubs can be found close to the Peak Forest canal terminus in Whaley Bridge. 100 yards from it, the **Navigation** in Wharf Street is a comfortable stone-built pub offering handpumped Boddingtons Bitter and lunchtime food. Across the old A6, the seventeenth century **Jodrell Arms Hotel** serves Websters Yorkshire Bitter, Wilsons Original Mild and Bitter and guest beers.

RIVER SEVERN and GLOUCESTER & SHARPNESS CANAL

Since mediaeval times, the River Severn has linked the industrial Midlands to the commercial docks of Gloucester and Sharpness. The Gloucester & Sharpness canal stretches from Sharpness docks and the Bristol Channel up to Gloucester where the Severn takes over, winding north through Tewkesbury (where there is access to the River Avon), Upton-on-Severn and Worcester to Stourport, the end of its navigable course and its junction with the Staffs & Worcester canal at Diglis Basin in Worcester.

APPERLEY
Coal House

Tel: Tirley 211
Gabb Lane, Apperley, Glos. East bank of the Severn north of Haw Bridge

✘ lunchtime and evening

🍴

☺

🍺 **Robinson's Best Bitter; Hook Norton Best Bitter; Wadworth 6X**

The Coal House is proud of its Steak on a Stone – the meat is served raw to the customer with a very hot, flat stone on which it can be "fried" to individual taste. If you can't quite imagine this, then try it. Another imported delicacy is on offer, even rarer in these parts – Robinson's Best Bitter from Stockport, which one only needs to drink and enjoy.

An old building with pebbledashed façade and a modern, though homely, single-bar interior, the Coal House is situated on a broad loop of the Severn in fine wooded countryside. It is the focal point of a small settlement that has grown up around the historic Coal House Wharf. As the name implies, coal was once traded here and the pub was home to the wharfinger.

Today, the wharf provides excellent moorings to the thirsty boater and a pleasant beer garden at the front with a relaxing view of the river.

ASHLEWORTH QUAY
Boat

Ashleworth Quay, Glos. West bank 3¼ miles south of Haw Bridge

✘ lunchtime sandwiches

🍴

☺

🍺 **Smiles Bitter; Arkells BBB; Westons Cider**

As the Severn winds its way through rural Gloucestershire the spire of Ashleworth church appears above steep banks heralding your arrival at the cluster of dove-grey fifteenth-century stone buildings that dominate Ashleworth Quay. The magnificent tythe barn once served the Priory of St. Augustine's in Bristol and is still a working barn looked after by the National Trust. The humble red brick cottage by the river bank is equally a piece of living, thriving history, for this is the incomparable Boat.

An uncompromising free house, it is run on simple lines by venerable sisters Irene and Sybil Jelf, scions of a family that goes back 600 years in Ashleworth. Legend has it that a grateful King Charles, assisted across the river in his escape from the Roundheads, granted to the Jelfs the right to work the important ferry that once operated here.

Nothing in the Boat detracts from the serious

business of well-lubricated relaxation. A dreamy air lingers in the cosy parlour where locals sit and chat in comfortable armchairs. The bar is furnished in wood with long table, chairs and high-back settles. A huge black cast iron range, beamed ceilings and undulating flagstones complete the timeless, unhurried scene. A tiny riverview terrace is also paved in flagstones, providing a delightful outdoor drinking space in the shade of the old brewhouse.

Self-publicity is not the way of the Boat. You take it as you find it. And, to confirm that life's pleasures must be earned, finding it is not easy. A brand new concrete staircase up the bank marks the point of embarkation. Tempting as this may appear, soundings should be taken and it may be necessary to moor up to trees in deeper water a few yards downstream. Having completed this hazardous pilgrimage, boat crews can enjoy the delights of a totally unspoilt pub, a rarity that is part of our diminishing national heritage.

GRIMLEY
Camp House Inn

Camp Lane, (off A443) Grimley Village, Worcs. OS ref. 835 592. Riverside below Bevere Lock

✕ lunchtime and evenings

🍴

☺

🍺 **Whitbread Flowers IPA, Original; Wadworth 6X or Marston Pedigree Bitter**

Bevere lock, below which the old Camp House Inn is situated, is one of the most attractive on the Severn, with a rose garden tended by the lock-keeper and his wife. This isolated riverside pub and its spacious rambling gardens are probably more accessible by boat than by motor vehicle. Nevertheless, its prime location, well-kept traditional beers and cider (it was in the 1990 Good Beer Guide) and far-reaching reputation for excellent home-made food ensures it gets very busy, especially at weekends in summer when river trade swells the numbers and barbecues are on the menu. Early evening it's chips, children and animals to the fore as meals and pets whizz by in numbers, while geese, ducks and peacock create their own inimitable background din.

Inside, the Camp House is largely unspoilt and enjoys the irregular and irreverent configuration of a pub which has evolved rather than been designed, with two separate but connected drinking areas, uneven floors and ceilings and not a trace of symmetry in sight. One area contains a dartboard, a fine high-backed wooden settle and some cosy alcoves overlooking the river, while the area directly around the bar is homely and traditional. Bar meals and snacks include giant French sticks while home-made pigeon and rabbit pies are available lunchtimes and evenings.

PURTON
Berkeley Hunt Inn

Tel: (0453) 811217
Purton, Glos. OS ref. 692 044. By Purton lower bridge on the Gloucester and Sharpness canal

✕ lunchtime and evening
🍴
☺
🍺 **Wadworth 6X; Marston Pedigree Bitter; Summer guest beer**

The Berkeley Hunt has a number of remarkable features, not least that it has survived the modern age so far intact. This may not be entirely evident from its outward appearance, upon which the tasks of re-roofing, re-glazing and stucco rendering have bestowed a singular rectangularity. Pass through the front door, however, and a wholly unexpected scene greets the visitor.

It is an interior dark but never gloomy. The tiny bar is straight ahead at the end of a short central corridor, beer being brought from the cellar at the back. To the right is a cheerful public bar with wooden benches round the walls and well equipped for darts, shove-ha'penny and cribbage. A snug bar is to the left with high-back settles, sofas and easy chairs, with a bar parlour beyond open to the public on busy sessions.

This was a farmhouse until the canal was dug alongside and to this day continues to function as such, possibly one of only two such pubs in the country.* Pony breeding with two stallions at stud is a notable activity.

* See the entry for the Holly Bush, Little Leigh, by the Trent & Mersey Canal.

With all the additional commitments that a working farm entails, it is small wonder that facilities on offer in the pub have their limitations. No advantage has been taken of extended opening hours and, though ploughman's lunches are available, this is no "foody" pub. Most eccentrically, however, the Berkeley Hunt must be unique in offering its customers no toilet facilities of its own. But fear not, public provision is to be enjoyed right next door and they conveniently remain open out of pub hours. I am unable to relate the history of this very interesting arrangement.

STOURPORT-ON-SEVERN
Tontine Hotel

Tel: (02993) 2048
Severnside, Stourport-on-Severn, Worcs. Waterside at Stourport Basin and at Severn lock

---

✕ lunchtime

🏠

◎

🍺 Banks's Mild, Bitter

The River Severn and Staffs & Worcester canal meet in the bustling commercialised waterways town of Stourport, an inland Rhyl of amusement arcades, bingo halls, fairgrounds and candy floss. Its river frontage is dominated by the imposing façade of the Tontine Hotel, built by the canal company in 1788 and a piece of waterways history. The pub itself forms the central part of the building and looks much the same today as it did in old prints dating from the late eighteenth century. Its front overlooks the river and the locks which connect it to the canal, while at the rear are the basins and boatyards off which the Staffs & Worcester canal begins its journey north towards Kidderminster and Wolverhampton.

The pub's name refers to the interesting method used to raise money for its construction. Of Italian derivation, a tontine meant that a group of fathers got together to invest money in the interests of their children. The money then remained untouched, gaining interest, until all but one of the children had died. The survivor took the lot.

Entering the Tontine's cavernous interior from the direction of the river, you are confronted by a long high corridor lined with fruit machines (at least it keeps them out of the drinking areas). To the left, a family room, to the right a spacious and comfortable Victorian-style lounge with dark green dralon, pale insets on the walls and some old photos. It ha just the faintest whiff of bygone grandeur. At the back of the pub is a vast and basic bar with tiled floor and pool table. In common with most Banks's pubs the Tontine is a managed house, and dispenses its cask-conditioned beers by their ubiquitous metered electric pumps. It's also a Banks's "Pint & Platter" pub, offering typical pub food from sandwiches, ploughman's lunches and burgers in various manifestations to salads and everything-with-chips, every lunchtime between 12 and 2. Special Sunday roasts are also served and occasionally a burgers and hot dogs catering van stations itself at the top of the vast two-tiered beer garden, its lawns leading down to the river edge.

Like the town itself, the Tontine is brash and raucous, and not for the sensitive or faint-hearted. Nevertheless it's extremely popular, drawing large numbers of customers especially at weekends in summer, when it's open all day.

TIRLEY
Haw Bridge Inn

Tel: Tirley 316
Haw Bridge (B4213), Tirley, Glos.
By bridge

✗ lunchtime and evening

🍴

🍺 **Whitbread Flowers IPA, West Country Pale Ale**

Seeing it at its normal peacetime level, it is hard to imagine the scene in the Spring of 1990 when the Severn declared war on the fields, houses, people *and* pubs with whom it shares this beautiful landscape. The river rose some thirty feet and inundated the Haw Bridge Inn for a full three months.

Discussing these events with the landlord, I was firmly reminded that three months' loss of trade is no laughing matter. This friendly, busy pub has survived the trauma remarkably well however – not even a hint of damp remains. In fact the feeling one gets here is that very little has changed over the 150-odd years the pub has nestled by the western abutment of Haw Bridge, or even the twenty-odd that it has been part of the estate of one of the less sensitive of the big brewers.

The two bars are unspoilt, comfortable and unpretentious. There are benches and tables outside for enjoyment of the river view, snacks are available, and try the WCPA – it's arguably a true local brew, tasty and *cheap*.

WORCESTER
Severn View
Hotel

Tel: (0905) 27600
Newport Street, Worcester.
Riverside near Severn Bridge

✗ lunchtime and evenings

🍴

⌷ Home Mild, Bitter; Younger
No. 3, IPA; Theakston XB

Many riverside buildings in the West Country suffered in the floods of February 1990, but not many poured 3,000 gallons of traditional beer down the drain as a result. The landlord of the Severn View Hotel, who has a no-nonsense approach to most things, decided that was the only safe solution once his cellars had been flooded to a depth of fifteen feet. "The beer is stored in barrels with porous wooden taps. I certainly wouldn't fancy drinking the beer after seeing some of the rubbish in that river."

Fortunately the damage done to this handsome and spacious old hotel was mostly cosmetic and temporary. Records show that in the 1890s it was known as the Hope & Anchor, although it certainly predates that. It wouldn't have had an open-plan interior in those days as it has now, but it still retains atmosphere, comfortable rather than plush and without bland hotel anonymity. It is divided into several distinct drinking areas including a darts corner, and has lots of old beams, a low ceiling and subdued lighting. Furnishings consist of dark varnished wood tables, patterned fabric upholstery, tie-back curtains and new carpet courtesy of the River Severn. The windows are part leaded, part frosted, part stained glass (there's also a part you can see through).

A good range of traditional beers from the Scottish & Newcastle group is available, along with the intriguingly-titled "Cuisine International" menu, available every lunchtime and every evening except Sundays. Its claim to be "Worldwide Fayre" is only fair if you're prepared to count standards such as steak as Canadian, pâté as French and the ubiquitous chili con carne as Mexican. Belgian broccoli and cream cheese pie is one for the veggies, while gooseberry and honey pie is apparently one of ours. Elsewhere, peppered chicken and Black Forest gâteau get Germany in on the act, lasagne and minestrone fly the flag for Italy while, curiously I thought, Nigeria gets the vote for swordfish steak. Cheeseboard takes no chances, and, in the new spirit of pan-European unity and cooperation, goes for "Europe" as its place of origin. Apart from Cuisine International, there are daily specials including ploughman's and "real" gammon ("not that plastic crap") and freshly baked cobs with cheese and ham off the bone. Next to the lounge is a small, narrow intimate restaurant, while outside there is seating for 30–40. The Severn View also claims to offer the best value accommodation in town, with fifteen rooms at less than £20 per head for B&B.

Almost next door, on North Parade, is the unusually-named **Old Rectifying House**, an unfortunately tasteless and gimmicky conversion of a handsome old building featuring the ghastly juxtaposition of black oak beams and cheap matchstick pine. Nevertheless it does offer a wide range of traditional beers – Marstons, Boddingtons, Ruddles, Brains – and food at all times. It's open all day.

SHROPSHIRE UNION CANAL

A typical Thomas Telford canal, wide and straight with comparatively few locks but spectacular deep cuttings and impressive high embankments (known as "cut and fill", an entirely different method of dealing with natural contours than that used by James Brindley on his much earlier waterways).

It runs from Wolverhampton in the south to Ellesmere Port in the north west, roughly parallel and to the west of the Trent & Mersey, passing through Staffordshire, Shropshire and Cheshire and the towns of Market Drayton, Audlem and Chester. It has junctions with the Staffs & Worcester canal at Autherley in Wolverhampton, the Llangollen canal at Hurleston and at Barbridge with the Trent & Mersey via the short Middlewich Arm.

In an age where we regard our canals as a harmonious part of the natural landscape, it is instructive to recall that, at the time of construction, the Shropshire Union, in common with many other canals, was greeted with the same kind of public outcry as those modern lines of communication, motorways and roads, are today.

Plus ça change plus c'est la même chose … perhaps in future there will be M25 Preservation Societies and relaxing trips around Spaghetti Junction?

AUDLEM
Bridge

Tel : (0270) 811267
12 Shropshire Street, Audlem,
Ches. Canalside at Bridge 78
(A525)

✕ lunchtime and evening

🍴

☕

🍺 Marston Burton Best Bitter,
Pedigree Bitter, Merrie Monk,
Owd Rodger (Winter)

OFF THE TOWPATH

The Bridge was built as a canal tavern in the 1830s and has been a popular and widely-known place of recreation for boating people ever since. Indeed it was the boatmen's insistence on tots of assorted spirits – purely for medicinal reasons! – which contributed to the conversion of the pub's beer-only licence to a full licence in the early 1940s. Around the same time it passed to the family with which it has remained ever since. Nearly fifty years of family continuity have helped maintain the Bridge's proud reputation as a genuine village local, unspoilt and unpretentious. A piano blends effortlessly with the darts, dominoes and table skittles ambience of the bar. Decoration includes splendid old canal photos and CAMRA mirrors. The Bridge has regularly appeared in the Good Beer Guide and was CAMRA's North West Region Pub of the Year in 1983/4. A wide range of food, from sandwiches and vegetarian to steaks, can be consumed either in the bar, dining room or on board the boat, as a meal service to boats is in operation during the cruising season. There is a garden and children's play area. Children are also allowed into the comfortable side room. The car park was once the stables. The gents' loos are outside.

This is very much a locals' and boaters' pub, a canalside classic.

CHESTER

The canal passes through the heart of the handsome historic Roman city of Chester, which has many fine pubs, restaurants and hotels. The pick of them from a beer drinker's point of view is probably the ancient **Olde Custom House** in Watergate Street, a quarter mile south of the Wharf. It has two lounges, one bar and no juke box, and offers a range of Marstons and Border traditional beers and lunchtime food. It is the meeting place for many local clubs and societies, including CAMRA.

GNOSALL
Boat

Tel: (0785) 822208
Wharf Road, Ghosall, Staffs.
Canalside at Bridge 34 (Boat Inn Bridge)

✗ lunchtime and evening

🍺 **Marston Burton Best Bitter, Pedigree, Owd Rodger (Winter)**

Like many pubs on the Shropshire Union, the Boat came in at around the same time as the canal was built. It was converted from a cottage, or cottages, and the old stables used to be below what is now the lounge.

Today it's a superb village local, bristling with life and character. The interior consists of one large, curiously-shaped room with a bay window overlooking the canal and an unusual curved wall at the end of the lounge. As the landlord observed: "You're tied to the brewery and there's not much you can do with the building. It'll never be a disco bar, and the locals would ignore it if it was. So it won't change much."

Collections abound in this quirky, idiosyncratic delight of a pub – brass taps, large copperware, teapots – for the landlady is a teapot fanatic, a species I was quite unaware of – baseball caps (a concession to modern times), and on the ceiling a collection of walking sticks and varnished oars.

The traditional beers are in tip-top condition and food is available at all times: a good menu of hot and cold meals, mostly home-cooked, during the boating season (generally Easter till the end of the children's summer holidays), and out of season pizzas and sandwiches are always there to fill the gap. It caters for children and vegetarians too.

There is a small canalside patio, and shops in Gnosall (pronounced "No-sull") village are about 100 yards away.

Navigation

Tel: (0785) 822327
Newport Road, Gnosall, Staffs.
Canalside at Bridge 35 (Gnosall Bridge)

✗ lunchtime

🍴

🛏 (next door)

🍺 **Courage Directors**

Yet another pub built specifically for canal custom, around 1860. Being on the towpath side, it had no stabling of its own and beer had to be delivered by fly-boats through a door into the basement. The Navigation is a good honest pub, cheerful, clean and well kept, having been the Best Kept Pub in the village no less than four times in recent years. It has a simple two-room layout, both of them narrow and elongated, and saddled with silly nautical names – the Gun Deck Bar and Crow's Nest Lounge. In truth, the seafaring theme is restricted solely to a few framed prints and owes more to the days of Nelson than the navigation. The vibrant bar is home to the raucous locals and their raffles, sweeps, wagers and draws, darts challenges and general banter. The lounge is quieter and comfortable. There is a good beer garden and separate children's play area with a Krypton Factor commando-style scramble net.

Food is restricted to lunchtimes only, Sundays included, and to the pizza/lasagne/curry/chili/sandwiches mould. Barbecues are sometimes held on summer evenings.

Reasonably priced bed and breakfast is available next door at Coton Mill, a converted nineteenth century flour mill, telephone (0785) 823483.

KNIGHTON
Haberdashers Arms

OFF THE TOWPATH

Knighton, Staffs. Half mile north-east of Bridge 45

Tiny isolated pub in tranquil rural setting. Banks's real ales, garden. Not to be missed.

MARKET DRAYTON

The canal skirts the town of Market Drayton, and only one pub is near to it. That is the **TALBOT** in Newcastle Road (tel 0630 4989), 100 yards from Bridge 62. It's a friendly, smartly-appointed locals' pub with Ansells Bitter, Ind Coope Burton Ale and a nice garden. Large bar with darts, pool and bagatelle and a real fire, comfortable lounge and tiny restaurant. Food served lunchtimes, and evenings in summer. Menu changes regularly.

SOUDLEY
Wheatsheaf

OFF THE TOWPATH
Tel: (063 086) 311
*Soudley, Shropshire. 1 mile east
of canal – accessible from
Bridges 48 (head north) or 52
(east, right and right again!)*

It's a fair trek to this remote rural pub but plenty of canal users make it to enjoy the full range of Marstons real ales. Lunchtime and evening food, bar skittles. The pub dates from 1784.

MIDDLEWICH

OFF THE TOWPATH

The short, tranquil Middlewich branch of the Shropshire Union connects with the Trent & Mersey at Middlewich. The pub to aim for is the **BADGER,** Church Minshull on the B5074, five minutes walk into the village from Bridge 14. It's a 200-year old building featured in the 1990 Good Beer Guide and offering a wide range of traditional beers from Marstons and Oak Brewery in Heywood, Lancs. It has a beer garden and a separate restaurant, and opens all day during summer and Saturdays throughout the year. It gets very busy at weekends.

STOAK
Bunbury Arms

OFF THE TOWPATH

Little Stanney Lane, Stoak (off A5117, near M53 junction 10), Cheshire. OS 422733. Quarter mile north of Bridge 136

Superb traditional pub with cosy low-roofed lounge and tiny old-fashioned bar. It offers lunchtime food (except weekends), beer garden, Higsons Sheffield-brewed Bitter on handpump.

WOODSEAVES
Anchor Inn

Tel: (078 574) 284
High Offley, Woodseaves, Stafford. OS 775255. Canalside at Bridge 42 (Anchor Bridge)

✗ lunchtime and evening

🍴

🍺 **Marstons Pedigree Bitter, Owd Rodger, Wadworth 6X, Oak Bitter plus cider**

Built around 1830, this isolated, plain-looking pub remains part of canal folklore – unconventional, uncompromising, unaltered. It was kept by the same landlady, Mrs Pascall, for seventy years, the majority of them after her husband died. The pub was known to them as "Sebastopol" and to the boatmen as the "New Inn". Boatmen and their families were virtually the only customers in those days, gathering to eat, drink and sing there, sometimes calling as early as six in the morning for a drink before moving on. With the decline of the working boats, trade almost disappeared but the pub was not allowed to die. Proper road access came around 1960, although it's still very difficult to find by car – fortunately some might say – and motorists and pleasure boaters began to replace the lost trade.

The Anchor remains a basic unspoilt pub without a hint of the synthetic or exploitative, unless you regard a towpath display of beermats and the availability of souvenirs, pottery, canalware and Anchor T-shirts at the nearby Anchor shop as rampant commercialism. Its two tiny rooms are still spartan and, it has to be said, less than spotless. Features include tiled floor, scrubbed wooden bench seating, a real fire and a grandfather clock. The bar is painted in roses and castles, canal style. You're likely to encounter folk music or an impromptu session on the squeeze-box on a Saturday night, or a travelling theatre. Informal snacks like sandwiches and rolls, toasties and pies can be produced more or less any time when the pub is open.

There is a beer garden between pub and canal, shielded by a towpath hedge, with bench seats and tables and an uncharacteristically well-manicured lawn. More typically, a dilapidated green corrugated hut stands in one corner, like a cricket score-box during winter. There is a caravan site to the rear of the pub.

Don't expect to be made a fuss of at the Anchor. There are no glib customer-care policy statements, easy smiles and "Have a nice day!" That's all from a different world. It attracts those who like things as they were and don't mind sacrificing a few creature comforts to attain it. It's a place for hardy outdoor types or incurable romantics, folkies and dreamers, the fringe and neo-Luddites. Poseurs, yuppies and the mainstream will find it primitive and outmoded and head for the next dralon boutique.

The New Inn, New Bradwell

GRAND UNION CANAL

STAFFS & WORCESTER CANAL

An early James Brindley canal, narrow and full of twists, turns and locks, the Staffs & Worcester was constructed to forge a link between the three great rivers Trent, Mersey and Severn. It runs from Stourport, where it locks into the River Severn, to Great Haywood Junction near Stafford and Stone, where it meets the Trent & Mersey, passing through Kidderminster, Stourbridge, Wolverhampton and Penkridge. There are junctions with the Birmingham Canal Navigations and the Shropshire Union in Wolverhampton.

GREENSFORGE
Navigation

Tel: (0384) 273721
*Greensforge, near Kingswinford,
W. Midlands. Canalside at
Greensforge lock*

✕ lunchtime and evening

🍺

🍺 **Davenports Bitter**

The Navigation was built around the same time as the canal was cut to take advantage of the new custom. From the outside, it still looks the part with its whitewashed frontage, leaded windows and old gas lamp above its front door, all set against a serene rural lockside setting. Some woody rustic garden furniture surrounds the front, with chunky sawn-off logs as stools.

Sadly, the interior is something of a disappointment. It was "done up" (i.e. spoilt) in the summer of 1988, converting it to open plan and robbing it of the intimacy suggested by its quaint exterior. Obviously-recent brickwork jars with old beams and inglenooks, and the attractive feature of stone chimney breasts at either end of the room with a settee and armchair gathered around one of them is again compromised by the curious rust coloured eggshell/mosaic pattern brickwork which frames them.

It's fully carpeted, has a few bar stools and modern matchstick chairs with dark varnish and fabric cushions. There's a fruit machine and on the occasion of our visit, the formula blandness of Radio 1. The food is pretty formula too, though quite acceptable, with pizza, steak, filled jackets, gammon, plaice, scampi, steak 'n' kidney pie and sandwiches and rolls. "Navvy Special" is a sort of ploughman's with cheese, pork pie and pâté, whilst "Gamekeeper's Lunch" is the same minus the pâté. Presumably gamekeepers prefer to preserve the ingredients in living form. Food is available lunchtimes except Sundays and early evenings till 8pm except Sundays and Tuesdays.

The pub is frustrating because it could so easily have been a canalside classic instead of merely adequate. I debated long and hard before deciding that its beer, food and delightful setting just about sway the decision.

PENKRIDGE
Boat

Tel: (0785) 714178
Cannock Road, Penkridge, Staffs.
Canalside at Penkridge lock and
Bridge 86

✘ lunchtime and evening

🍴

☺

🍺 **Ansells Bitter, Ind Coope
Burton Ale**

A listed building dating from 1779, the Boat was probably built for the canal trade and continues to enjoy considerable canal custom. It's a homely and friendly locals' pub, although it could hardly be described as unspoilt following several refurbishments. Its style hovers midway between mock Victorian and imitation rancho, with a farm cottage feel to the single-room interior which verges on the rustic twee, contrived but ultimately quite pleasing. There is both oak- and pine-panelling a plenty and, to one end, a traditional old range framed by exposed brickwork. The wall space here is fiercely competitive, with plenty of brass and bric-à-brac – artificial nostalgia bought by the yard. Tiled floor gives way to carpet, burgundy PVC seating to plusher button-backed fabric, the dartboard to piped music, your indications that you are now entering the area designated as "lounge". (I would like to balance any suspicions of criticism with the observation that there are many worse examples than this, and that to demand 100 per cent authenticity would at a stroke eliminate virtually every pub in the land.)

There is also a small narrow corridor containing a bar skittles table and in which children are allowed, and some pleasantly situated tables and chairs alongside the canal. The Star Theatre Group perform here annually.

Pub food is available every lunchtime between 12 and 2 and every evening except Sunday between 6.30 and 8.30. Chili, pizzas, excellent home-made pies, snacks, everything-with-chips are at the core of the safe, reliable menu.

STOURPORT-ON-SEVERN
Black Star

Tel : (02993) 2404
I Mitton Street, Stourport-on-Severn, Worcs. Canalside at Bridge 5 (Low Mitton Bridge)

✗ lunchtime and evening

🍴

☺

🍺 **Marston Burton Best Bitter, Pedigree Bitter**

There are some pubs whose picture-postcard exteriors flatter to deceive, concealing interiors of open-plan dralon-infested mediocrity. Then there are others that get it just right and you know it instinctively the moment you enter. The Black Star is one of the latter. It's long and narrow, flanked along its length by the canal to one side and the neatly manicured lawns of the Remembrance Gardens to the other. The end nearest the road bridge was seemingly an old low-roofed cottage at some time, and probably constituted the whole of the pub. The part above what is now the lounge was clearly a separate building one, with a much higher roof and resembling an old church or chapel.

The real delight of the Black Star is its low-beamed, two-part tap room. At one end it has a wood fire, tiled floor and dartboard, and a bay window facing the road. This gives way to a cosy and welcoming carpeted seting area, with views out over the gardens. Games and draw results, postcards and hand scrawled notices are pinned to the wall, which is always a good pointer as to whether it's a proper community pub or a contrived business expressly designed to make you part with your money.

Beyond the central servery is a pleasant, comfortable but mildly anonymous lounge with some canalware and photos and a piano. In addition there is a narrow pathway for outdoor drinking between the side of the pub and the brick wall at the side of the canal. Typical pub food is available at lunchtimes and evenings between 7 and 9, including mixed grills, pizzas, filled jacket potatoes, scampi, lasagne, chili sandwiches, salads and sweets. Live music is sometimes staged, usually on Tuesday evenings.

If you only have time for one pub stop in Stourport, this is the one. It's only a short towpath walk from the basins in the centre of town.

SWINDON
Green Man

OFF THE TOWPATH
Tel: (0384) 287138
High Street, Swindon, Staffs. 100 yards west of Bridge 40

A friendly old village local with Banks's beers, garden, games room and excellent value pub food (except Sundays). Live entertainment most Fridays, "free and easy" nights Sunday and Tuesday.

WOLVERLEY
Lock

Tel: (0562) 850581
Wolverley Road, Wolverley, near Kidderminster, Worcs.

✕ lunchtime and evening

🍴

🍺 **Banks's Mild, Bitter**

Picturesquely situated alongside the lock and pretty canalside terrace, this famous canal pub was once a pair of sixteenth-century cottages which was only converted into a pub in the late 1760s. A brewhouse was later added, now incorporated into the building. Tales relating to a previous landlord, one Harry Davies who held the licence for 55 years, have passed into canal folklore. He and the boatmen who regularly visited the pub found it convenient for payment for beer to be made with coal or whatever cargo happened to be on board – so convenient that they often ended up "over refreshed" on the floor, their money intact but their cargoes much reduced. Historically, however, the Lock has never been solely dependent on canal trade. Its attractive white front with hanging baskets, flower tubs and old brewery sign faces not the canal but the busy road, a former drovers' route from the Black Country to Wales and a reminder of where most pub custom comes from these days.

Inside the Lock is friendly and lively, with a traditional plain beamed tap room with a log fire and quarry tiles, and a small parlour with wooden settles and lots of canal scenes on the walls. As a Banks's Premier Pint 'n' Platter pub the Lock is popular for eating out. Food is available every lunchtime and evenings except Sundays and Mondays. The menu offers starters, snacks, sweets, daily specials and Lock Inn specialities. Apart from standard items like rump steak, gammon, scampi, plaice, trout, steak and kidney, chicken Cordon Bleu or Kiev and three-egg omelettes, there are Lock Inn grills (a he-man carnivore feast with steak, beefburger, sausage and bacon), all-day breakfasts and traditional Sunday roasts. Children's and vegetarian options are also available. Expect good value and large portions.

The Mikron Theatre regularly perform here and the pub's fame can be further spread by wearing "Lock at Wolverley" T-shirts, designed and printed by the local school.

STOURBRIDGE CANAL

The Stourbridge leaves the Staffs & Worcester at Stourton Junction north of Kinver, and ends at Delph bottom lock in Brierley Hill, where the Dudley canal takes over. At Wordsley Junction the Stourbridge Town Arm leads into the centre of Stourbridge.

AMBLECOTE
Moorings Tavern

Tel: (0384) 374124
*Lower High Street, Amblecote,
Stourbridge, Worcs. At end of
Stourbridge Town Arm*

✕ lunchtime and evening

🏠

🍺 Theakston XB; Cotleigh
Tawny Bitter; Exmoor Gold;
Old Merlin Mild; Hook Norton
Old Hooky; Stones Best Bitter;
regular guest beers

The Town Arm of the Stourbridge canal terminates just a few minutes walk from Stourbridge town centre. Overlooking the terminus is the splendid late eighteenth-century bonded warehouse building, now HQ of the Stourbridge Navigation Trust. The rear of the Moorings Tavern faces the terminus. There are no prizes for guessing the major reason for its inclusion here. Its range of traditional beers is exceptional, with many of them rare to the West Midlands region. The guest list changes constantly, with the choices available chalked on a board. Premier Ales sold the pub in 1990, but retain a toehold in the supply of beers – Old Merlin is the company's mild.

The pub itself is pleasant if unremarkable, with a reasonable atmosphere when the charty music isn't too intrusive. There is one large U-shaped room with several distinct areas including one with a pool table. Beamed, carpeted and burgundy dralon-ed throughout, it's a fairly predictable scene, with only token acknowledgement of the canal's proximity by way of a few artefacts (and, of course, its name).

A comprehensive range of food is available including daily specials, snacks and sandwiches and a main menu featuring steaks and grills, a range of pizzas, filled jackets, chip butties and seasonal seafood. Giant Yorkshire puddings with a choice of hot fillings are served on Sundays. Summer barbecues are held on the rear terrace overlooking the water. There is a Chinese takeaway nearby and the Wordsley Crystal shop is opposite.

WORDSLEY
Samson & Lion

Tel : (0384) 77796
*Brierley Hill Road, Wordsley, W.
Midlands. Canalside by Lock 5 on
the Stourbridge 16*

✕ all day every day

🍴

☺

🍺 **Ansells Bitter; Bathams Bitter;
guest beers**

The Samson & Lion first became a pub in the mid-eighteenth century, although the building itself predates that. It used to be sister pub to the Bottle & Glass, painstakingly reassembled on site at the Black Country Museum at Dudley. Its most dramatic transformation, however, came as recently as 1989 when its dynamic new owners began injecting ambition, enthusiasm and cash in equal measure. The result is an enterprising free house which manages to balance its evident commercial drive with an active involvement in the community and with the canal. In conjunction with other local agencies and canal organisations, a number of worthy community projects have been initiated including a nature trail and towpath and lock restoration and preservation schemes.

Between pub and canal is a pleasant terraced beer garden where barbecues take place most Fridays, Saturdays and Sundays. The L-shaped bar is pleasant if unremarkable save for a tiled area with pew-style seating and a fine uncovered and renovated wood-burning stove with brick surround. More recent additions include an uncommonly plush lounge with drapes and luxurious seating, a well-appointed children's room and a skittle alley and lounge in the cellar.

A rotating list of guest beers has already brought the diverse delights of Burton Bridge, Clarks, Jennings and Elgoods to the pub, as well as the inevitable Samson Bitter from Vaux in Sunderland. For those with an eye for a bargain (or a gimmick), there are "Early Bird Specials" from Monday to Thursday between 5 and 7pm offering a selection of reduced price beverages and three Happy Hours between 5 and 8. An interesting range of food is available at all times and features brilliant sandwiches – the name doesn't really do them justice – with imaginative salad accompaniment (if you have a fetish for limp lettuce, a tomato segment, a twist of

cucumber and a sprinkling of mustard and cress,
eat elsewhere) and intriguing "filled cases",
which turn out to be like mini patties, and very
good too.

Provided it does not stray into the karaoke
and "Dress to Impress" zone or spontaneously
combust from its own ambition, the pub should
continue to be highly popular with canal users.

STRATFORD CANAL

The Stratford leaves the Worcester & Birmingham Canal at Kings Norton to the south of Birmingham and winds south-eastwards to meet the River Avon in central Stratford. Kingswood Junction near Lapworth provides access to the Grand Union canal.

LOWSONFORD
Fleur de Lys

Tel: (05643) 2431
Lowsonford, near Henley-in-Arden, Warwicks. Canalside north of Lock 31 and Bridge 41

✗ lunchtime and evening

🍴

🍺 **Whitbread Boddingtons Bitter, Flowers Original; Marston Pedigree Bitter; Wadworth 6X**

The Fleur de Lys was fashioned from three thirteenth century cottages incorporating a bakehouse, and became a pub in the fifteenth century. Today this ancient beamy pub promotes a sense of calm and timelessness, with a classy, almost bistro ambience. As you enter its long low buildings, you step sharply down, probably banging your head on the first of many low oak beams, into a dimly lit interior with an unusual split-level L-shape featuring leaded windows, brass and copper and a lovely old inglenook stone fireplace. The upper level has quarry tiled floor and rugs, wooden tables and chairs. For the most part it is mercifully free of piped music or mechanical intrusion.

The famous Fleur de Lys pies were created here long ago but moved to factory mass production at the end of the Fifties. Catering at the Fleur de Lys has become substantially more sophisticated since then, with food now available throughout the day, Monday to Saturday, as well as Sunday both sessions. It ranges from snacks to full à la carte, and features such unusual and tempting dishes as poached smoked haddock with fresh asparagus, chicken breast with brie and honey, and chicken, avocado and prawn lasagne.

The pub's canalside gardens are delightfully unmanicured and unhusbanded, with sturdy wooden benches and chairs dotted haphazardly around. It is almost possible to moor in the pub car park. There is also a well-equipped children's play area, and a water point, post office and stores. It's a lovely area and tranquil. Despite the pub's well-accented clientele and the odd Merc or BMW in the car park, it's not prohibitively expensive or off-puttingly pretentious, and there's no ban on jeans.

PRESTON BAGOT
Crab Mill

OFF THE TOWPATH
Tel: (092 684) 3342
*Preston Bagot (on B4059),
Warwicks. 400 yards east of
Bridge 47a*

A beautifully preserved rural pub, a three hundred years old ex-cider mill. Subdued lighting, cosy corners and olde worlde charm, for which you pay heavily on the beers. The food however is reasonably priced and of a good standard. There is a children's menu.

✘ lunchtime and evening

🍴

🍺 **Marston Pedigree Bitter;
Wadworth 6X; Whitbread
Flowers IPA, Original**

STRATFORD UPON AVON
Shakespeare Hotel

OFF THE TOWPATH
Tel: (0789) 294771
*Chapel Street, Stratford upon
Avon, Warwicks. In town centre,
250 yards from Stratford basin*

A smart, timbered town hotel, with expensive real ale in the Froth & Elbow bar. Mixed clientele – tourists, families, thespians and local bar billiards hustlers. Full restaurant facilities throughout the week, plus hot and cold bar meals and snacks.

✘ lunchtime and evening

🍴

☺

⛵

🍺 **Courage Directors;
Donningtons SPA; Hook
Norton Best Bitter; Guest
beers**

WILMCOTE
Swan House
Hotel

OFF THE TOWPATH
Tel: (0789) 267030
The Green, Wilmcote, Warwicks.
West of Bridge 59

✖ lunchtime and evening

🍴

🛏

🍺 **Hook Norton Best Bitter,**
Theakston XB

Small, comfortable eighteenth century hotel in attractive old village. Listed building, close to Mary Arden's cottage. Friendly, lively and popular with canal users. Families welcome. Terraced beer garden, Good Beer Guide standard beers, excellent bar and restaurant food.

RIVER THAMES

By dint of its geography and long history the Thames is England's premier waterway. Today it provides superb amenities for pleasure craft of all types and its variety is immense. From the viewpoint of the small boater the river is effectively navigable from Limehouse Basin, which affords a connection with the river Lee and the Regents Canal branch of the Grand Union, to Lechlade in Gloucestershire, a distance of some 140 miles. Below Teddington Lock the Thames is tidal and care must be taken and permission sought for passage and mooring. The main navigable tributaries on the upper reaches are the River Wey at Weybridge and the Kennet at Reading, which provides a direct link to Bristol via the Kennet and Avon Canal.

ABINGDON
Old Anchor Inn

Tel : (0235) 521726
*St Helen's Wharf, Abingdon,
Oxon. North bank 300 yards west
of Abingdon bridge*

✗   lunchtime and evening

◉

🛏

🍺   **Morlands Bitter, Old Masters**

I've yet to meet a soul who has visited the Old Anchor and not enthused wildly about it. It was surely, until very recently, the Thames's least spoiled, most unpretentiously basic and best loved pubs. Tony and Pauline Griffiths ran the place for many years until retiring in 1990 to their native Merseyside. In this time they had the wisdom to realise the source of the pub's popularity and kept everything the way it was.

Now that they have gone, Morlands (with the best intentions, I'm sure) have completed an ambitious exercise in renovation which is as depressingly predictable as it is, I believe, ultimately misguided. To be fair this is not the vandalism visited upon old pubs in the sixties and seventies. The bar parlour at the back might even be said to have seen some improvement. The benches round the wall, black painted of yore, are now pleasantly stripped and varnished and the Griffiths' stone-effect wallpaper has been relegated in favour of magnolia emulsion. The cast iron range in the fireplace may or may not be the original but it certainly belongs and the lovely flagstoned floor thankfully remains uncarpeted.

The tap room at the front, however, with its charming bar counter with white painted shelving behind has gone forever. The new servery, inappropriately constructed of brick and coarse timber, is resited in a large open plan area that replaces a rambling collection of corridors and rooms. The decor is neo-Victorian – floral patterns, old prints, bric-à-brac and brass light fittings.

All this said, you still have a pretty good pub. The food has been upgraded, accommodation is newly available and someone has dredged the moorings so that you can now tie up right outside on the elaborate cast-iron railings. With the fine old almshouses and the entrance to the defunct Wilts and Berks canal nearby, the riverfront setting is superb, and the attractive Victorian brick exterior with the pub's name carved on a masonry band on the façade is preserved intact.

While newcomers to the Old Anchor will be aware that much has recently changed, their overall impression will be favourable. Those of us who knew the pub before can only bemoan the fact that the brewers seem to enjoy the same immunity from historic building legislation as the Church of England and British Rail.

CLIFTON HAMPDEN
Plough

OFF THE TOWPATH

Clifton Hampden, Oxon. Half mile north of Clifton Hampden bridge

Tetley Bitter, Ind Coope Burton Ale

The Plough is a classically picturesque, heavily thatched, free house. There are some fine old tiled and black weatherboarded outbuildings (including toilets) around a gravelled yard, while three small, attractively homely and unspoilt bars comprise the pub's characterful interior.

ETON
Waterman's
Arms

OFF THE TOWPATH
Tel: (0753) 861001
Brocas Street (off High Street), Eton, Berks. 150 yards west of Windsor bridge behind Eton College Boathouse

✗ lunchtime and evening meals (not Sun evening)

⊛

◎ dogs also welcome

Courage Best Bitter, Directors Bitter; John Smiths Bitter; Wadworth 6X

If my critical faculties had become jaded by visiting more pubs in a lunchtime than I normally do in a month then my apologies are due to the brewers and publicans concerned; but, despite the grandeur and history among which they are situated, the pubs of Eton and Windsor seemed soulless and uninviting. Hidden from the river by the Eton College Boathouse and lurking clandestinely down a narrow byway was the exception I was seeking.

The Waterman's Arms claims the date of 1542 though what we see today from the outside is probably a century or so later, still very old. Despite its modest size and cottagey air, the symmetry of the pub's façade gives it a look of some importance. It has a pleasantly intimate interior with separate drinking areas in one open plan bar, which is populated by a cheery throng of appreciative locals. There are some interesting prints and photographs on the walls, mostly with views of the Thames in Victorian times. There is an attractive high-tec addition to the pub at the back in the form of a conservatory which opens in summer to provide an all-weather "outdoor" drinking area.

Getting to the Waterman's Arms by car, as with many town centre pubs, is fraught with difficulty. Approach from the south and you'll find Windsor bridge has been pedestrianised. There are three parking meters in Brocas Street but you'll be lucky to find these available, and then there's the tourists to deal with. For the boater, though, there are convenient public moorings at the water meadow just to the west. Those by Eton College boathouse are strictly private.

HAMMERSMITH, LONDON W6
Dove

Tel: (081) 748 5405
19 Upper Mall, Hammersmith, London W6. North bank between Chiswick Eyot and Hammersmith Bridge

✗ lunchtime and evening

🍴

🍺 **Fullers London Pride, ESB**

The tidal Thames is frequently navigated by the crews of hired craft, usually on a one-way dash to link up with more placid waters at Teddington, Brentford or Limehouse, and also for a unique view of the sights of London. Most hire companies in the area are happy to advise on the correct procedure and which authorities to contact. Few of the capital's riverside pubs offer safe or convenient moorings but although your timing needs to be immaculate this, the prettiest, the most intimate and the least spoilt of these invariably historic inns, offers real possibilities for a brief embarkation.

There are many stories of the Dove's historical associations, some apocryphal and some undoubtedly true. It is hard to believe that Charles II and Nell Gwynne met here regularly; but that "Rule Britannia" was composed in one of the upstairs rooms one can more readily accept. It is certainly the case that the pub has belonged to Fuller, Smith and Turner since 23 November 1796.

The pub's modest Georgian frontage and the little alleyway it faces are genuinely evocative of old London. The two front rooms are pure early Victorian – a tiny public bar/snug with room enough for five or six drinkers, a slightly more commodious low-ceilinged saloon with old benches, prints on the walls, and a fine bank of 19th century beerpump handles. Some structural alteration is evident between here and the small riverside patio, with its excellent views of a broad loop of the Thames. Two small rooms with a central corridor have made way for a large bar where buffet lunches are served and consumed. Apart from this sop to convenience and modernity, the Dove is an historically intact gem and inbued with real atmosphere.

With deep cellars and a short dray-trip from the brewery, it also offers Fuller's beers at their pristine best.

HENLEY-ON-THAMES
Little White Hart Hotel

Tel: (0491) 574145
Riverside, Henley-on-Thames, Oxon. West bank just north of Henley bridge

✗ lunchtime and evening

🍴

◎

⋈

◲ **Brakspear Bitter, Special Bitter, Old Ale (winter)**

The Little White Hart comprises a group of structures of similar vintage but very different in style. The main building is classically Victorian and designed in the style of riverside buildings of that era, its appearance being that of a huge three-storey boathouse. The ground floor rooms have large picture windows through which they can be seen to stretch far back as if to accommodate stacked ranks of sleek rowing eights. The roof line consists of two large, elaborately barge-boarded projecting gables sheltering spacious balconies below.

To the right of this opulent structure a row of early nineteenth-century cottages has been incorporated into the hotel to provide a large and very pubby room appropriately named the

Cottage Bar and easily mistaken as a quite separate establishment.

The final flourish of this interesting assembly is a barn-like function room with a large plate glass window in which is displayed the Henley Brewery's old horse-drawn fire engine.

The Little White Hart faces the river across a road and a narrow quayside. There are moorings here for patrons, but these seem to get very crowded in the high season, so it is as well that the town is copiously supplied with alternative sites on both sides of the Thames.

HENLEY-ON-THAMES

OFF THE TOWPATH

A lot can be deduced about Henley and its pubs by reference to the character of its Member of Parliament, the Rt. Hon. Michael Heseltine. Populist, successful, tastefully groomed and rather rakish on the outside, there lies beneath a fierce integrity and a deep respect for traditional values. There is also a capacity to move with the times if the times are moving your way.

A tour of the local hostelries is *de rigeur* for anyone finding themselves in this delightful market town. The great majority of them belong to the borough's own Brakspear's Henley Brewery in one of the beer scene's most cherished monopolies.

Not to be missed under any circumstances, in Market Place, 400 yards up the High Street from the bridge, is the renowned **Three Tuns**. This truly classic town centre boozer has the familiar floor plan of the tap room at the front and central saloon with common servery, both accessed from a side corridor which eventually leads to the Ladies and Gents and a most attractive patio in the back yard. The interior is well preserved, beamy and atmospheric. The beer here, served by unusual modernistic chromium-plated handpulls, and also the food are of the highest standard, and the Three Tuns has one of England's most charismatically eccentric publicans.

Also worth a visit is the nearby **Old Bell** in Bell Street, a pub very similar in appearance to the Three Tuns but with a somewhat more genteel air about it. Back near the river there is the excellent **Anchor** in Friday Street and the nearby **Royal Hotel**, less majestic than the name implies but nevertheless a comfortable and friendly establishment. Both do good value food and accommodation. There is even a very acceptable alternative to all this Brakspear's. While all other brewers seem to have given up the ghost, Morlands of Abingdon raises the flag of competition at the mock-Tudor **Argyle** just up Market Place from the Three Tuns.

KINGSTON UPON THAMES
Bishop out of Residence

Tel : (081) 546 4965
2 Bishops Hall, Thames Street, Kingston upon Thames, Surrey. East bank 50 yards south of Kingston bridge

✗ lunchtime

🏛

🍺 **Youngs Bitter, Special Bitter, Winter Warmer**

The unusual name of this pub was suggested by a company shareholder at one of Young's famously bibulous annual general meetings. It is a clever reference to its position on the site of the fourteenth-century Bishop's Palace, which I assume disappeared long before the Bishop out of Residence and its neighbouring shopping development were planned and not, I'm sure, demolished to make way for it.

The pub was built in 1979, its red brick exterior devoid of ornament but interestingly terraced. The decor of the interior, with its two large bars on separate decks, is quite extraordinary in concept and can only be described as Louis Quattorze meets High Street Odeon – all chandeliers and velvet drapes. The Bishop out of Residence is a fascinating twentieth century architectural contrast to the Gazebo next door, and both pubs should be visited in tandem.

Contrasting draught beers, equally traditional and expertly tended, make such an experimental comparison doubly worthwhile.

Boaters Inn

Tel: (081) 541 4672
*Canbury Gardens, Lower Ham
Road, Kingston upon Thames,
Surrey. East bank ¼ mile north of
Kingston railway bridge*

✗ lunchtime and evening (not
Sun evening)

▨

☺

◁ **Boaters Bitter; Whitbread
Boddingtons Bitter;
Brakspears Special Bitter;
Fullers London Pride; Greene
King Abbot Ale**

The Boaters Inn has an interesting history, all of it very recent. Built originally as tea rooms for the municipal park in which it is situated, its boxy, single-storey exterior of pine and white weatherboarding blends discreetly with its silvan riverside surroundings. After a further incarnation as a licensed restaurant it became a flourishing public house some five years ago.

The atmospheric interior is full of natural wood and untreated brickwork, with lots of alcoves and bric-à-brac. The style is traditional without aping the past, and those familiar with the winter sports scene may detect an Alpine influence at work. A series of seating bays gives an excellent aspect of the river via large sliding picture windows. These can be opened in the summertime when the pub becomes an extremely popular venue both for local people out for a stroll in the park and for those on the river attracted by the excellent moorings.

The range of beers may change during the high season due to the experimental introduction of other products but in winter should stabilise at the selection listed. The house beer is brewed for the pub by Courage.

It is gratifying to see that a place recently established for other purposes can succeed so well simply by enthusiastically upholding the grand traditions of the English public house.

Gazebo

Tel: (081) 546 4495/547 3968
*Thames Street, Kingston upon
Thames, Surrey. East bank 200
yards south of Kingston bridge*

✗ lunchtime and evening

🍽

☺

🍺 **Samuel Smith Old Brewery
Bitter, Museum Ale**

Some years ago Samuel Smith of Tadcaster decided to sally forth from their Yorkshire fastness and introduce Londoners to their distinctive brews by building up an estate in the capital. Their London pubs are either historically old and impressively refurbished or, like the Gazebo, brand new. Other brewers, unsuccessfully bidding for these sites, have been heard to mutter "where do they get the money?" To rub this point home the Gazebo is placed smack next door to locally based rival Young & Co's *Bishop out of Residence.*

The style of the Gazebo is modern but with a lot of traditional details, including a fine glazed cast iron stairway on the outside. There are excellent moorings with a sort of ceremonial landing stage – broad stone steps flanked on either side by decorative Victorian gazebos which give the pub its name. The building itself is of yellow brick with white painted woodwork and most impressive. The lounge bar, airy and luxuriously furnished with leather Chesterfields, is on the first floor, with a large balcony giving scenic views of this pleasant and busy stretch of the river. On the ground floor is a fun-looking children's room and the saloon bar, more simply furnished than the lounge and a bit gloomy by comparison.

You takes your pick which bar is for you but remember that the lounge is only open during old-style pub hours, before three o'clock in the afternoon and after seven in the evening.

LECHLADE
Trout Inn

Tel: (0367) 52313
St John's Bridge, Lechlade, Glos.
Riverside by bridge

✗ lunchtime and evening
(restaurant Thur, Fri, Sat)

🍴

☺

🍺 **Courage Best Bitter, Directors Bitter**

The sign of the trout hangs above the doorway of numerous pubs on the banks of the Thames, but none exploit the name as a running theme so effectively as the Trout at Lechlade. There's trout on the menu, prepared in a plethora of different ways, there's stuffed trout in glass cases around the walls, trout everywhere, in fact, except in the saloon bar fish tank. This freshwater aquarium is nevertheless home for many of the noble fish's cousins – carp, roach, loach, minnow, whatever river fish survive such captivity. "If the pub was in the tropics we might consider keeping tropical fish," said the landlord.

This is effectively the last pub on the navigable Thames and a grand place for that half-way point in a there-and-back cruise. It has a delightful, oft-photographed, Cotswold stone exterior and a large garden where marquee functions can be arranged and boules and Aunt Sally are played in sylvan surroundings, with good moorings alongside. The interior is superbly atmospheric with undulating stone floors, open fires and old beams aplenty. As the name of the nearby bridge suggests, the trout has ancient monastic origins.

If you are a jazz enthusiast make sure to arrive here on a Tuesday evening – the idiom is usually traditional but the occasional modern ensemble has been known to perform. If you like to play darts avoid Monday and Thursday evenings in winter as the board will be in use for league matches, which is fine if you just enjoy watching.

The town of Lechlade is about a mile upriver from the Trout. The limit of navigation is at the junction with the disused Thames and Severn Canal, in the heyday of which Lechlade was a thriving inland port. St John's lock is the highest on the river and there stands nearby the statue of Old Father Thames.

NEWBRIDGE
Maybush Inn

Tel: (0865) 300624
Newbridge, Standlake, Oxon.
Riverside south of bridge on the A415

✘ lunchtime and evening

🍽

☺

🍺 **Morlands Bitter, Old Masters**

The Maybush would be the most poetically named pub for many miles around were it not for the Rose Revived just across the river. There may seem a danger that its grand and historic neighbour might overshadow it but the Maybush holds its own in more than just the name stakes.

The exterior is modest but very attractive. It is single-storeyed in cottage style with an upper floor in the loft lit by big dormer windows. The walls are of rough stone with brick arched windows, an interesting reversal of the common arrangement in areas where stone is less plentiful. The interior is low-ceilinged and atmospheric with fine old oak furniture. The beer is most palatable and the rapid turnover of bar meals during my brief visit attested to the popularity of the pub's cuisine.

The Maybush sits between the famous thirteenth-century New Bridge and a single arch and equally narrow bridge over a subsidiary channel. Severe traffic jams and serious accidents are avoided by a complex series of traffic lights which confusingly control one's exit from the pub's car park. The visitor by boat has a far easier time of it with ample convenient moorings and no electronic restriction to navigation.

Rose Revived

Tel: (0865) 300221
Newbridge, Standlake, Oxon.
Riverside north of bridge

✘ lunchtime and evening

🍽

☺

🛏

🍺 **Morlands Bitter, Old Masters**

The story behind the Rose Revived's delightful handle is that, whilst enjoying a spot of rest and recuperation here during one of his campaigns, Oliver Cromwell was inspired to test the claimed revitalising qualities of the landlord's ale. He dunked into his foaming tankard the stem of a rather moribund rose, which miraculously regained its bloom and vigour. It would be mean-minded to doubt such a charming story, so well illustrated on the pub's sign; but other accounts have it that an incoming landlord many years ago decided to revive the original name which his predecessor had abandoned. The original name was the Rose, hence we have the Rose Revived.

Little is known of the early history of this inn but, as far as the fabric goes, the handsome outer shell is of the 1930s, of Cotswold stone with moss-covered Stonesfield slate roof and a large semi-circular bay window overlooking the river. Inside the old layout is partially intact with many original features including a large inglenook fireplace. The whole is very well, even luxuriously furnished and furbished while, despite an up-market approach, the feel of a genuine pub is maintained.

The Rose Revived is renowned for its high-class accommodation and excellent catering. There is a full à la carte menu in the separate restaurant and the bar provides waitress-served snacks. The staff here can take large functions such as weddings and conferences in their stride without losing that essential human touch so often absent in such establishments.

OXFORD
Isis Tavern

Tel: Oxford 247006
Mill Lane, Iffley, Oxford.
Riverside 250 yards up from Iffley Lock

✕ lunchtime and evening (hot meals weekends only)

🍴

🍺 **Morrells Best Bitter, Varsity**

At some point in history the city and university of Oxford adopted the Thames as their own and named it the Isis, to distinguish it from the dirty, dead and dangerous body of water that flows through the capital, or perhaps they simply failed to realise it was the same river. Different rivers they certainly could be and nowhere is the contrast more acutely evident than at Iffley Lock. Among the trees is the superbly tended lock itself, gates and balance beams immaculate in battleship grey. There is the weir and its subsidiary buildings roofed in oak shingle, and the boat roller with its stone Palladian and timber Chinese bridges. Nearby, again in a kind of subdued Palladian style, is the Isis Tavern, one of those waterside pubs to which no road goes. By foot or by bicycle, access is by a little pathway from the village and suburb of Iffley. This crosses between the weir and lock on a twisting tree-lined causeway. There are plenty of moorings above the lock for private or hired cruisers, and, should you be passing by on one of Messrs Carter's steamers, leave the tourists behind for a rewarding visit to this most interesting pub.

The Isis may at first appear visually quite ordinary until you realise how perfectly square in plan and symmetrical it is, with only the chimney stacks and Morrell's signage out of unison. Seen as a box, the two sides observed from the river are identical in every detail with three large sash windows up and two down flanking a central doorway beneath semi-circular fanlights. The remaining blind sides of the building are surely the same but I did not feel moved to skulk suspiciously round the back to confirm this. At the front is a spacious and attractive garden dominated by a large evergreen tree at its centre.

The interior of the pub is split directly down the middle between saloon and public bar with a central servery. The decor and furnishings are modern but of good quality and there are plenty of items of interest including an old clinker-hulled racing sculler suspended from the high public bar ceiling. There is much for amusement here as well with facilities for darts, shove-halfpenny and bar billiards.

In the winter, as you might expect, there's not a lot going on around here so the pub is likely to close prematurely if there is no trade. Therefore, when visiting this part of the Thames, it is well worth ensuring some likelihood of the doors of the Isis being open. You can then enjoy the comings and goings and the sights of one of the river's loveliest and most popular stretches while savouring superb locally brewed beer in unique surroundings.

Waterman's Arms

Tel: (0865) 248832
7 South Street, Osney Island, Oxford. West bank between Osney Lock and bridge

✖ lunchtime and evening (not Sun, mon evening)

🍴

☺

🍺 **Morlands Bitter, Old Masters**

This modest back-street corner boozer is located in workaday but most attractive riverside surroundings. The nearby streets and the terrace of Victorian cottages that face the water have a kind of Coronation Street feel about them. The Thames here, with the tall factory wall on the opposite bank, looks more like a broad urban canal but the whole scene is transformed by the procession of trees that lines the towpath. Here can be found the most tranquil and convenient moorings in central Oxford.

The Waterman's Arms is somewhat more ornate than its neighbouring dwellings. The yellow brickwork is relieved by window arches, decorative quoins and longitudinal bands of red, and there is a nice little corner main entrance with two stone corbels forming an archway above. The modern extension is considerably less interesting but, only one storey in height, it is sufficiently unassuming to blend with the older part of the building, and its large picture windows offer pleasant river views from the saloon bar.

Even though the casual visitor may have little opportunity for involvement, the pub evidently enjoys an important role in the local community, which enhances its appeal. There is much homespun decor in the two bars and the trophies and team photos attest to a thriving cricket team. All in all a friendly, interesting little pub with excellent beer and a warm welcome.

PANGBOURNE
Swan

Tel: (0734) 844494
Shooters Hill, Pangbourne, Berks.
South bank riverside above
Whitchurch lock

✗ lunchtime and evening

🍴

☺

🍺 **Courage Best Bitter, Directors**

When an old pub is taken into one of the diverse chains of pubs/restaurants (Beefeater, Barney's Carvery) it is generally set to lose all vestige of history and charm. Not that these chains don't provide a convenient family venue and often reasonable draught beer. Very occasionally even these conversions are quite sensitively done.

The Swan has for a while now been a Trusthouse Forté "Trencherman" eatery. Prior to this it was just an ordinary (if such a quaint and historic place could be so described) Courage pub. Preferring that it had remained as such, I would nevertheless aver that it is still a pub of great character, in as much as it can still be called a pub, and that the new facilities will be much appreciated by those that seek them out.

This beautiful stretch of the river is well worth a visit and was much loved by those two great chroniclers of the Thames, Kenneth Grahame and Jerome K. Jerome. The Swan itself was twice visited by the Three Men in a Boat, latterly to abandon their craft after two solid days of rain, to continue their journey to London by train.

The rambling brick and stone cream painted exterior with its fine tiled roofs and pretty Victorian porch has been left very much intact while within many of the original features survive. There has been no excessive knocking-through or beam exposure and the decor is relaxing and tasteful.

The word *trencherman* defines somebody who basically enjoys his food. Such a person would seem well catered for at the Swan. The menu is traditional and reasonably priced and food is served at your table, there being no separate restaurant (the company blurb describes this sensible arrangement as "exciting"), and the beer is very good. With so much in life coming in packages these days it is nice to find examples where the packaging is done well.

RADCOT
Swan Hotel

Tel: (036 781) 220
Radcot Bridge, Radcot, Oxon.
Riverside by Navigation Bridge

✖ lunchtime and evening

🍺

☺

🛏

🍺 **Morlands Bitter, Old Masters**

The contemporary peace of this quiet hamlet belies a most violent past. As a strategic and ancient crossing point of the Thames, it has seen a series of bloody contests for its control. As far back as 1141 King Stephen thwarted the ambitions of Matilda, Countess of Anjou, the earthwork remains of whose castle lie to the north of Radcot Bridge. The barons held out against King John here in 1387 and there were a number of skirmishes during the Civil War.

The bridge over the main course of the Thames at Radcot is the oldest on the river, built around 1154, while the one which crosses the navigation channel by the Swan is newer by some 600 years.

The history of the pub itself is less well documented but the present building dates from 1873 and is constructed of the same local stone which used to be trans-shipped from the nearby wharves down the Thames to London and thence even to Paris. The Swan occupies a small tree-lined island with a superb garden, excellent moorings and facilities for camping and cara-vaning. In the yard is an attractive Victorian stable block and dovecote, due for conversion into premises for the licensee and family, freeing space in the pub for additional guest accom-modation.

Inside, the single bar is subdivided according to floor surface – carpet in the lounge section and flagstones for the darts area. The walls are covered in a most impressive collection of stuffed fish, emphasising the attraction this stretch of the river holds for anglers.

Fans (such as myself) of Morland's oft-underrated ales will not be disappointed by the condition in which they are served at the Swan, and indeed some doubters might even be converted to their subtle distinction. Food is available for most of each lunch and evening session, while in the summer the pub remains open in the afternoon if there is sufficient trade.

The history of this place is chronicled in a grand little booklet entitled "Radcot and its Bridge" by E. A. Pocock. You should find this available behind the bar although its 1966 date and price of 2/6 suggest it is long out of print.

RICHMOND UPON THAMES
White Cross Hotel

Tel: (081) 940 6844
Water Lane, Richmond upon Thames, Surrey. East bank 200 yards north of Richmond bridge

✕ lunchtime and evening

🍴

☺

🍺 **Youngs Bitter, Special Bitter, Winter Warmer**

Richmond's riverfront is famous worldwide for its new housing and office development in the authentic classical manner by the architect Quinlan Terry. Much criticised in the style wars that have recently bedevilled British architecture, this skilfully varied group of buildings is to my objective eye a magnificent success. The joy is that the adjacent old buildings, such as the mid-Victorian but Georgian inspired Grade III listed White Cross, far from being dominated, or worse still demolished, by the new development, have become integral to it.

Because of the sloping riverbank on which it stands the basement of this fine three-storey yellow brick and stucco building tapers from the back to form virtually a ground floor at the front, with a grand stairway leading up to the main entrance above. On this lower level there is a fully equipped servery, complete with hand-pumped draught beer, for drinkers on the attractive river-view terrace – much more convenient than tackling those steps to the indoor bar with a tray load of drinks.

There is a restaurant on the first floor while the ground floor consists of a series of cosily furnished interconnected rooms with a very fine central island bar surrounded by sash windows. An interesting feature is the fireplace on one wall with a window directly above it, the chimney flues passing either side.

The name of the pub derives from the Convent of the Observant Friars (whose symbol it was) that stood on this site between 1499 and 1534. Today this thriving tavern observes the highest standards of service to the customer and is justly very popular.

SANDFORD-ON-THAMES
King's Arms

Tel: (0865) 777095
Church Road, Sandford-on-Thames, Oxon. By Sandford lock

✕ lunchtime and evening (not Sun evening)

🅱

☺

🍺 **Courage Best Bitter, Directors Bitter; John Smith's Bitter**

A building historian could have fun in the King's Arms working out the old plan and assessing the number of rooms the pub once had. The evidence for such an inquiry is clear from the different materials used for the flooring. There is an area of chequered quarry tiling laid diamond-fashion and yet another where it is plain. There are flagstones nearby and timber flooring of both the parquet and common board variety. If all these represent separate rooms this must not so long ago have been a veritable warren. Now that the public area is open plan but wisely left uncarpeted, the remaining patchwork of flooring helps preserve a unique character.

The interior decor is very much in the nostalgia idiom of today – Victorian cottagey with some transatlantic influences. There are areas of exposed brickwork next to "nicotine" painted embossed wallpaper; sturdy new settle-ended benches; floral chintzy patterns and lots of bric-à-brac and old books on the overhead shelving. There's a marvellous display of several years of formally posed nineteenth-century Oxford University Boat Race crews, rank upon rank of steely eyes over waxed moustaches.

The King's Arms is superbly situated by a small lockside basin. This was once the stream feeding the adjacent mill's waterwheel, an unholy place for a dip, accidental or otherwise, while too hurriedly leaving the pub. The fabric of the building is seventeenth century or earlier with a fine pitched roof of multi-hued old tiles.

There is an extensive menu here, of which the pub is justly proud and they specialise in all kinds of smoked cuisine, products of their very own "smokerama".

STAINES
Swan Hotel

Tel: (0784) 452494
The Hythe, Staines, Middx. South bank just east of Staines bridge

✖ lunchtime and evening

⊛

◎

⋈

⊲ **Fullers London Pride, ESB**

It would not be helpful of me to describe in detail the interior of the Swan because major refurbishment is due for completion by the time this guide appears. In its present state it is comfortable and pleasantly laid out, if slightly tatty, and has as a central feature a magnificent old inglenook fireplace which appears recently to have been exposed. This is most likely a survival of the original early seventeenth-century building which Samuel Pepys frequently visited.

Little else of the fabric inside is of genuine antiquity, so Fullers, with a good reputation in this department, need not be too restrained in effecting some necessary improvements. It will be no great loss if the beer pump handles on the toilet doors are replaced by more conventional doorknobs for instance.

The company abandoned manual beer engines in most of their pubs for a period in the seventies and this was presumably thought of as a suitable alternative use for what is now regarded as the visible evidence of the availability of real ale.

The Swan offers a pleasant aspect to both river and road. On the latter side we have a typically Georgian formal frontage with a superb carved swan nesting atop the well-proportioned classical porch. The river frontage has a more rambling appearance with a large five-sided bay projecting on to the towpath and a colonnaded balcony overlooking the willow-shaded terrace.

As you would expect of a well-appointed hotel the food at the Swan is an excellent bet. There is a restaurant and a good value and delicious bar buffet selection which is available throughout the afternoon.

TADPOLE BRIDGE
Trout Inn

Tel: (0367) 87382
*Tadpole Bridge, Buckland Marsh,
Oxon. 50 yards south of bridge*

✕ lunchtime and evening

🍺

☺

🛌

🍺 **Archers Village Bitter; Gibbs
Mew Local Line Bitter,
Salisbury Bitter**

It is nice to find a free house offering an adventurous choice of real ales from brewers who lack the discounting clout to get their beers into as many pubs as we, and no doubt they, would like. Archers comes from a tiny but thriving set-up in Swindon over the Wiltshire border, while the same county is host to the long established Gibbs Mew of Salisbury, whose Local Line Bitter was originally brewed by the now sadly defunct Chudley in Maida Vale, West London.

The range of beers would be enough to tempt one to this attractive stone built pub, but the appeal here is not just to the serious drinker. The food is excellent – either snacks in the friendly bar or sit-down meals in the small dining room. Anglers can enjoy the pub's two miles of riverbank fishing rights and the excellent moorings will be most welcome to those arriving by boat. Indeed, with the river here passing through one of its bleaker rural stretches – flat water-meadows stretching uninterrupted to the valley's distant edge – the Trout, with the attractive eighteenth-century bridge adjacent, is something of a beacon of civilisation.

THAMES DITTON
Albany

Tel: (081) 398 7031
*Queens Road, Thames Ditton,
Surrey. South bank, east of
Thames Ditton Island*

✕ lunchtime and evening
(evenings Wed–Sat)

🍺

☺ (lunchtime for food)

🍺 **Draught Bass, Charrington
IPA, occasional guest beer**

The Albany is highly evocative of the Thames during the Victorian era. Its white painted gabled river frontage looms close to the water's edge with a narrow terraced garden descending in two stages to the pub's own moorings. Albany Reach was a popular berth for houseboats in the nineteenth century. It is easy to picture the elegant parties hosted by residents of these boats (many of whom were leading music hall artists of the day) with guests arriving in a profusion of small craft and resplendent in garish blazers and laced crinolines. Swaying magnificently in the breeze, tall trees surround the pub to give a suitably gothic air.

The interior is due for imminent refurbishment but it is possessed of many original features and an authentic atmosphere.

Evidently the Albany was not at first built as a public house. Theories as to its original purpose suggest either that it was a farmhouse, which seems awfully unlikely; or that it was built by an aristocrat (whose name I dare not divulge) as a residence for his mistress. There is apparently documentary evidence for this second, far more appealing, conjecture.

Queens Road is a cul-de-sac that goes no further than the Albany on the river's edge, implying perhaps that a ferry once plyed these banks. The sign of the Albany stands at the junction with Summer Road, a quarter mile from the pub itself, but of great assistance to the terrestrial visitor.

Old pubs need all kinds of modern facilities to attract today's discerning customer but the best of them retain strong historical links. One can sit here in the Albany, sup some fine draught beer and dreamily conjure up vivid images of times past.

WALTON-ON-THAMES
Swan

Tel: (0932) 225964
Manor Road, Walton-on-Thames, Surrey. South bank 1 mile east of Walton bridge

✗ lunchtime and evening

🏠

◎

🍺 **Youngs Bitter, Special Bitter, Winter Warmer**

This pleasant nineteenth-century tavern boasts the most attractive garden perhaps of any Thames-side pub. From the rear of the building it sweeps a hundred yards to the towpath edge in a series of shallow terraces and is abundantly bedecked in flowers and shrubs of every description. There is also a small cottage, separate from the main building and somewhat older, which serves as a private function room.

The Swan itself is typically Victorian, of white painted brick with a half-timbering effect on the upper floor frontage. It has two little timber porches and an unusual turret on one corner. The bar windows, with their boldly striped awnings, are of lead latticework and incorporate decorative swan motifs in finely crafted stained and painted glass.

The interior is divided into three bars, a small public, large saloon and lounge-cum-restaurant. The latter is appropriately named the "Cygnets Bar" while the non-smoking saloon is known as the "Cob and Puffin Bar". I am at a lost to discover the significance of this last bird.

The whole interior has something of the feel of a well-kept genteel small hotel, with accommodation the only missing ingredient.

WOLVERCOTE
Trout

Tel: (0865) 54485
Godstow Road, Wolvercote, Oxford. By Godstow Bridge

✗ lunchtime and evening (no food Sun evening; restaurant meals but not snacks on other evenings)

🏨

☺

🍺 **Draught Bass, Charrington IPA**

This historic inn has as many of the attributes of a country manor house as it does those of a pub, the chief distinction being that it is in the hands of a national brewer rather than the National Trust. It is grandly proportioned, with walls of Cotswold stone and roof of local Stonefield slate. It retains its original leaded casement windows, and a giant ivy creeper cascades over one gable-end. A flock of peacocks strut, display and screech on the spacious tree-lined lawns, providing an exotic element in the pub's menagerie of rabbits and guinea pigs. There is an attractive patio overlooking the weir stream, across which can be observed an elaborate island garden bedecked in grottos and classical statuary. The Chinese-style Victorian wooden bridge that once provided access from pub to island is in a state of advanced dereliction, but there are plans to make this venerable span structurally sound in the near future.

The interior consists of three beautifully furnished old bars and two restaurants, one in a sympathetic modern extension. There are some superb carved wood furnishings including an elaborate back bar fitting which looks as old as the pub itself and possibly older. There are fireplaces and flagstones and ancient doors with massive wrought iron hinges. The walls and ancient roof beams display a profusion of antique bric-à-brac – old pewter beer tankards, sporting tropies and prints and vintage weaponry.

The present building dates from soon after 1646 when its predecessor on the site was destroyed in the Civil War by General Lord Fairfax. This had once been a hospice for the nearby Benedictine nunnery and the last resting place of Rosamund Clifford, tragic rival of the redoubtable queen Eleanor for the affections of Henry II.

In more recent times the Trout has been a favourite haunt of Oxford academia, whose gleaming towers provide a romantic view in the near distance. Far from being a time-warp, this fine tavern offers all the amenities that today's customer expects, including excellent draught beer.

RIVER TRENT

One of England's most historic inland arteries, the Trent connects the Midlands with the Humber ports and the North Sea. It has many junctions; after its navigable origin at Derwent Mouth in south Derbyshire where it joins the Trent and Mersey canal, it soon traverses a complicated waterways junction at Trent Lock where the Soar Navigation enters the Trent and the entrance to the Erewash canal is passed. In Nottingham an unnavigable six-mile stretch of river is bypassed by the Nottingham canal. Another bypass takes in the fair town of Newark, while towards its northern end the Trent skirts Gainsborough on its way to junctions with the Fossdyke Navigation at Torksey, the Chesterfield canal at Stockwith and the Stainforth and Keadby canal at Keadby before reaching the Humber.

OFF THE TOWPATH
BEESTON

The **Boat & Horses** in Trent Road, Beeston, just north of Beeston lock, is a large estate pub which used to be a change-over station for barge horses. It offers electric-pumped Home Mild and Bitter, lunchtime and evening food and summer barbecues and a beer garden. Attenborough nature reserve is close by.

FISKERTON
Bromley Arms

Tel: (0636) 830789
Main Street, Fiskerton, near Southwell, Notts. Riverside at Fiskerton wharf

---

✘ lunchtime (not Sun)and
   evening

🍴

🍺 **Hardys & Hansons Best Mild, Bitter**

Dating back from the eighteenth century, the Bromley Arms took its name from the auspicious Bromley family (seemingly comprised entirely of rear admirals and viceroys) who lived at nearby East Stoke Hall on the opposite bank and were the first to buy the pub. It still enjoys a lovely rural setting, with its attractive crop of outbuildings, unbroken fields and greenery opposite and at its feet the broad sweep of the mighty Trent, kept in check by a newish flood wall. There is a path at the front of the pub on to which you can wander with your pint, watch the river and contemplate infinity.

Its cask beers have earned the Bromley Arms frequent inclusion in the Good Beer Guide. Unusually, it's the Mild that emerges from the handpumps, whilst the Bitter is electric-pumped. Sandwiches and rolls are always available and there is also an above-average quality lunchtime menu (except Sundays) featuring steak and kidney pie, seafood platter, various salads and fish dishes and a range of sweets.

The pub's simple two-room interior consists of a small basic bar and a riverside lounge which has two wall-mounted displays of some interest; an RAF feature including some action shots of mid-air refuelling, and a glass-fronted cabinet containing a Nottingham-made Gunn & Moore cricket bat donated by former Notts opening batsman Paul Todd and autographed by the team. His county caps are also displayed, along with a miniature bat autographed by Western

Australia's state side. The lounge also has a small electric organ in the corner. A separate function room is used for meetings, by the local CAMRA branch among others. There is mooring at the wharf.

OFF THE TOWPATH
HOVERINGHAM

In the village of Hoveringham, a ten minute walk north of the river, are two pubs worthy of your attention. Both are in the Main Street and offer Marston's beers and excellent food lunchtime and evenings. Set back from the road, the **Reindeer** has an attractive, cosy two-roomed interior and backs on to the village cricket pitch. Virtually opposite is the **Marquis of Granby**, which offers a range of guest beers and something for everyone, including an outdoor drinking area.

OFF THE TOWPATH
NEWARK

It's certainly worth the short detour to visit the historic town of Newark, with its handsome castle overlooking the river. It has several good pubs too. The most noteworthy for those who enjoy a good pint and traditional pub atmosphere must be the **Old Kings Arms** in Kirkgate in the town centre, a lively, boisterous Marston's pub offering virtually the full range of their traditional beers along with a varied lunchtime and evening menu including fresh vegetables and real bread. Nearer to the river are the **Newcastle Arms**, a quarter mile north-east of Trent Bridge in Appleton Gate, a small traditional two-roomed local with handpumped Home Mild and Bitter and lunchtime food (except Sundays), and the **Malt Shovel** in Northgate, a one-room free house with Taylors Landlord, Wards Sheffield Best Bitter and a range of guest beers, as well as an imaginative menu which changes constantly.

NOTTINGHAM
Narrow Boat

Tel : (0602) 501947
*Canal Street, Nottingham. 50
yards from the Navigation at
Wilford Street Bridge*

✗ lunchtime

🍺 **Shipstones Bitter**

From Wilford Street bridge and lock and the Navigation pub, head towards the traffic lights and turn right – the Narrow Boat is on the right, just before the interesting canal museum at Fellows, Morton & Clayton Wharf and close to the renowned Broadmarsh shopping centre. The rear of the pub virtually backs up to the water's edge, but there is no access from there.

Not entirely unexpectedly, the Narrow Boat has a strong canal theme, from its pub sign and fascia, painted in roses and castle lettering to the slightly tacky servery painted to resemble the side of a boat and punctuated with a row of portholes. There are canal paintings and photos too, and a collection of plates in the bustling main bar.

Not that this friendly, lively pub's appeal is narrowly channelled towards the waterway; these days it attracts a broad mix of customers, and has become a popular live rock music venue – there is a function room and a rock-orientated jukebox featuring Pink Floyd, Rush, U2, the Stones and the like (all of which beats the living daylights out of dance and pop as far as this writer is concerned).

Monday night is quiz night, while pool enthusiasts can indulge themselves in a side bar off the impressive wall- and floor-tiled vestibule. There is also a small quiet back room with a TV.

Good value bar food is available every lunchtime including Sundays, and ranges from chip cobs to chili, salads, sausage casserole, cannelloni, spring rolls and seafood platter. There are good options for vegetarians, such as vegetable curry, vegetable casserole and cheese and vegetable pie. There is also an unusual Chef's Special – "Poll Tax Pie: fishy, half-baked and hard to swallow". I'll have some of that.

Navigation

Tel: (0602) 417139
Wilford Street, Nottingham.
Canalside at Wilford Street
Bridge and lock. Good moorings

✗ lunchtime

🍴

🍺 **Banks's Mild, Bitter**

Once a run-down city pub, the Navigation acquired new owners and a new lease of life in the mid 1980s when Wolverhampton-based Banks's took it over, refurbished and converted it to a managed house. What emerged is a thriving one-room pub, brash and boisterous but the right side of naff, and sometimes very noisy courtesy of the raucous regulars, the CD jukebox or both. There is some instant canalia courtesy of some old prints and assorted canal-related artefacts. The battery of primary colours – blues, yellows, reds – with which your senses are assaulted are presumably designed to echo the canal theme. A raised area houses a pool table, and outside are some wooden benches and tables alongside the lock, so you can sit, sup and watch others do the hard work.

Food is served lunchtimes only, six days, and is advertised as "Galley Grub". This turns out to be sandwiches and cobs, burgers, pies and everything-with-chips, salads and the faithful old retainer for vegetarians, veggie lasagne. The Navigation opens all day on Saturdays and for all but one hour on Fridays, and allows children in at lunchtimes all week. It is also supposedly haunted. The manager once saw a dark, shadowy figure flit across the bar, but said nothing, fearing mass scepticism and derision. A few days later, unprompted, a pale, fearful, quaking customer confided in him that he thought he'd seen a ghost in the bar a few days before – a black shadow. Happy drinking!

NOTTINGHAM
Trip to
Jerusalem

OFF THE TOWPATH

1 Brewhouse Yard, Castle Road, Nottingham

Nottingham's most famous pub, and yet another claimant to the "oldest pub in England" title, although its claim would seem more realistic than that of many others. Built into the steep rock face below Nottingham castle, it's no longer a free house but a Hardys & Hansons tied house offering their traditional Bitter along with Marston's Pedigree and lunchtime food. An essential visit.

TRENT & MERSEY CANAL

One of the major arteries of the inland waterways system, the Trent & Mersey originates at the confluence of the rivers Derwent and Trent near Shardlow in Derbyshire, and runs north westwards through Staffordshire and Cheshire to Preston Brook where it meets the Bridgewater canal. Along the way it passes through the hearts of the brewing, potteries and salt extraction industries (Burton-on-Trent, Stoke-on-Trent and Middlewich respectively).

It has numerous junctions – the Coventry canal can be joined at Fradley near Lichfield, the Staffs & Worcester canal at Great Haywood, the Caldon canal in Stoke-on-Trent, the Macclesfield canal at Hardings Wood near Kidsgrove, the Shropshire Union at Middlewich via the Middlewich Arm, and finally the River Weaver via the awesome (though currently still inoperative) Anderton Boat Lift.

ALREWAS
George & Dragon

OFF THE TOWPATH
Tel: (0283) 790202
Main Street, Alrewas. 10 minutes walk into village from canal, via Bridges 46, 47 or 48

✗ lunchtime and evening

🍴

🅰 **Marston's Pedigree Bitter**

Comfortable and popular pub in main street of attractive village. Known for good food and beer.

BARTON-UNDER-NEEDWOOD
Barton Turn

Barton Turn, Barton-under-Needwood, Staffs. Canalside at Barton Lock

✗ lunchtime

🍴

🅰 **Marston's Pedigree Bitter**

Barton Turn is a tiny settlement on the edge of the large, thriving village of Barton-under-Needwood. It has been bypassed by the thunderous A38 trunk road, leaving the street between pub and lock, the old Roman road Ryknild Street, blissfully quiet and traffic-free.

Known until recently (and still known locally) as The Vine, the Barton Turn is a small, friendly, straightforward boozing pub, relying not on music, food (it only offers sandwiches and rolls), a theme or a Laura Ashley interior for its trade, but on beer sales and locals. It seems to be a successful formula.

The building itself has been traced back to at least 1880, though it probably predates that, and has served as a Marston's pub for most of that time. Whether it remains so must be open to question; the brewery has just acquired a big eaterie in the village a mile away, and invested telephone numbers in giving a pub in the next village a facelift, leaving the Barton Turn stranded and perhaps surplus to requirements in between. Where, I wonder, does a pub so dependent on beer sales and local trade figure in the grand corporate design?

For now, the pub has a simple single L-shaped room layout, with an extension harbouring a bar billiards table and a further annexe serving as a pool room. There is a dartboard, fireplace, vinyl floor covering and wine-coloured PVC seating. A mix of wooden copper-topped tables, paintings and pen-and-ink drawings of the pub and canal, mirrors and hanging lanterns complete the picture. There is a small and slightly ramshackle beer garden, unfortunately at the rear of the pub, facing the A38 rather than the canal at the front.

BRANSTON Bridge

Branston, Staffs. Canalside, Bridge 34

✕ lunchtime and evening

🍴

🍺 **Marston's Pedigree Bitter**

Next to the pub stands an old box tree, the original sign of a canalside pub. It would be difficult to imagine a better example of the species, for here is a canalside classic.

Situated on the outskirts of Burton-on-Trent close to the thunderous A38 trunk road, the Bridge aims to be the star mooring for the Burton area. Its structure is as old as the canal itself, the main building having been used as a store shed during the canal's construction. It was converted to a pub once the canal was established. Today a number of services have been introduced specifically for canal users, including basic provisions, a telephone, frozen portions of the pub's excellent food to take on board, coin operated washing machines and tumble dryers and cycle hire.

Good quality hot food and snacks are available lunchtimes and early evenings, and range from the chili/lasagne type fare to various grills including a formidable full English breakfast. Meanwhile, ale connoisseurs can savour fruity, delicious Marston's Pedigree in the way nature would have intended – straight from the casks in the cellar adjoining the bar. It probably has little bearing on the actual taste, but does wonders for the romantic imagination.

The bar itself is small, homely and friendly, usually dominated by the babble of conversation or the raucous clatter of dominoes. There is also a piano. A small, plusher area off the main bar houses diners. Outside a splendid and frequently crowded canalside beer garden provides plenty to occupy the kids. A compulsory stop if you're in the area.

BURTON-ON-TRENT
Burton Bridge Brewery

OFF THE TOWPATH
Tel: (0283) 36596
24 Bridge Street, Burton-on-Trent. 25 yards west of river, on bridge. Journey into central Burton from canal

✗ snacks lunchtime and evening

🍺 **Burton Bridge XL Bitter, Bridge Bitter, Porter, Festival Ale, Old Expensive; guest beers on Sunday**

The brewery tap (and only tied house) for Burton's smallest (and arguably best) brewery. Small, friendly and traditional. Skittle alley, jazz club Thursdays, occasional mini beer festivals.

CHURCH LAWTON
Red Bull

Tel: (0782) 782600
Congleton Road South, Church Lawton, near Kidsgrove, Staffs. Canalside at lock 43 in the Red Bull flight

✗ lunchtime and evening

🍺 **Robinsons Best Mild, Best Bitter**

The Red Bull doesn't quite know where it is. Despite a Stoke-on-Trent postcode and telephone number, and proximity to Kidsgrove, undeniably a Staffordshire town, it is actually situated in Cheshire, taking its licensing laws from Crewe and paying its local tax to Congleton. Despite the confusion, the Red Bull has served canal travellers since the canal was built, making a welcome stop amid the flight of locks which bears its name.

Its slightly bland open-plan interior is divided into two distinct areas, both comfortable and plush, dimly lit, carpeted throughout and nicely decorated. The small lounge bar at the front with corner servery has beams, lots of brasses, glossy dark wood tables, a CAMRA mirror, some rather tawdry fairy lights and piped pop which verges on the intrusive. Behind it is a mirror image bar with a small alcove to the side and a separate restaurant beyond. Indeed food is what the Red Bull tends to be dominated by these days, in common with an ever-increasing number of licensed premises – I'm reluctant to term most of them "pubs". There is a bar menu including a daily special and a restaurant menu which can also be used in the main body of the pub. Available every session, food ranges from sandwiches, salads and filled jackets to steaks, home-made pies, fish dishes, chicken Kiev and so on. In addition, a hot and cold table is provided on weekday lunchtimes and traditional Sunday roasts on the day of rest.

The pub has an attractive grassed beer garden alongside the lock, and an upstairs room with dartboard and pool table, used for private functions when there's one booked and as a family room when there isn't. Children must be accompanied and be off the premises by 9 pm. There is a telephone for customers' use.

The licensee has been a Robinson's tenant for nearly thirty years and knows a thing or two about looking after traditional beers – the Best Mild is her preferred tipple, which speaks volumes. She tried all-day opening but it didn't really work out and is now confined to Saturdays only.

In truth the Red Bull is not outstanding in as much as nothing really leaps out at you for either praise or criticism. But what it lacks in individuality, character and "pubness", it makes up for in friendliness and the quality of its food and beer.

FRADLEY JUNCTION
Swan

Tel: (0283) 790330
Fradley Junction, near Lichfield, Staffs. Canalside at Fradley Junction where the Coventry canal meets the Trent & Mersey

✗ lunchtime and evening

🍺 **Ind Coope Burton Ale, Ansells Bitter**

The junction of the Coventry and Trent & Mersey canals is a justly famous waterways landmark and popular meeting place, as busy with canal life as it is isolated from the other world outside. It fairly bristles with canal life in all its colourful aspects – boats moored and moving, an attractive flight of locks and, the focal point of it all, the Swan pub. There are few more vivid canal scenes.

The Swan has a good traditional public bar with a real coal fire, ornate mirrors and old canal prints. The lounge area is pleasant if unremarkable, but the subterranean cellar bar is worthy of note; it almost gives the impression of a canal tunnel with its arches and gaudy red-and-white painted bare brick finish. Framed Lockmaster canal maps decorate the walls.

Food is available at the Swan every lunchtime and evening – yes, it is still possible to eat out on a Sunday evening. Steaks, fish, gammon and grills form the basis of the menu, while the carvery-style Sunday lunches are renowned locally for their value for money. This and the pub's attractive location mean that it often becomes extremely hectic, so aim to get there around opening time if you want Sunday lunch.

The ramped track that runs between the pub's frontage and the canal exists only to serve the pub and the handful of adjacent cottages, so you can sit or stand outside in safety and enjoy a drink right by the canal, which can be very congested. It may be necessary to moor some distance from the pub.

HANDSACRE
Crown

Handsacre, Staffs. Canalside by
Bridge 58

✗

🍺 Draught Bass

Despite its unexceptional exterior, here is a pub which has in abundance the quality which many sadly lack – character. It begins, as it should, behind the bar and radiates outwards to the mixed assembly of exiled Geordies and Scots who came here to work the coal mines, natives of the villages, canal users and other travellers who come to enjoy the unfailingly cheerful lively atmosphere and excellent Draught Bass.

There is a small, plain bar, a larger comfortable lounge with occasional live organ music and a bright, basic games room. Food is limited to snacks like hot pies, sandwiches and the ever-multiplying explosion of things-in-a-bag. There is also a fish and chip shop nearby.

The Crown is uncompromising but warm, welcoming you without making a fuss of you. Take it on those terms and you will unearth an uncomplicated, friendly English village local serving the community and its patrons in time-honoured fashion.

KIDSGROVE
Blue Bell

Tel: (0782) 77399
Hardings Wood, Kidsgrove,
Staffs. Canalside at Hardings
Wood junction

✗ lunchtime

🍺 Marston's Pedigree Bitter;
Whitbread Boddingtons
Bitter; Castle Eden Ale

Here's a strange state of affairs: a pub that's over 200 years old with authentic old beams, low ceiling and wooden settles, but with a clientele drawn largely from the younger end of the market – not so much lager louts as the rock fraternity, with their Iron Maiden and White-snake T-shirts. It has a rock-orientated juke box and more than its share of fruit machines for such a small place. In truth, however, it does attract a cross-section of ages and types, and is quite quiet at lunchtimes.

Inside it has three small connected drinking areas as well as a pool room at the rear. The area around the servery is cosy and traditional and has a CAMRA mirror on the wall and a small TV in the corner. The other two areas have matching dralon stools and upholstery. There are also a few benches and tables both at the front and rear of the pub for outdoor drinking. The Blue Bell is in the unusual position of having different canals on either side of the building: to the front, the Trent & Mersey, beyond the rear car park the Macclesfield. By road the pub can be reached by a short gravel track off the road by the canal bridge.

Elementary but reasonably priced pub food consists of sandwiches, burgers, pizzas, chicken, scampi and fish and chips all served lunchtimes only.

In this down-to-earth, untypical rock meeting place you will find a decent pint and a raucous, rough-hewn friendly welcome along with the ZZ Top and Rolling Stones.

LITTLE LEIGH
Holly Bush

OFF THE TOWPATH

Little Leigh, Cheshire. Ten minutes walk east of Bridge 209, on the A49

◁ Greenalls Mild, Bitter

An historic, rustic, thatched gem, a working museum and, sadly, an endangered species. The owners, in a breathtaking demonstration of irresponsibility and short-sightedness, applied for planning permission to flog off their treasure and turn it into a private house, thus depriving the public of its cosy tap room, public bar oozing with character and warmth, and tiny corridor fronting the serving hatch. However, at the time of going to press, it had won a hard-earned reprieve, though for how long is unclear. Enjoy it while you still can, before the likes of Greenalls deluge us all in a lamentable tidal wave of uniformity.

LONGPORT
Pack Horse

Tel: (0782) 815934
Station Street, Longport, Stoke-on-Trent. Canalside by Bridge 126

✘ lunchtime and evening

▨

▨ **Ansells Mild, Bitter; Ind Coope Burton Ale; guest beers**

The Pack Horse once belonged to the former Parkers Brewery of Burslem, and until recently had its own brewhouse. The extensive stables, once used for barge horses, are now the Stable Bar, a private function room. Today the pub is clean, comfortable and popular with all ages, a lively focal point for a diverse cross-section of the local community, hosting a folk music club on Fridays, music and trivia quizzes on Thursdays and the local IWA.

Though essentially a single room, the Pack Horse has several quite distinct areas. As you enter, with the bar directly ahead, a left turn will take you into a small public bar/games room area, with a dartboard, pool table and some plain old wooden tables for dominoes and crib. The fireplace is host to an unreal fire, but makes an attractive feature nonetheless, set off nicely by the old clock on its mantelpiece.

The L-shaped lounge area has a pleasant almost rustic feel with its exposed brickwork column, floral tie-back curtains, velour seating and hotch-potch of wall-mounted plates, prints, mirrors and photographs. It, too, has a fireplace with a clock on the mantelpiece to balance the one in the bar opposite. There is also a jukebox. The enclosed courtyard outside contains a small garden.

The Pack Horse's all-day menu is excellent value and includes steak, fish, home-made steak and kidney pie (beef cooked in ale with crispy flaky topping), omelettes, daily specials and vegetarian specials which are always available. The menu is complemented at lunch times by another snackier menu, with soup, filled jacket spuds and some tasty triple-decker sandwiches. Food is not available on Sunday evenings. Beware Karaoke on Friday evenings!

MIDDLEWICH
Boars Head

Tel : (0606) 843191
Kinderton Street (A54),
Middlewich, Cheshire. 50 yards
east of Bridge 172

✖ lunchtime

🛏

☺

⋈

🍺 **Robinsons Best Mild, Best Bitter**

This is a large, spacious, brick built hotel with four rooms and no trace of the pretentious. It's a typical northern boozer, unassuming and friendly, with touches of faded elegance mixing none too comfortably with more recent refurbishments and embellishments in the bar and lounge.

The TV room at the rear houses a piano and serves as a family room. There is a pleasant simple bar, a large games room with two pool tables, and a lounge through an arch framed by wrought iron and containing pew seating, bricked-up fireplace, anaglypta wall covering and an epidemic of spider plants. I suspect it will always look as though they haven't quite finished decorating, a suspicion not intended as a criticism. In the case of the primitive gents' toilet, they never even started.

The traditional beers, central to the pub's appeal, are in consistently prime condition though the handpumps are merely decorative. It's electric pumps that deliver the beer from cellar to glass. And I don't feel that the high volume Jason Donovan from the juke box enhanced the flavour any.

Straightforward snacks and bar meals (on weekday lunchtimes only) range from sandwiches and burgers to roast meats, home-made pies, fish, chili, chicken, all with chips and veg, plus a special of the day. The Kinderton Hotel next door is under the same ownership, so use is permitted of their limited outdoor drinking area. Both places offer accommodation. There are shops, a supermarket and two boatyards close by.

Newton Brewery Inn

Tel: (0606) 843502
Webbs Lane, off Pepper Street, Middlewich, Cheshire. Canalside between Middlewich Big Lock and Bridge 172

✗ lunchtime and evening

🍺 Marston Burton Bitter, Pedigree Bitter, Merrie Monk

A small, brick-built pub backing onto the canal, the Newton Brewery is one of those comforting, safe, unspectacular pubs that contain no surprises, no gimmicks, no theme, unobtrusively modernised and full of homely virtues.

It came under new management in April 1990, but with no discernible change in direction. It has a friendly, thriving traditional locals' bar with vinyl tiled floor, a small TV and lots of pub games including darts and table skittles. It looks out onto the large lawned beer garden and kids' play area leading down to the canal. There are donkey rides during the summer.

At the front facing the road is a plain comfortable lounge where food is served at every session, until 9.30 pm. Children are allowed in with dining adults until 8.30 pm. The deservedly popular giant Yorkshire pudding makes another welcome appearance here, with a choice of beef casserole, chicken in wine sauce or onion gravy as a filling. Elsewhere on the menu you can find all the usual stuff – burgers, ploughman's, toasted sandwiches, scampi, chicken Kiev, pizzas, chili, a daily special, sweets, a Kiddies' Korner. Above all, the Newton Brewery is a proper pub with a fine bar, and makes an ideal informal stop while on a cruise.

SHARDLOW
Canal Tavern

Tel: (0332) 792844
Hoskins Wharf, London Road (A6), Shardlow, Derbys. Canalside at Hoskins Wharf

✗ lunchtime and evening

🍺 Hoskins Beaumanor Bitter, Penn's Ale, Premium, Hoskins Old Nigel (Nov–Mar); guest beer

Shardlow is a well-preserved traditional canal port, with the Trent & Mersey as its main artery. Many fine examples of canal architecture survive, including boatyards, workshops and pubs. Perhaps the best-known, the eighteenth-century Trent Mill or Clock Warehouse, was acquired in the spring of 1987 by Hoskins, the small Leicestershire brewers, and a major restoration project began. As a result, this Grade II listed building in a superb setting has been imaginatively and sympathetically transformed into a successful and thriving business without detracting from its character and appearance. The use of original materials has played a significant part in the tasteful conversion, including traditional beams and stone floor.

The large central arch through which boats used to enter and unload now serves as the division between the single-bar pub and the restaurant, which together form the Hoskins Wharf complex. The pub offers a range of hot dishes in the lasagne/moussaka mould at lunchtimes from Monday to Thursday with an expanded range on Friday and Saturday, while the adjoining restaurant, open lunchtimes and evenings seven days a week, offers a much wider range including vegetarian options and Sunday lunches. Advance booking at weekends is recommended.

Plenty of attractive and comfortable outdoor drinking space and a good adventure playground add to this pleasant pub's appeal, which has lured such noteworthies as Edwina Currie, MP, Aussie actress Val Lehman (Bea in Prisoner Cell Block H, apparently) and the BBC's Tomorrow's World team. You have been warned.

Ambitious plans for the future include canalside barbecues, all-day opening in summer, a two-storey hotel and a floating restaurant. A pub in the traditional sense it's not, but it does offer a good range of traditional beers and all the advantages of its fine location, with splendid views out over the canal basin.

Malt Shovel

Tel: (0332) 792392
The Wharf, Shardlow, Derbys.
Canalside near Bridge 2

✗

🍴

Marston's Mercian Mild, Pedigree Bitter

Built in 1799, the Malt Shovel originally formed part of the malt rooms of the long-deceased Zachariah Smith brewery, only becoming a pub in 1904, some years after Marstons had acquired the Smith's brewery. Much of the building has remained intact, retaining many of its original features. Reference to the Smith's brewery is included in the rare collection of framed old advertising prints and mirrors which adorn the walls of the small, cosy, low-beamed bar. Ceiling space is congested and fiercely competitive – one part houses a selection of brassware, kettles, lamps, trumpets and bugles, while in another area swords and daggers battle for space, and beer mugs and jugs jostle in yet another. From the outside the place looks a picture with its black and white façade fronting the canal and its prize-winning hanging baskets. There is also a pleasant canalside patio.

The food and beer are of a high standard. All the beers are traditional, while the daily (except Sundays) specials conjured in the kitchen are outstanding, and good value, like chicken Wellington, malted steak, rolled leg of lamb with cheese and mint, and seasonal game dishes like fowl duck pie, a concoction of duck and guinea fowl cooked in port and Guinness. The specials are complemented by a comprehensive standard menu ranging from steaks to sandwiches. The Malt Shovel fully merits its place in the Good Food Guide.

But that's not the only guide in which you'll find it listed. The "Haunted Inns of England" refers to the pub's ghost, a vagrant in the old Zachariah Smith days who was murdered in the malt rooms – the area now occupied by the small, lower-level bar. It is there that "Humphrey", as the landlord has called him, makes his very convincing appearances, sufficiently convincing to induce in the landlord a particularly physical reaction the first time he witnessed one. The BBC once did a Halloween broadcast from the pub.

STOKE-ON-TRENT
Blacks Head
OFF THE TOWPATH

16 North Street, Stoke-on-Trent, Staffs. 10 minutes walk from canal on the edge of Stoke town centre

---
🍺 **Draught Bass, Theakston Old Peculier**

Traditional Potteries pub, 200 years old, serving Draught Bass and a continually changing range of guest beers (over 300 in the last two years). Near Stoke station.

Rose & Crown
OFF THE TOWPATH
Tel: (0782) 280503
Etruria Road, Hanley, Stoke-on-Trent, Staffs. East of Bridge 117

✗ lunchtime and evening

---
yy Usually closed Sat lunchtime and all day Sun

🍺 **Ansells Mild, Bitter; Gibbs Mew Wiltshire Bitter; Ind Coope Burton Ale; guest beers**

Former Parker's brewery showpiece pub, opposite the site of the National Garden Festival. Superb traditional bar, comfortable food-orientated lounge. Booking for food is essential on Saturday evenings.

STONE
Star

Stafford Street, Stone, Staffs. Canalside, Stone bottom lock

✗ lunchtime and evening

🍴

☺

🍺 **Banks's Mild, Bitter**

This traditional, cottagey old pub looks inviting enough from the outside, with its whitewashed exterior and attractive lock-side location. But to take a step down from the towpath through the pub's stable door is to enter another world. For the Star is a quirky gem, an irregular and intriguing concoction of, apparently, 13 rooms, most of them seemingly on different levels. Of the three which will be of most interest to the visitor, the friendly bar is highly recommended. It oozes character with its beams, tiled floors, varnished wooden tables, open fire grate and collection of Toby jugs hanging from the ceiling. There are no electronic devices here to bug you, although there is a gaming machine lurking in the corridor that leads off.

Immediately to the right as you enter the pub, the Canal Bar is a touch plusher and more loungey but essentially in harmony with the pub's image, whereas the Trent & Mersey Room, a comfortable family room off the corridor, lacks a little atmosphere, probably because of its isolation from the sunken serving area in the public bar.

Food is available every lunchtime and evening. It's standard pub fare for the most part — chip and sausage butties, fish and chips, pies, chili, filled jacket spuds, salads, chicken Kiev, various curries — but does feature one unsung regional speciality among the "starters and snacks". Staffordshire oatcakes are not cakes at all but savoury oat pancakes served hot with melted cheese and quite delicious.

Claimed to date from the fourteenth century, the Star is very much a canal pub and a magnet for waterways enthusiasts. It used to provide stabling, now replaced by a large car park. The pub is an ideal place to sit, sup and soak up the atmosphere, perhaps sparing a thought for the poor souls racing by on the elevated road bridge alongside the pub.

WHEELOCK
Cheshire Cheese

Tel: (0270) 760319
466 Crewe Road, Wheelock,
Ches. Canalside at Bridge 154

✗ lunchtime and evening

🍴

☺

🍺 Tetley Dark Mild, Bitter

Among many favourable entries from all around the world in the pub's visitors book, one in particular catches the eye. It reads "The Tetley family, Malton, Yorkshire. My great grandfather would have been pleased." Whether authentic or not, I'm sure the old man would have taken delight in this small friendly old pub, where licensee and locals share a roguish twinkle in the eye. Its small open-plan interior strikes the right balance between impersonal and intrusive, offering the choice of a quiet drink or joining the ensemble.

The main area has wood-panelled bench seating and some original beams, and the walls feature one old and one more recent photograph of the pub, a collection of old bottles (acquired by the landlord by following a JCB on its destructive course around town) and an unusual glass-fronted brewing display case. In one corner there is a collection of old barrel taps. Inevitably this has become known as the tap room. The window behind the servery used to be used to serve beer to the working boatmen. There is a lower-level area containing a dartboard and jukebox.

Barge horses used to be led up the covered passageway outside the back door and it still contains a hoist above a trapdoor into which the beer barrels used to be lowered. It leads to a small beer garden with children's play facilities. Unfortunately the old stables are due for demolition.

Word always spreads quickly along the waterways grapevine and more and more are getting to know about the excellent value meals at the Cheshire Cheese. In addition to the daily specials, which are a real plateful, there are various home-made pies, fish dishes, jacket potatoes as well as salads, snacks and a kids' menu.

Theoretically the pub closes in mid-afternoon and stops taking food orders at 9 pm, but you won't be turned down or turned away – it's that sort of place. Wheelock Wharf has a water point, sanitary station and useful local information board. There are plenty of moorings nearby.

Commercial

Tel: (0270) 760122
Crewe Road (A354), Wheelock, Cheshire. Canalside, Bridge 154

Marston's Burton Best Bitter, Pedigree Bitter, Whitbread Boddingtons Bitter, Thwaites Bitter

---

Oh the agony of choice! So much to do at Wheelock, and so little time. Well, if it makes it any easier, the Commercial is only fifty yards north of the Cheshire Cheese; if you want food or if it's any lunchtime other than Sunday between 12 and 2, make for the Cheshire Cheese.

If, however, it's a choice of good, well-kept

traditional beers you're after, seek out the Commercial instead. In addition to the splendid listed selection there are occasional and varying guest beers and a traditional cider.

Other than that there's really very little to say about the Commercial. It's a simple, quiet, uncomplicated free house that time forgot, an old Georgian house with an old-fashioned atmosphere. Wicker seats and an old Birkenhead Brewery notice in the gents add individuality, and there's a nice traditional bar area that positively encourages quiet contemplation and lively conversation.

RIVER WEY AND BASINGSTOKE CANAL

The Wey is an ancient waterway. Its commercial use predated the river's canalisation with modern style pound-locks as long ago as the seventeenth century. The town of Godalming, $19\frac{1}{2}$ miles cruising from the confluence with the Thames at Weybridge, is the limit of navigation and the furthest point south on the present inland waterway system. The Basingstoke canal leaves the Wey at Woodham junction and is navigable for $30\frac{3}{4}$ miles to just east of the collapsed Greywell tunnel. The latter's occupation by some rare bat species has put a question mark over plans for its repair, and unfettered use by powered craft of the remainder of this recently restored waterway is opposed by some conservationists.

ASH VALE
Swan Hotel

Tel: (0252) 28259
Hutton Road, Ash Vale, Surrey.
Canalside at Heathvale Bridge

✗   lunchtime

🍴

🍺   **Courage Best Bitter, Directors Bitter**

Much of the land hereabout is owned by the Ministry of Defence and used by the army to hone its particular skills. The distant clatter of automatic weapons as you approach the Swan can either alarm or reassure you according to your point of view. The mother and father of a mock battle that seemed to be taking place nearby on my visit to this large Victorian hostelry was in stark contrast to the placid canalside surroundings in which it is situated.

From the outside the Swan has that sort of identity crisis suffered by one or two other pubs in this book: where's the front? Rather than presenting equally grand elevations to all sides the Swan tackles the problem by being really quite plain all round. The focus of attention is, quite correctly, within.

Recent conversion has created a single large U-shaped room with a central bar, but there remains a distinct difference in mood and furnishing between the two halves. To add interest there are lots of canal photographs and a whole flock of stuffed birds in glass cases around the walls.

The Swan has a large garden by the canal with entertainment for the kids provided in the form of a wendy house and a helter skelter. The strange vessel moored in the car park is the pub's contender in the annual charity raft race held on this stretch of water on August bank holiday. This must create unusual problems of navigation for passing boats. Best, I think, to moor up, visit the Swan and watch the fun till it's all over.

CROOKHAM
Fox and Hounds

Tel: (0252) 615980
*Crookham Road, Crookham,
Hants. North bank of the canal
between Coxheath Road bridge
and Reading Road South bridge*

✗ lunchtime and evening

🍴

☺

🛏

🍺 **Courage Best Bitter, Directors Bitter**

The tradition of pleasure boating on our canals is an older one that we sometimes realise and was common enough in the last century even as commerce ruled the waterways. At this time the proprietor of the Fox and Hounds not only provided stabling for the canal carriers' horses but also hired out rowing boats for those whose reasons to be afloat were purely recreational.

Today, trade from the canal is still attracted to the friendly little inn, which enjoys an excellent waterside location against a low embankment with good moorings, and set against a verdant background of huge trees on the opposite bank.

The name of the Fox and Hounds has been interpreted on pictorial signs in almost as many ways as there are pubs that bear it. There is the direct approach with the latter in pursuit of the (doomed) former. The humorous approach has the sly fox outwitting his tormentors, often by slipping into the pub as the hounds race by. Here, though, the Fox is seen arm in arm with two hounds (apparently female) while jigging in happily subversive collaboration. The interesting history of this design's conception is catalogued beside the original sketch in a frame over the fireplace.

Hopefully this will be used as reference for a repaint as the flaking varnish and the dulled pigments are not a good advertisement for the pub's spruce and comfortable two-bar interior.

FARNCOMBE
Ram Cider
House

OFF THE TOWPATH
Tel: (04868) 21093
Catteshall Lane (off Catteshall Road), Farncombe, Surrey. 400 yards south of Catteshall Lock on the Wey

✗ lunchtime

🍴

🍺 **Bulmers Extra Dry, Dry, Medium and Sweet Traditional**

The Ram Cider House totally confounds the commonly held image of such establishments. Far from being "a bit of a dive" it's very smart indeed. It is housed in a classic sixteenth century timber-frame building, and there has been no expense or effort spared in suitably decorating and furnishing its three characterful bars. The servery has a hatch opening on to two acres of superb garden.

Until recently owned by Bulmers the Ram is now a free house. Other ciders, such as Westons, are now available in traditional form other than on draught but there is, of course, no beer whatsoever. There are plans to extend the place to accommodate family room and restaurant in the near future.

GUILDFORD
Britannia

OFF THE TOWPATH
Tel: (0483) 572160
9 Millmead, Guildford, Surrey. By Mill Mead Lock on the Wey

✗ lunchtime and evening

🍴

🍺 **Friary Meux Best Bitter, Ind Coope Burton Ale, Gales HSB**

At Mill Mead lock the Wey finds itself the central feature of some attractive and well-manicured municipal parkland, heartening to those boaters travelling south who will have found some parts of the river's course through Guildford town centre rather less than endearing. Overlooking this verdant scene, across a small car park from the weir stream is the Britannia, an interesting architectural quirk from the inter-war period.

The dominant features are the big red brick Dutch gables at either end of the façade. The roof itself encloses the second floor of the building and the prominent dormer windows are anything but Dutch in inspiration. The loggia at the front is furnished with a bench for sheltered outdoor drinking and contains the entrances to the two bars. There are benches and tables on the front terrace for taking in the view and parking the children in fine weather, and a homely walled beer garden at the back where barbecues take place.

The interior has recently been redecorated in the busy, slightly cluttered style now fashionable, but it blends well with the feel of the place and advantage has been taken of the canal/river theme with rose decorated ornaments and interesting old photographs.

With luck the Britannia will be open all day by the time this guide appears, so there will be no need for precise timing if you wish to stop off here to enjoy some fine beer in friendly, pleasant surroundings.

NEW HAW
White Hart

Tel: (0932) 842927
New Haw Road, New Haw, Surrey. By New Haw lock on the Wey

✗ lunchtime

⊗

⊞ **Courage Best Bitter, Directors**

These southern suburbs are hardly the most inspiring, even to a North Londoner such as I, but every so often a shallow humped bridge appears signalling the course of the River Wey. The view from the parapet of these bridges is of a totally different world. This tranquil, idyllic and superbly maintained waterway, so detached from the suburban sprawl that is never far away, sums up the joy of inland waterway travel. Only the occasional stop for replenishment and refreshment brings one into contact with the world beyond. Sadly, in this context, the Wey is endowed with too few pubs of character, but the White Hart is certainly one of them.

This attractive Regency building is deceptively squat for its two storeys. It has the typical shallow pitched roof of the period and the lower floor, with its large chequerboard windows, projects out slightly to provide a convenient little balcony for the publican's living quarters. There is a pretty grass covered and willow shaded beer garden overlooking the weir stream, with plenty of children's play facilities. The interior is split laterally between saloon and public bar with a central servery, a most sensible traditional arrangement. Add to all this some excellently kept draught beer and you have one of the River Wey's best service areas.

The White Hart is expected to undergo a big

refurbishment soon, employing the decorative tradition of the waterways as a theme. This should work wonders if not overdone.

PYRFORD LOCK
Anchor

Tel: (09323) 42507
Lock Lane, Pyrford Lock, Ripley, Surrey. By Pyrford Lock on the Wey

✘ lunchtime (Mon–Fri)

🖾

☺

🍺 **Courage Best Bitter, Directors Bitter, John Smiths Bitter**

The Anchor is a large building of the 1930s. Its classic roadhouse style seems somewhat inappropriate for its remote location by the River Wey and approachable only by narrow lanes. It has a large terrace out front for al fresco drinking, which also provides an ideal surface for the Morris dancers who visit the pub in the summer months. "You either like them or you hate them," said the landlord. Personally, having joined the Greenwood Men for just one dance in my local pub, I can only say how much I admire their considerable stamina and athleticism, skilfully disguised as it is behind much hair and large beer bellies.

The exterior of the pub pays homage to its surroundings only in the discreet canal-style signage, but inside it's another story.

The old thirties interior is long gone to be replaced by a sort of Scandinavian style of decor, festooned in canalania of every description. The bar, the ceilings, the floors, doors and furniture are all of natural pine, and part of the attic has been opened out to provide a large and interesting family room with access via an open stairway. This odd combination of themes and styles is actually quite characterful.

The pub is certainly popular. For the boater the nearby lock and boatyard make it a natural stopping place. The landlubber will not only visit the Anchor for its excellent lunches and beer but also for its charming rural setting. After West Byfleet the urban sprawl begins to thin out and the River Wey here is beginning to take on a more rustic character.

To explain how to reach the Anchor by road

would require several pages of directions, but the simplest route is to approach it from the Wisley turning on the A3 and perhaps take in the gardens of the Royal Horticultural Society while you're about it.

WEYBRIDGE
Lincoln Arms

Tel: (0932) 842109/842844
104 Thames Street, Weybridge, Surrey. Riverside just south of the Thames/Wey confluence

✕ lunchtime and evening (not Sun evening)

🛏

☺

🍺 **Friary Meux Best Bitter, Ind Coope Burton Ale, Tetley Bitter; Youngs Special Bitter**

The Lincoln Arms won a CAMRA award for refurbishment back in 1983. A visit here today will show how well this work has survived, both fashion-wise and physically, and how richly deserved was the recognition.

The most interesting new feature is the enclosure of the bar servery with sash windows. This arrangement has some Victorian antecedents in south London but is much more common in island bars up north. Its disadvantage may be that it adds a certain sad finality to closing time as the windows slide down, but it looks most attractive. Apart from this the interior has loads of stripped pine, nice patterns and lots of appealing bric-à-brac.

The exterior, equally tastefully done, has an unusually broad classical stuccoed façade with four large bay windows, an imposing porch at one corner and a fine centrally placed roofboard sign. There are substantial gardens back and front, the latter surrounded by a low white-painted picket fence. Friendly staff, good beer (the manager is a member of Ind Coope's Guild of Master Cellarmen), and a wide choice of appetising food combine to make the Lincoln Arms an appealing package. On Tuesday evenings in winter meals are not available due to the popular weekly pub quiz.

The confluence of the Thames and Wey presents a confusing picture from the land. The Lincoln Arms faces the most easterly channel of this mini-delta. There are plenty of nearby moorings but many of them may be restricted.

The visitor by boat may get a clearer picture of all this and will certainly be rewarded by arranging an embarkation to visit this fine pub.

Old Crown

OFF THE TOWPATH
Tel : (0932) 842844
*83 Thames Street, Weybridge,
Surrey. 250 yards south from the
Lincoln Arms*

✕ lunchtime and evening

🏢

🍺 **Courage Best Bitter, Directors**

Built, I suppose, in the seventeenth century, the Old Crown has an exterior of white-painted weatherboarding and undulating pantiled roof of great character. It also has an unusual, if not unique, miniature gallows sign over the pavement (as opposed to the normal arrangement crossing the road). The inside of the pub possesses equal charm. There are three separate cream-painted bars. These have fine tongue-and-groove ceilings supported by old cast iron columns, giving the sensation of being aboard a Victorian battleship. The wooden beer pump handles appear to have been made from policemen's truncheons.

For once all the clichés are wholly apt. The Old Crown can only be described as a lovely rambling old pub.

WINCHFIELD
Barley Mow

Tel : (0252) 617490
*The Hurst, Winchfield, Hants.
Just east of canal at Barley Mow
bridge.*

✕ lunchtime and evening

🏢

🍺 **Courage Best Bitter, Directors
Bitter, John Smiths Bitter**

The Barley Mow is one of those splendidly isolated pubs whose isolation attracts customers from miles away. On a Friday night, like bees to a flower of exceptionally sweet nectar, swarms of drinkers descend upon this quiet location. A large overflow car park, provided by the council, not only serves the pub but also car-borne sightseers to the canal towpath. It does seem ironic that boaters are, and will probably continue to be, to some extent discouraged from using this waterway.

This is a large pub with a fine early nineteenth century façade. A smart saloon bar is contained within the ground floor of the main building and a sumptuous lounge to the side leads to a large beer garden, the whole brilliantly floodlit at night. The pub also has its own cricket pitch which must provide an idyllic arena for this most gentlemanly of games.

If the people of Aldershot, Basingstoke and Farnborough have no trouble finding the Barley Mow, a stranger in these parts will possibly face problems in this large but thinly spread village. It has a railway station so there must be a lot of people around somewhere. Once you have found the station carry on along the road to Dogmersfield and the canal bridge signals your arrival.

WORCESTER & BIRMINGHAM CANAL

From its junction with the River Severn in the bustling Diglis Basin in Worcester, the Worcester & Birmingham progresses north eastwards to terminate in Gas Street Basin in the heart of Birmingham. It has a junction with the Stratford canal at Kings Norton in Birmingham.

STOKE POUND
Queens Head

Stoke Pound, off A4024 between Stoke Heath and Bromsgrove. Canalside at Bridge 48, near Tardebigge bottom lock

✖ lunchtime and evening

🍴

🍺 **Courage Best Bitter, Directors, John Smith's Bitter**

Once a modest-sized structure, the Queen's Head has been extended time and again over the years to accommodate its burgeoning popularity, particularly as an eating establishment. Unfortunately, among the hordes it sucks in are a fair number of loud yuppies in their designer shades and fuel-injection Bermuda shorts. The side car park and huge low-level overspill car park are liberally sprinkled with the stereo-powered BMWs, XR2s and 3s, Turbos and GTIs.

Like some of its clientele, the pub itself verges on the ostentatious and can be a bit pricey, but it consistently attracts canal users in large numbers as well as motorists. From the canal it certainly looks a picture with its waterside terrace and beer garden with parasols and lanterns, and a line of moored boats virtually pressing against the bar windows.

There is an extensive open-plan interior, a mix of the old and the recent, the authentic and the contrived. Old beams mix with some much more recent brickwork and the obligatory burgundy dralon upholstery in the area nearest the bar. The rest is food-dominated, with a raised dining area and large separate restaurant with carvery counter. Along one wall stands a row of fruit machines and an old red telephone kiosk. There is also a TV, a birdcage (with trilling occupants) and some slightly tacky prints of assorted animals and birds.

Catering, though, is where the Queen's Head really scores. It is highly recommended for its food, with a splendid carvery complemented by a comprehensive bar menu, with a wide and imaginative choice of everything from snacks to full three-course meals. Reasonable prices and generous portions make for excellent value for money. Last orders for food is 9.30 pm.

With a groceries store next door, the Queen's is a handy place to steel yourself for the rigours of the Tardebigge locks, or alternatively reward yourself for completing them. The food and beer are worth tolerating a few yuppies for.

STOKE WORKS
Boat & Railway

Tel: (0527) 31065
Shaw Lane, Stoke Works, near Bromsgrove, Worcs. Canalside just south of Bridge 42

✗ lunchtime and evening

🍺 **Banks's Bitter, Hansons Mild**

This small but busy village local is a real focal point for a wide cross-section of the local community, and is the meeting place of the Worcester & Birmingham Canal Society. The assorted clientele recalls the days when all pubs were like this, before the loathsome concept of niche marketing arrived to torment us. The Boat & Railway (the pub is lodged between the canal and the main Birmingham–Bristol train line) is also an established real ale haunt, with a long record history of inclusion in the Good Beer Guide. The beers are in fine condition. The pub was converted to open plan in recent years, to the regret of the landlord who favoured the intimacy conferred by its former separate bar/lounge layout. Nevertheless, it remains cosy and friendly and retains its essential "pubness". It has a wood-panelled bar, fabric covered bench seating, a few dark wood beams, copper-topped tables and some cane chairs and stools. The upholstery is not burgundy coloured, but more a sort of mucky gold. It makes a change.

Clearly no interior designer has been let loose here. It has the random, chaotic mix of styles, colours, patterns and finishes that often characterises plain, homely, informal boozers like this. There is a skittle alley with its own bar, and an upstairs function room hosting live rock and blues on alternate Thursdays. Alongside the canal, a narrow and basic terrace nestles beneath a cover of corrugated perspex.

Typical pub grub is offered all day Monday to Friday and Saturday lunchtimes and consists of steaks, pies, salads, sandwiches, and chips. No sign of chili, but I expect it's there somewhere. Vegetarians are also catered for.

TIBBERTON
Speed the Plough

OFF THE TOWPATH
Tel: Spetchley (090 565) 602
Plough Road, Tibberton, Worcs.
100 yards south of Bridge 25

✗ lunchtime and evening

🍴

🍺 **Banks's Mild, Bitter**

A small, cottagey village pub with a friendly atmosphere, primarily a boozer. It has a bar, lounge and tiny dining room. Evening food only if the pub isn't too busy. There are tables and chairs at the front and side of the pub for outdoor drinking. The pub name is an abbreviation of "God Speed the Plough", an agricultural blessing from bygone days. "God" was dropped more recently.

WORCESTER
Anchor

Tel: (0905) 351094
54 Diglis Road, Worcester.
Alongside Diglis Basin

✗ lunchtime and evening

🍴

🍺 **Banks's Mild, Bitter**

Diglis Basin, at the junction of the River Severn and the Worcester and Birmingham canal, is a fascinating though not especially picturesque clutter of boatyards, old warehouses, workshops and a dry dock, with an adjoining industrial estate and a faintly run-down air. It also houses a pub which the Good Beer Guide described as "a gem of a traditional pub". The Anchor is indeed a good honest traditional boozer, in truth more of a man's pub than a target for a family outing, particularly in its busy, smoky tap room where crib and dominoes dominate. It has a tiled floor and not-too-obtrusive maritime flavour, with a ship's wheel and lanterns and mock portholes above the bar, behind which mirrored panels help create atmosphere. Elsewhere there is a small snug at the front in which children are allowed, an upper level rear lounge with its own bar and a skittle alley/function room, connected to the pub via a small beer garden.

Snacks are available at lunchtimes and early evenings, while the traditional beers have the Banks's hallmarks – dependable and consistent if a little unspectacular, and comparatively inexpensive.

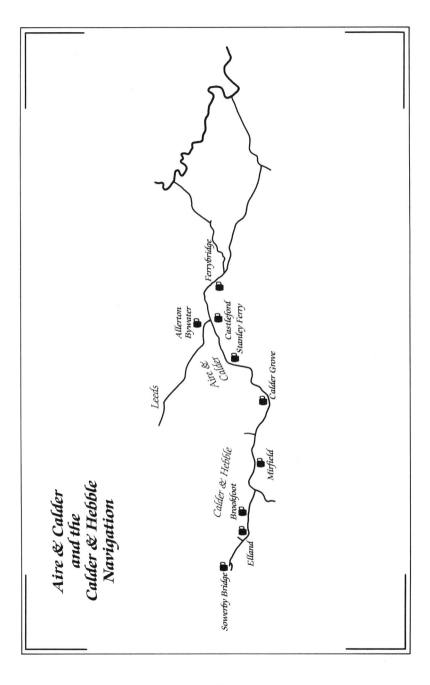

Aire & Calder
and the
Calder & Hebble
Navigation

Leeds

Ferrybridge

Allerton
Bywater

Castleford

Stanley Ferry

Aire &
Calder

Calder Grove

Mirfield

Calder & Hebble

Brookfoot

Elland

Sowerby Bridge

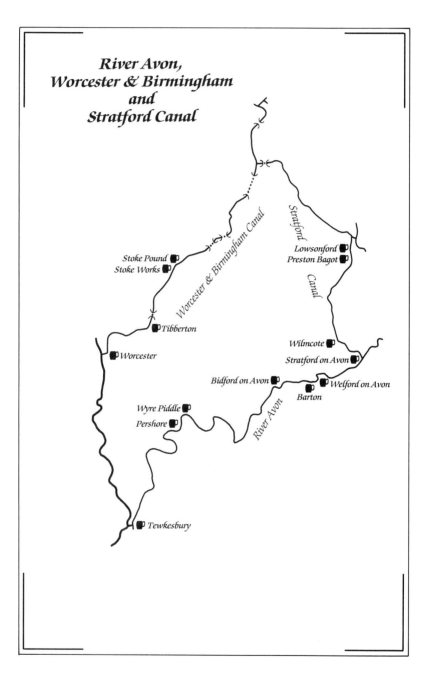

River Avon, Worcester & Birmingham and Stratford Canal

Stratford Canal

Worcester & Birmingham Canal

Stoke Pound
Stoke Works

Lowsonford
Preston Bagot

Tibberton

Canal

Worcester

Wilmcote

Stratford on Avon

Bidford on Avon

Welford on Avon

Barton

River Avon

Wyre Piddle

Pershore

Tewkesbury

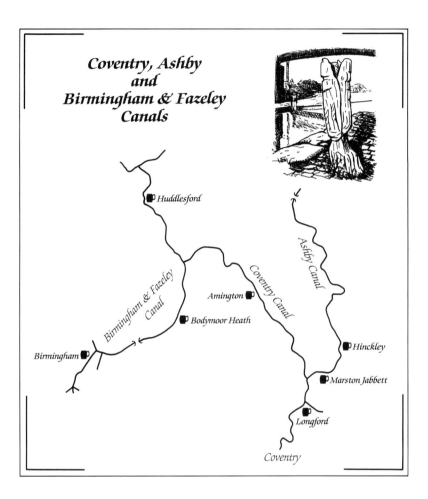

**Coventry, Ashby
and
Birmingham & Fazeley
Canals**

Huddlesford

Birmingham & Fazeley Canal

Coventry Canal

Ashby Canal

Amington

Bodymoor Heath

Birmingham

Hinckley

Marston Jabbett

Longford

Coventry

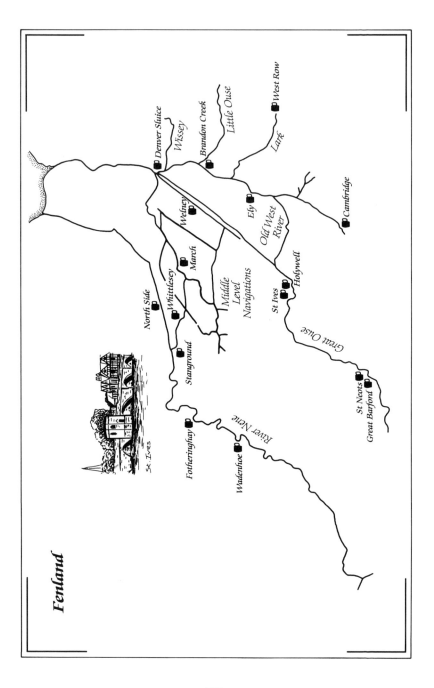

Fenland

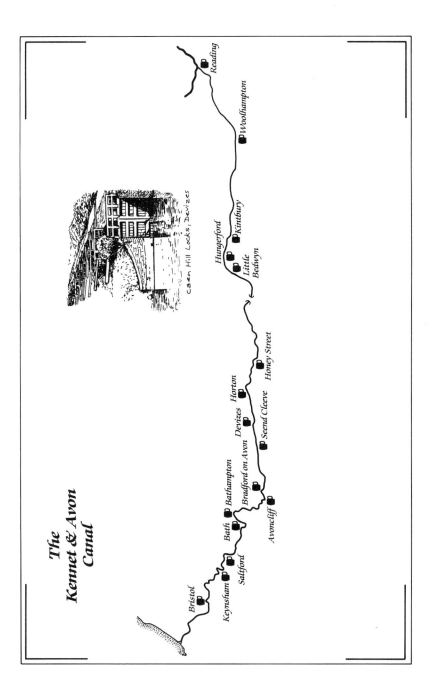

The
Kennet & Avon
Canal

Bristol
Keynsham
Saltford
Bath
Bathampton
Bradford on Avon
Avoncliff
Devizes
Horton
Seend Cleeve
Honey Street
Little Bedwyn
Hungerford
Kintbury
Woolhampton
Reading

Caen Hill Locks, Devizes

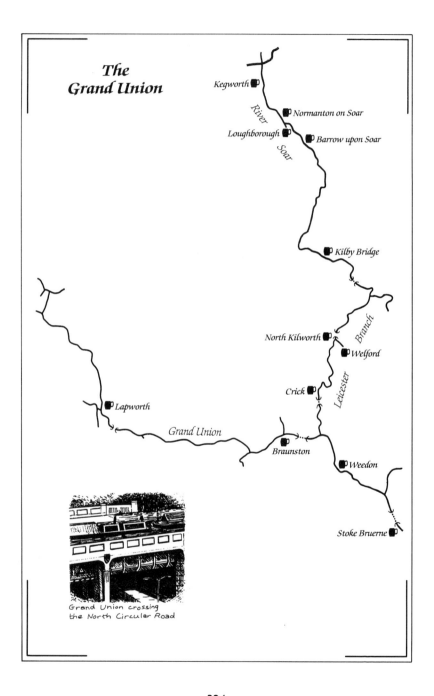

The Grand Union

Kegworth

River Soar

Normanton on Soar

Loughborough

Barrow upon Soar

Kilby Bridge

North Kilworth

Leicester Branch

Welford

Crick

Grand Union

Braunston

Weedon

Lapworth

Stoke Bruerne

Grand Union crossing
the North Circular Road

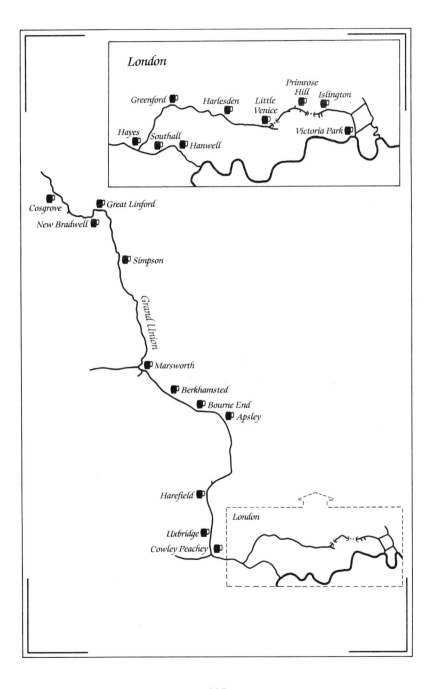

London

Greenford Harlesden Little Primrose Islington
                        Venice   Hill

Hayes Southall Hanwell   Victoria Park

Cosgrove Great Linford

New Bradwell

Simpson

Grand Union

Marsworth

Berkhamsted

Bourne End

Apsley

Harefield

London

Uxbridge

Cowley Peachey

Lee & Stort Navigation

Bishop's Stortford

Hertford
Ware

Cheshunt
Waltham Abbey
Enfield Lock

Tottenham Hale
Upper Clapton
Lea Bridge
London

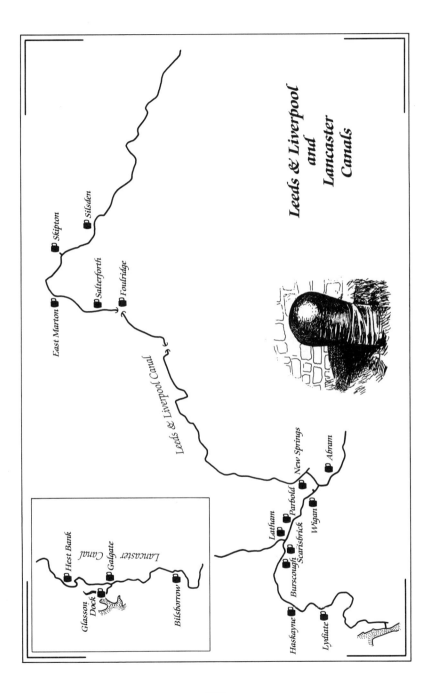

Leeds & Liverpool
and
Lancaster
Canals

Leeds & Liverpool Canal

Skipton

Silsden

East Marton

Salterforth

Foulridge

New Springs

Parbold

Abram

Latham

Wigan

Burscough

Scarisbrick

Haskayne

Lydiate

Hest Bank

Lancaster Canal

Galgate

Glasson Dock

Bilsborrow

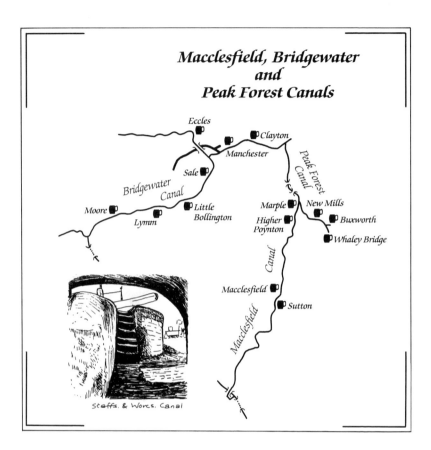

Macclesfield, Bridgewater and Peak Forest Canals

Eccles

Clayton

Manchester

Sale

Bridgewater Canal

Moore

Lymm

Little Bollington

Marple

Higher Poynton

New Mills

Buxworth

Whaley Bridge

Peak Forest Canal

Macclesfield

Sutton

Macclesfield Canal

Staffs. & Worcs. Canal

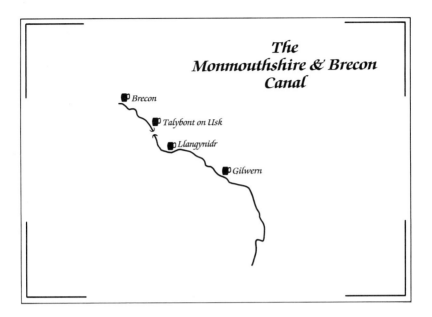

The Monmouthshire & Brecon Canal

Brecon

Talybont on Usk

Llangynidr

Gilwern

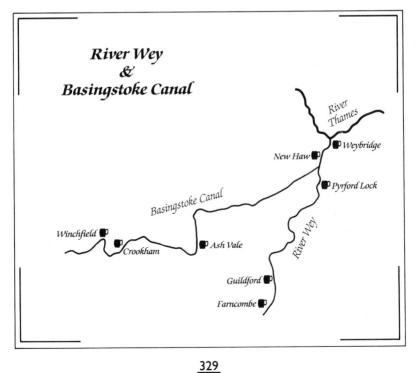

River Wey & Basingstoke Canal

River Thames

Weybridge

New Haw

Pyrford Lock

Basingstoke Canal

River Wey

Winchfield

Crookham

Ash Vale

Guildford

Farncombe

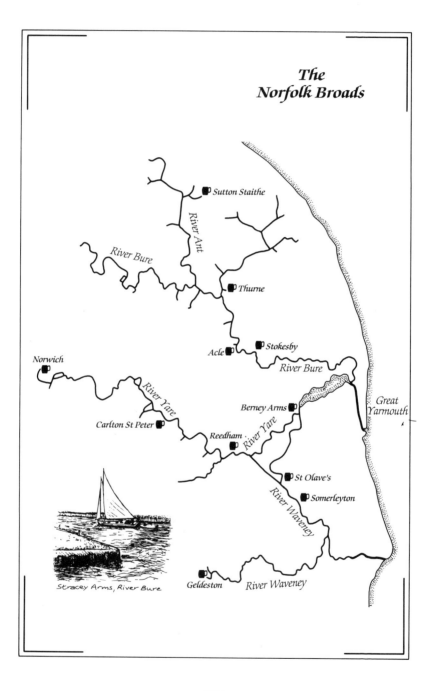

The
Norfolk Broads

Sutton Staithe

River Ant

River Bure

Thurne

Acle Stokesby

River Bure

Norwich

River Yare

Berney Arms

Great
Yarmouth

Carlton St Peter

Reedham

River Yare

St Olave's

Somerleyton

River Waveney

Geldeston River Waveney

Stracey Arms, River Bure

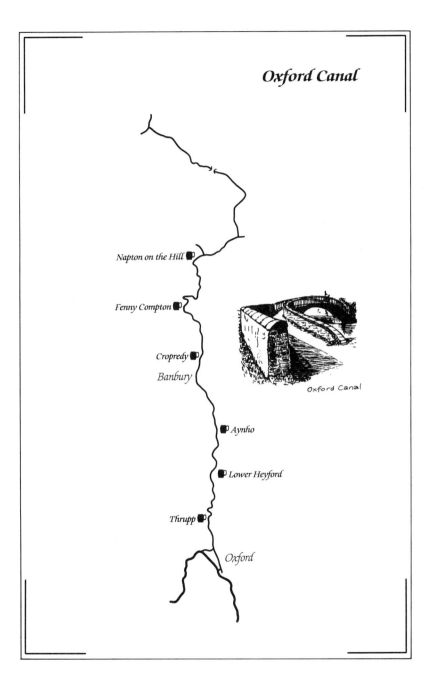

Oxford Canal

Napton on the Hill

Fenny Compton

Cropredy

Banbury

Aynho

Lower Heyford

Thrupp

Oxford

Oxford Canal

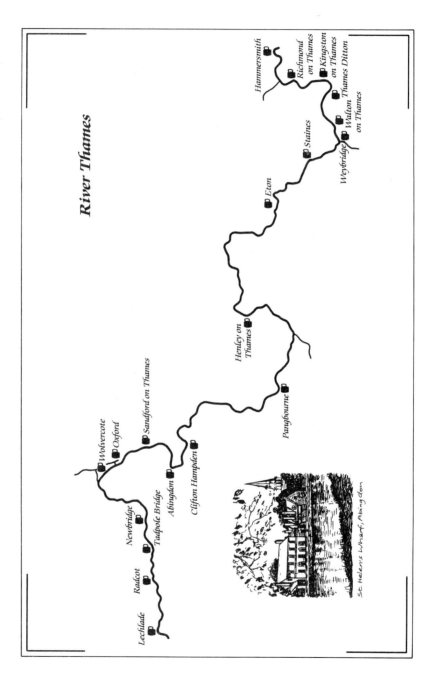

River Thames

Lechlade

Radcot

Newbridge

Tadpole Bridge

Wolvercote

Oxford

Sandford on Thames

Abingdon

Clifton Hampden

Pangbourne

Henley on Thames

Eton

Staines

Weybridge

Walton Thames Ditton on Thames

Kingston on Thames

Richmond on Thames

Hammersmith

St. Helen's Wharf, Abingdon

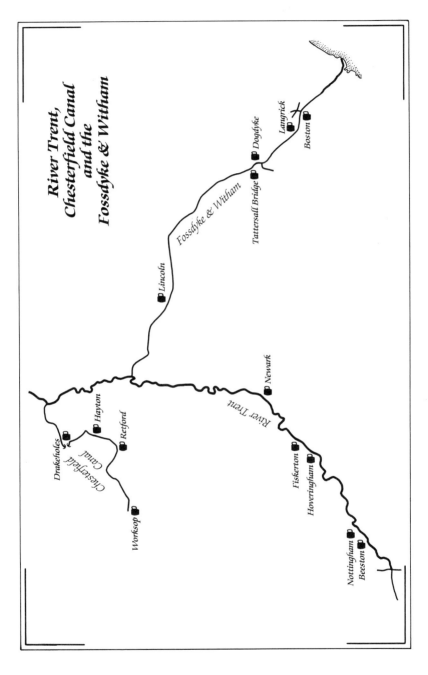

River Trent,
Chesterfield Canal
and the
Fossdyke & Witham

Boston
Langrick
Dogdyke
Tattersall Bridge
Fossdyke & Witham
Lincoln
Newark
Hayton
Retford
Drakeholes
Chesterfield Canal
Worksop
River Trent
Fiskerton
Hoveringham
Nottingham
Beeston

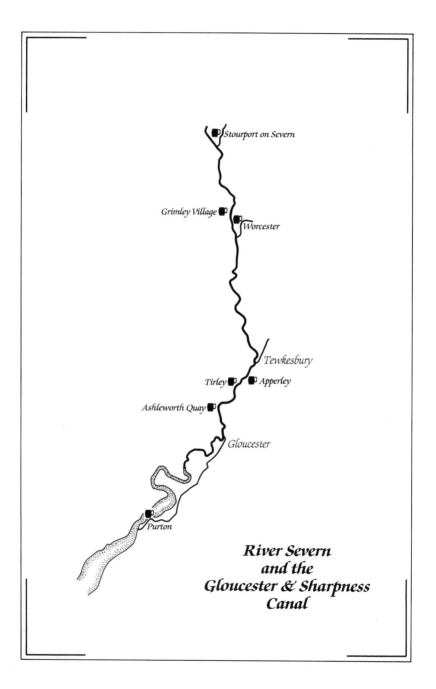

Stourport on Severn

Grimley Village

Worcester

Tewkesbury

Tirley Apperley

Ashleworth Quay

Gloucester

Purton

**River Severn
and the
Gloucester & Sharpness
Canal**

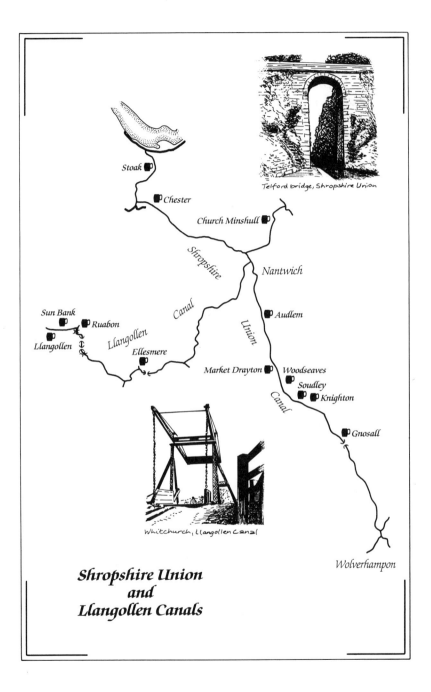

Telford bridge, Shropshire Union

Stoak

Chester

Church Minshull

Shropshire

Nantwich

Sun Bank
Ruabon
Llangollen
Llangollen
Ellesmere

Canal

Union

Audlem

Market Drayton
Woodseaves
Soudley
Knighton

Canal

Gnosall

Whitchurch, Llangollen Canal

Wolverhampon

Shropshire Union
and
Llangollen Canals

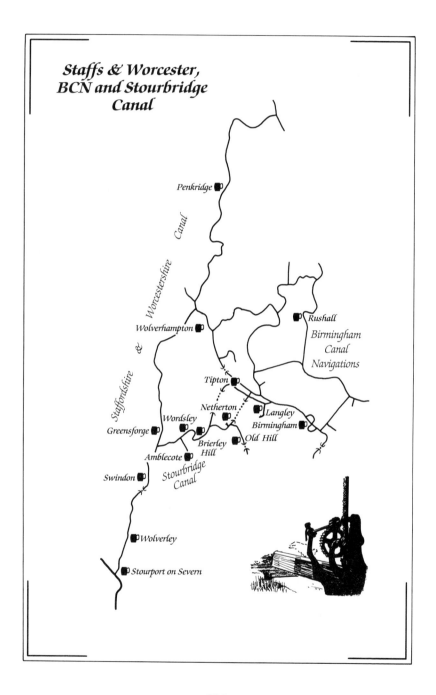

Staffs & Worcester, BCN and Stourbridge Canal

Penkridge

Worcestershire Canal

Wolverhampton

Rushall

Birmingham Canal Navigations

Staffordshire &

Tipton

Netherton

Greensforge

Wordsley

Langley

Birmingham

Old Hill

Brierley Hill

Amblecote

Swindon

Stourbridge Canal

Wolverley

Stourport on Severn

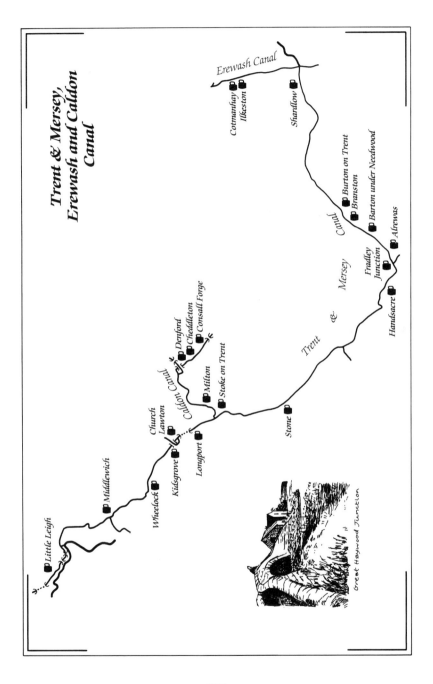

Trent & Mersey, Erewash and Caldon Canal

Erewash Canal

Cotmanhay
Ilkeston

Shardlow

Burton on Trent
Branston
Barton under Needwood

Alrewas

Fradley
Junction

Mersey Canal

Handsacre

Trent

&

Stone

Stoke on Trent

Milton

Consall Forge
Cheddleton
Denford

Caldon Canal

Church
Lawton

Longport

Kidsgrove

Wheelock

Middlewich

Little Leigh

Great Haywood Junction